Conversation Analysis

Conversation Analysis

PRINCIPLES, PRACTICES AND
APPLICATIONS

*Ian Hutchby
and Robin Wooffitt*

Polity

First published in 1998 by Polity Press in association with Blackwell Publishing Ltd.

Reprinted 1999, 2001, 2002, 2003, 2004, 2005

Editorial office:
Polity Press
65 Bridge Street
Cambridge CB2 1UR, UK

Marketing and production:
Blackwell Publishing Ltd.
108 Cowley Road,
Oxford OX4 1JF, UK

Published in the USA by
Blackwell Publishing Inc.
350 Main Street
Malden, MA 02148, USA

A catalogue record for this book is available from the British Library.

Library of Congress Cataloging-in-Publication Data
Hutchby, Ian.
    Conversation analysis : principles, practices, and applications /
  Ian Hutchby and Robin Wooffitt.
        p.   cm.
    Includes bibliographical references and index.
    ISBN 0–7456–1548–1 (alk. paper). — ISBN 0–7456–1549–X (pbk. :
  alk. paper)
    1. Conversation analysis.   I. Wooffitt, Robin.   II. Title
P95.45.H88   1998
    302.3'46—dc21   98-2890
                                                          CIP
Typeset in 11 on 12.5 pt Times
by Wearset, Boldon, Tyne & Wear
Printed in Great Britain by Athenæum Press Ltd, Gateshead, Tyne & Wear
This book is printed on acid-free paper.

For further information on Polity, please visit our website: http://www.polity.co.uk

Contents

Transcription Glossary

The transcription symbols used here are common to conversation analytic research, and were developed by Gail Jefferson. A more detailed discussion of the use of these symbols and others is provided in chapter 3.

(0.5)	The number in brackets indicates a time gap in tenths of a second.
(.)	A dot enclosed in a bracket indicates a pause in the talk of less than two-tenths of a second.
=	The 'equals' sign indicates 'latching' between utterances. For example:

```
S1:  yeah September ⌈seventy six=
S2:                 ⌊September
S1:  =it would be
S2:  yeah that's right
```

[ ]	Square brackets between adjacent lines of concurrent speech indicate the onset and end of a spate of overlapping talk.
.hh	A dot before an 'h' indicates speaker in-breath. The more h's, the longer the in-breath.
hh	An 'h' indicates an out-breath. The more h's the longer the breath.
(( ))	A description enclosed in a double bracket indicates a non-verbal activity. For example ((banging sound)). Alternatively double brackets may enclose the transcriber's comments on contextual or other features.
-	A dash indicates the sharp cut-off of the prior word or sound.
:	Colons indicate that the speaker has stretched the preceding sound or letter. The more colons the greater the extent of the stretching.
!	Exclamation marks are used to indicate an animated or emphatic tone.

( )	Empty parentheses indicate the presence of an unclear fragment on the tape.
(guess)	The words within a single bracket indicate the transcriber's best guess at an unclear utterance.
.	A full stop indicates a stopping fall in tone. It does not necessarily indicate the end of a sentence.
,	A comma indicates a 'continuing' intonation.
?	A question mark indicates a rising inflection. It does not necessarily indicate a question.
*	An asterisk indicates a 'croaky' pronunciation of the immediately following section.
↓ ↑	Pointed arrows indicate a marked falling or rising intonational shift. They are placed immediately before the onset of the shift.
a:	Less marked falls in pitch can be indicated by using underlining immediately preceding a colon:

S: we (.) really didn't have a lot'v cha:nge

a:	Less marked rises in pitch can be indicated using a colon which itself is underlined:

J: I have a red shi:rt,

Under	Underlined fragments indicate speaker emphasis.
CAPITALS	Words in capitals mark a section of speech noticeably louder than that surrounding it.
° °	Degree signs are used to indicate that the talk they encompass is spoken noticeably quieter than the surrounding talk.
Thaght	A 'gh' indicates that the word in which it is placed had a guttural pronunciation.
> <	'More than' and 'less than' signs indicate that the talk they encompass was produced noticeably quicker than the surrounding talk.
→	Arrows in the left margin point to specific parts of an extract discussed in the text.
[H:21.3.89:2]	Extract headings refer to the transcript library source of the researcher who originally collected the data.

Introduction

What do we do when we talk?

Talk is a central activity in social life. But how is ordinary talk organized, how do people coordinate their talk in interaction, and what is the role of talk in wider social processes? Conversation analysis (CA) has developed over the past thirty years to address these questions. The answers it provides, and more particularly the means by which it provides those answers (its assumptions, methods and procedures, together with the findings these enable us to generate), are the subject matter of this book.

Conversation analysis is characterized by the view that how talk is produced and how the meanings of that talk are determined are the practical, social and interactional accomplishments of members of a culture. Talk is not seen simply as the product of two 'speaker-hearers' who attempt to exchange information or convey messages to each other. Rather, participants in conversation are seen as mutually orienting to, and collaborating in order to achieve, orderly and meaningful communication. The aim of CA is thus to reveal the tacit, organized reasoning procedures which inform the production of naturally occurring talk. The way in which utterances are designed is informed by organized procedures, methods and resources which are tied to the contexts in which they are produced, and which are available to participants by virtue of their membership in a natural language community. The analytic objective of CA is to explicate these procedures, on which speakers rely to produce utterances and by which they make sense of other speakers' talk.

CA originates in the path-breaking lectures given by Harvey Sacks in the sociology departments of the University of California at Los Angeles, and later Irvine, between 1964 and 1972.

Sacks, who was killed in a car crash in 1975, was a highly original, often iconoclastic thinker whose ideas have, since his death, radically influenced researchers in fields as diverse as sociology, social psychology, linguistics (especially sociolinguistics and pragmatics), communication studies, human–computer interaction and speech therapy.

For many people, the present authors included, Sacks's work was first encountered in the form of mimeographed copies of the virtually unedited, typed transcripts which Sacks had made of his tape-recorded lectures. For a long time these mimeographs, circulated freely among those who (a) knew of their existence and (b) knew where to get them from, were the only means by which the great bulk of Sacks's work could be accessed. In 1992 this was changed when the lectures were edited by Gail Jefferson and published in book form (Sacks 1992).

Even so, in reading the book one still readily gets the frisson of excitement that emerged from those earlier, often scrappy A4 pages: a sense of the ongoing creation of a radically new form of social science. Like Saussure and Wittgenstein before him, two other revolutionary thinkers who had used the freer form of lectures in preference to the constraints of finished publications as the principal means for putting their ideas across, Sacks must have been well aware that the contents of his lectures constituted a break with the way things had been hitherto. In fact, Sacks's awareness of this was something that he did not try to hide. In many ways, this consciousness of his own originality is crystallized in the following remarkable exchange between Sacks and one of his students, which occurs late in the series of lectures. Sacks has been lecturing in his usual way, based around a fragment of recorded conversation. The student interrupts the lecture to ask a question:

> *Student:* I was just wondering if we're ever going to get around to topics of conversation.
>
> *Sacks:* That's an amazing question. I wouldn't know what you're- What do you have in mind?
>
> *Student:* I just think that we should get some content. I feel very frustrated about it.
>
> *Sacks:* ... What would be some content?
>
> *Student:* I don't know. I expected at least that you're going to analyse conversations ...

Sacks: Often you can do that kind of thing and figure that it will work. But as weird as it may be, there's an area called the Analysis of Conversation. It's done in various places around the world, and I invented it. So if I tell you that what we're doing is studying conversation, then there's no place to turn, as compared to experimental psychology where you can say 'I want to know what the mind is like' and then you can choose to study humanistic psychology or something like that. There is no other way that conversation is being studied systematically except my way. And this is what defines, in social science now, what 'talking about conversation' would mean. Now surely there are other ways to talk about conversation. But in social science there isn't. And people take it that they have to learn from listening to the sort of things I say, what it could possibly mean to talk about a particular conversation, how a conversation works, or how the details of conversation work. Nobody has ever heard a characterization in that detail, with that abstractness, of a fragment like that. It's just never been done. It's been done here for the first time. (Sacks 1992, vol. 2: 549)

To some, this may come across as mere arrogance. But what is remarkable about these comments for us is the extraordinary awareness Sacks shows of the originality of his thinking. As we outline in chapter 1, it was in fact quite accurate at that point for him to say that no one else in social science was studying conversation systematically. In sociology, Sacks's 'home' discipline (even though he had started off studying law), there was virtually no interest in any aspect of language, let alone the mundanities of everyday conversation. And though the focus on conversation may suggest that Sacks would have most in common with researchers in linguistics, we will also show that his particular approach – especially the alluded-to focus on detailed, abstract description of fragments of naturally occurring talk – distinguishes him from the predominant methodologies in that field also.

In fact, CA lies at a unique interface between sociology and other major disciplines within the social sciences: principally, linguistics and social psychology. This interdisciplinarity has been a feature of CA from the beginning; it is reflected, for example, in the fact that the earliest major publications appeared not in sociology journals but in others such as the *American Anthropologist* (Schegloff 1968) or the major linguistics journals *Language* (Sacks et al. 1974; Schegloff et al. 1977) and *Semiotica* (Jefferson 1973; Schegloff and Sacks 1973). Throughout this book we will show that CA addresses a range of substantive issues, both theoretical and methodological, which readers from backgrounds in a wide variety of social sciences will be able to identify with.

For instance, CA's sociological lineage draws on affinities with Erving Goffman's explorations of the interaction order and with Harold Garfinkel's programme of ethnomethodology (we discuss this in chapter 1). One of the key sociological issues that CA, like these perspectives, addresses is that of intersubjectivity. How do we share a common understanding of the world and of one another's actions in the world? From Schutz onwards, various responses have been given to this question. CA's distinctive contribution, as will become clear in chapters 1 and 2, is to show that analytic access can be gained to the situated *achievement* of intersubjectivity by focusing on the sequential organization of talk: in other words, on the management of turn-taking.

A further issue is addressed by conversation analytic research on talk in institutional settings. This work makes a distinctive contribution to recent developments in the 'agency–structure' debate (Knorr-Cetina and Cicourel 1981; Boden and Zimmerman 1991), which have sought to transcend the traditional sociological distinction between micro and macro levels of social order in order to reach a new understanding of how social action is related to social structures. In a similar way to some of Anthony Giddens's (1984) theories on this subject, CA takes the view that 'structure' should not be viewed as an objective, external source of constraint on the individual. Rather, 'structure' is a feature of situated social interaction that participants actively orient to as *relevant* for the ways they design their actions. Thus, while analysts may want to assert that some feature of social structure, such as class or power, is relevant for the way in which particular interactions are managed, the more difficult task proposed by CA is to show that such features are relevant for the participants themselves, as displayed, for example, in the design of their talk (Schegloff 1991). This issue is discussed at length in chapter 6.

In the field of linguistics, CA is relevant for three main areas: the ethnography of communication, which has aimed to analyse the patterns of language in use and the ways in which these relate to social and cultural patterns (Gumperz and Hymes 1972); pragmatics, with its interest in how meaning is communicatively established (Levinson 1983); and discourse analysis, with its concern for the structural and sequential properties of spoken language (Brown and Yule 1982; Sinclair and Coulthard 1975). With these perspectives CA shares the view that everyday talk is a phenomenon that is worthy of analysis in its own right, rather than the disorganized and flawed manifestation of linguistic competence that Chomsky (1965) believed it to be. One of the most important contributions made by CA here is in terms of methodology. CA emphasizes that analysis should be based entirely on closely transcribed examples of actual talk recorded in naturally occurring settings, extracts from which are made available as part of published research. In this way, the claims of the analyst are open to test by the reader or other researchers on the basis of the data (or at least, a transcription of it: in chapter 3 we discuss the distinction between data and transcription). This stance has had a major influence on research in what is now known broadly as interactional sociolinguistics, leading to a move away from the reliance on intuitively invented examples of talk as data which typified some earlier work, especially in speech act theory (Schegloff 1988a).

A further contribution stems from the position conversation analysts take on the question of how talk is related to contextual and sociological variables. In line with its stance on the agency–structure debate in sociology, CA takes issue with the standard sociolinguistic notion that there is an intrinsic and causal relationship between language and the social contexts in which it is produced. Again, rather than assuming such a relationship exists, CA demands that the relevance of sociolinguistic variables for the participants themselves must be demonstrated on the basis of the data. This does not mean that variables such as gender, class or authority are irrelevant; but it does require the analyst to pay close attention to empirical phenomena and to begin from the assumption that participants are active, knowledgeable agents, rather than simply the bearers of extrinsic, constraining structures. In chapter 6 this issue is addressed in terms of interaction in institutional settings; but we also relate the argument to more 'mundane' forms of talk in chapters 4 and 5.

Within social psychology, CA's contribution relates to similar methodological and conceptual questions. For instance, a great deal of research on interpersonal communication has been based on data generated in experimental settings in which the researcher seeks to control for certain variables, such as gender. Once more, such an approach is criticized for paying too little attention to the relevance of such variables among the partici- pants themselves, effectively seeking to create a situation in which the phenomena the researcher has decided are important can be observed. Similarly, social psychological studies in which interactional phenomena such as interruption are encouraged to occur through experimental control, then quantified and corre- lated with variables like the gender of the participants, run the risk of generating invalid findings by categorizing certain events as 'interruptions' when closer examination reveals that the par- ticipants in fact may display no recognition that an 'interruption' actually took place at all. This issue is discussed in chapter 4.

Conversation analysis also plays a role in the area of social psychology known as discourse analysis (Potter and Wetherell 1987). There is a difference between this and discourse analysis in linguistics. While the latter is mainly concerned to develop a theory of spoken discourse as a structured phenomenon, often using the model of grammar as its basis (Sinclair and Coulthard 1975), discourse analysts in social psychology have been critical of the ways in which their discipline has tended to treat language as a passive or neutral means of communication. Drawing not only from CA but also from ethnomethodology and semiotics, they stress instead that language is both functional and construc- tive; in other words it can only be seen as a medium which people use to accomplish specific communicative tasks, and it is a vehicle through which our sense of the world itself is actively con- structed. Consequently, one of the main concerns has been to develop a research programme in social psychology which takes full account of the dynamic properties of language use, both spo- ken and written. This issue becomes the focus of our attention in chapters 7 and 8 when we discuss the design of people's accounts of experience and their descriptions of states of affairs in the world. What our discussions there suggest is that while there has been much criticism of discourse analysis by conversation analysts, and vice versa, the two approaches actually have many similarities and may benefit from further serious cross-fertilization.

However, having made these points about contacts with other perspectives, our view is that conversation analysis has now developed to the extent that it represents a distinctive subdiscipline in its own right, with its own methodological and conceptual armoury, which owes no primary allegiance to any particular field. For this reason, our aim in this book will be to introduce the principles, practices and applications of CA in such a way as to be readily understandable to readers from whatever background, whether or not they have a working knowledge of any of the social sciences mentioned above.

This is only possible because Sacks's way of applying his vision did not result in an idiosyncratic, one-off body of work. Rather, Sacks invented a *method* by which others could take up and develop his findings, and, more importantly, generate new ideas and findings of their own. In short, conversation analysis is a generative method for the study of a wide range of aspects of the social world. Since Sacks's death, conversation analysis has continued to develop, and the number of practitioners has continued to grow, so that now the body of work within the field is truly diverse, both in terms of its substantive themes and of its increasingly global distribution. Conversation analysis, which began in the USA, is now being widely practised in the UK, and has a growing presence in Germany, Italy, the Netherlands, Denmark, Finland, Sweden, Australia and Japan.

Moreover, practitioners do not just analyse the social organization of 'ordinary' conversation, the casual interactions in which we routinely engage on a daily basis; but also, through studying how people use specialized forms of talk, the nature of institutions and organizations, the properties of mass communication, the structures of conflict in interaction, as well as issues such as the role of gender differences, power, the importance of ordinary talk in legal and educational decision-making processes, and more.

Yet on a methodological level, that diverse body of work is recognizably consistent. This is because conversation analysis is an approach which incorporates general procedures for data collection and transcription, as well as techniques for data analysis. Part of our aim in this book is to introduce those general techniques and basic procedures in such a way as to provide the reader with some of the practical tools for doing conversation analysis.

However, this is not a 'cookbook' which will provide rules and recipes for the easy production of a piece of conversation analysis. Although the procedures and techniques are quite general, they are not the same as the formulae which one might apply to data in statistical analysis. Conversation analysis, first and foremost, represents a distinctive sociological vision, a way of seeing the world and of approaching data, which derives ultimately from the exemplifications provided by Sacks in his original lectures.

In this book we emphasize both the methodological distinctiveness and social scientific applications of CA. We will focus not only on what CA is, and on how to do it, but also on what can be done *with* it. The book is designed to work on three interrelated levels:

- On the first level, we will present CA as *methodologically distinctive*. A major part of the significance of CA lies in its approach to the production of social scientific research, and in the practical research methods which are associated with that methodological perspective. The chapters of this book are intended both to explain and to exemplify that methodology.
- A second level of significance is found in what has been described as the *conversation analytic mentality* (Schenkein 1978): the distinctive way of seeing and thinking about the social world to which CA introduces us and which is essential to the application of its methods. Our approach to this will be to exemplify the CA mentality by practically working through examples of conversation analytic work, since an essential feature of CA is that concepts are developed from, and securely rooted in, empirical observations of recorded, naturally occurring talk-in-interaction.
- On a third level, we will introduce the range of *social scientific applications* which emerge out of CA research. A criticism that is often levelled against CA, as against other qualitative methods, is that it only deals with the 'small-scale' features of social life, the 'mere details' of interaction, and does not connect in any meaningful way with what are seen as the major questions of the social sciences. Linked with this is the view that CA has no practical relevance in the world beyond scholarly research.

However, as is suggested by the first few sentences of this introduction, one of our aims is precisely to demonstrate the relevance of CA for social science more generally, and to illustrate some of its practical applications.

In line with these aims, the early chapters of the book are designed to focus on the methodology of CA, while later chapters concentrate on the main applications of the conversation analytic method. In chapter 1 we provide an introduction to the intellectual and disciplinary context in which CA came into being, focusing principally on the early development of the field in Harvey Sacks's lectures. Chapter 2 goes on to give an account of the foundational studies in CA, with the aim of introducing some basic analytic concepts and their application. In chapter 3 we begin to introduce the reader to the analytic techniques of CA, by means of a detailed discussion of the key issue of transcription and its close relationship with the analysis of data. Chapters 4 and 5 continue this practical thread by demonstrating a number of analytic techniques used in CA, ranging from the analysis of large collections of data to the detailed study of single cases.

The remaining chapters concentrate on how these analytic techniques and perspectives can be applied to various problems in the social sciences. Chapter 6 discusses the analysis of interaction in institutional or organizational settings. Here we demonstrate the power of CA as a technique for analysing a whole range of forms of talk using a single method. Chapter 7 addresses the issue of how CA can contribute to the analysis of data produced in social scientific interviews. Here we discuss key methodological questions both for standard interview-based social science research and for CA itself in the form of how to analyse extended monologues such as interviewee responses in unstructured interviews. Following on from this, chapter 8 provides a discussion of the relevance of and techniques for analysing accounts of the 'facts' produced in settings ranging from interviews to everyday telephone conversations. Finally, in chapter 9, we provide an introduction to a number of other practical applications of CA, focusing on areas ranging from the persuasiveness of political communication, to the design of interactive computer systems, through to therapy for speech disorders.

PART I

Principles

CHAPTER 1

What is Conversation Analysis?

We begin with a question: 'What is conversation analysis?' In a sense, the book in its entirety represents our answer to that question, because conversation analysis is best defined in terms of what it does, how it enables us to view the social world and to analyse social interaction, and that is what our subsequent chapters focus on. But it is useful to begin with a brief definition, an overview, of what CA is. We start out in this chapter with such a definition, which then leads us into a discussion of the fundamental assumptions informing CA. The most central of these assumptions is that ordinary talk is a highly organized, ordered phenomenon. We trace this claim as it emerged in the early researches of CA's founder, Harvey Sacks. Finally, we discuss the distinctively sociological background to the conversation analytic approach.

A definition of conversation analysis

To put it at its most basic, conversation analysis is the study of talk. More particularly, it is the systematic analysis of the talk produced in everyday situations of human interaction: *talk-in-interaction*. Throughout this book, we will refer to talk-in-interaction, rather than conversation, as the object of study for conversation analysts. The reason for this is simple. Although the field has adopted the name 'conversation analysis', practitioners do not engage solely in the analysis of everyday conversations. As we will demonstrate in later chapters, the range of forms of talk-in-interaction that have been subject to study within CA is far larger than the term 'conversation' alone would imply.

Another way of approaching the definition of CA is to look at what CA *does*. If CA is the study of talk-in-interaction, how do its practitioners go about that study? Perhaps the most distinctive methodological trait of CA, and certainly a policy that underpins all its analytic findings, is that research is based on transcribed tape-recordings of actual interactions. Moreover, what is recorded is 'naturally occurring' interaction; in other words, the activities which are recorded are situated as far as possible in the ordinary unfolding of people's lives, as opposed to being pre-arranged or set up in laboratories. Researchers make extensive use of transcripts of these naturally occurring events, both in generating analyses and in presenting those analyses in published form. The issue of transcription is the subject of chapter 3.

Overall, then, CA is the study of *recorded, naturally occurring talk-in-interaction*. But what is the aim of studying these interactions? Principally it is to discover how participants understand and respond to one another in their turns at talk, with a central focus being on how *sequences* of actions are generated. To put it another way, the objective of CA is to uncover the tacit reasoning procedures and sociolinguistic competencies underlying the production and interpretation of talk in organized sequences of interaction.

In relation to this, there is a further significance in saying that CA is the study not just of talk, but of talk-in-interaction. On one level, talk involves language. In fact, it might be said that talk is the verbal instantiation of language. But CA is only marginally interested in language as such; its actual object of study is the *interactional organization of social activities*. CA is a radical departure from other forms of linguistically oriented analysis in that the production of utterances, and more particularly the sense they obtain, is seen not in terms of the structure of language, but first and foremost as a practical social accomplishment. That is, words used in talk are not studied as semantic units, but as products or objects which are designed and used in terms of the activities being negotiated in the talk: as requests, proposals, accusations, complaints and so on. Moreover, the accomplishment of order, and of sense, or coherence, in talk-in-interaction is seen as inextricably tied to the local circumstances in which utterances are produced.

The upshot of all this is that CA's aim is to focus on the production and interpretation of talk-in-interaction as an orderly

accomplishment that is oriented to by the participants themselves. CA seeks to uncover the organization of talk not from any
exterior, God's eye view, but from the perspective of how the
participants display for one another their understanding of 'what
is going on'. As Schegloff and Sacks put it in an early summary:

> We have proceeded under the assumption (an assumption borne
> out by our research) that in so far as the materials we worked with
> exhibited orderliness, they did so not only to us, indeed not in the
> first place for us, but for the co-participants who had produced
> them. If the materials ... were orderly, they were so because they
> had been methodically produced by members of society for one
> another, and it was a feature of the conversations we treated as
> data that they were produced so as to allow the display by the co-
> participants to each other of their orderliness, and to allow the
> participants to display to one another their analysis, appreciation
> and use of that orderliness. (Schegloff and Sacks 1973: 290)

This is what underlies the focus on sequences: throughout the
course of a conversation or other bout of talk-in-interaction,
speakers display in their sequentially 'next' turns an understanding of what the 'prior' turn was about. That understanding may
turn out to be what the prior speaker intended, or not; whichever
it is, that itself is something which gets displayed in the next turn
in the sequence. We describe this as a *next-turn proof procedure*,
and it is the most basic tool used in CA to ensure that analyses
explicate the orderly properties of talk as oriented-to accomplishments of participants, rather than being based merely on the
assumptions of the analyst.

As an illustration of this, consider the following utterance,
which is from an exchange between a mother and her son about a
forthcoming parent-teachers' association meeting (our discussion
is based on that found in Schegloff 1988a):

(1)   [Terasaki 1976: 45]
    1   Mother: Do you know who's going to that meeting?

Mother's question 'Do you know who's going to that meeting?'
can be interpreted as doing one of two types of action. It could
represent a genuine request for information about who is attending the meeting; or she could be using it as a 'pre-announcement'
(Terasaki 1976), that is, as a preliminary to some information *she*

wishes to announce about who is going. In the first case, the required response would be an answer to the question; whereas in the second case, the response would be something like 'No, who?', which would provide the opportunity for the news to be announced.

Thus, taken in the abstract, Mother's utterance is ambiguous, and on a purely analytical level it would be problematic to assign a meaning to it. However, for CA, the issue is how the *participants* understand, or make sense of, any given utterance. Conversation analysts pay serious respect to the fact that their raw data were not produced in the first place for the purposes of social scientific analysis, or under the aegis of any special research project. Rather, they were produced for the specific people present at the time, whether face to face or on the other end of a telephone line. Therefore what we have to do is look to see how the recipient(s) of such utterances interpreted them.

When we do that, this is what we find:

```
1  Mother:  Do you know who's going to that meeting?
2  Russ:    Who?
3  Mother:  I don't know!
4  Russ:    Oh, probably Mr Murphy and Dad said Mrs
5           Timpte an' some of the teachers.
```

In the next turn, line 2, Russ responds with 'Who?', thereby displaying that his interpretation of Mother's initial utterance is as a pre-announcement. But Mother's next turn, 'I don't know!', displays that Russ's inference was in fact incorrect: she was actually asking an information-seeking question. Notice that following this turn, Russ responds with the information his mother was seeking, thereby displaying even more powerfully that he interpreted line 1 as a pre-announcement, because he in fact knows quite a lot about 'who's going to that meeting'.

The very turn-by-turn unfolding of interaction therefore assists the process of analysis. As Sacks, Schegloff and Jefferson put it:

> while understandings of other turns' talk are displayed to coparticipants, they are available as well to professional analysts who are thereby afforded a proof criterion (and a search procedure) for the analysis of what a turn's talk is occupied with. Since it is the parties' understandings of prior turns' talk that is relevant to their construction of next turns, it is *their* understandings that are

wanted for analysis. The display of those understandings in the talk of subsequent turns affords ... a proof procedure for professional analysis of prior turns – resources intrinsic to the data themselves. (1974: 729)

As such, the next-turn proof procedure will be key to many of our discussions in subsequent chapters.

These, then, are the crucial features of a definition of conversation analysis. In the rest of this chapter, in order to begin unpacking this series of assertions, we move to a discussion of the intellectual origins of CA, and of the fundamental assumptions about talk and its analysis that conversation analysts work with.

Harvey Sacks: order at all points

Conversation analysis emerged in the pioneering researches of Harvey Sacks into the structural organization of everyday language use, carried out at the University of California in the period from 1964 to 1975, when Sacks was killed in a car crash. Although Sacks was the initiator of this research programme, his work quickly began to attract a growing number of adherents in various places; most significantly, during his lifetime, his principal collaborators Emanuel Schegloff and Gail Jefferson.

Sacks originated a radical research programme which was designed to investigate the levels of social order that could be revealed in the everyday practice of talking. The hypothesis with which this programme was begun was that ordinary conversation may be a deeply ordered, structurally organized phenomenon. This question could best be explored, in Sacks's view, by using recorded data of naturally occurring talk, which could thus be observed repeatedly. This would get round a problem endemic to other naturalistic methods used to study interaction, such as participant observation in ethnography, which relies on after-the-event reconstructions of interactional occasions written by the researcher in his or her notebook. Thus, as Sacks put it:

It was not from any large interest in language or from some theoretical formulation of what should be studied that I started with tape-recorded conversations, but simply because I could get my hands on it and I could study it again and again, and also, consequentially, because others could look at what I had studied and make of it what they could, if, for example, they wanted to be able to disagree with me. (Sacks 1984a: 26)

With this in mind, Sacks worked on whatever data became available to him. At first, this was a corpus of telephone calls to a 'suicide prevention centre', to which Sacks had gained access through a research post in the Los Angeles Center for the Scientific Study of Suicide. It was during his observations of these calls that a question occurred to him which turned out to be the starting point for CA.

Sacks had observed that, in the majority of cases, if the person taking the call within the organization started off by giving their name, then the 'suicidal' person who was calling would be likely to give their name in reply. But in one particular call, Sacks noticed that the caller (B) seemed to be having trouble with the name of the answerer:

(2)   **[Sacks 1992, vol. 1: 3]**
      A: This is Mr Smith, may I help you
      B: I can't hear you.
      A: This is Mr <u>Smith</u>
      B: Smith

And, Sacks observed, for the rest of this conversation, the agent taking the call had great difficulty in getting the caller to give a name.

Now, for the personnel of the suicide prevention centre, this unwillingness of some callers to give their names constituted a particular kind of problem: part of the way they worked involved them wanting to establish some kind of personal identity for the caller. Therefore they wanted to know whether anything could be done about this. For Sacks, however, a quite different question began to suggest itself: namely, 'where in the course of the conversation could you tell that somebody would not give their name?' (Sacks 1992, vol. 1: 3). It was this question, and this sequence, that led to Sacks's unique approach to the study of talk. In a later memoir, Schegloff recounts this period:

It was during a long talking walk in the late winter of 1964 that Sacks mentioned to me a 'wild' possibility that had occurred to him. He had previously told me about a recurrent and much discussed practical problem faced by those who answered phone calls to the Suicide Prevention Center by suicidal persons or about them – the problem of getting the callers to give their names ... On the one hand, Sacks noted, it appears that if the name is not forthcoming at the start it may prove problematic to get. On the other hand, overt requests for it may be resisted. Then he remarked: Is it possible that the caller's declared problem in hearing is a methodical way of avoiding giving one's name in response to the other's having done so? *Could talk be organised at that level of detail? And in so designed a manner?* (1992a: xvi–xvii, emphasis added)

Three key points result from this '"wild" possibility'. The first is that utterances may be viewed as objects which speakers use to *accomplish* particular things in their interactions with others. That is, rather than taking an utterance such as 'I can't hear you' at its apparently straightforward face value, we might analyse it to reveal how such an innocuous statement is being strategically employed to achieve a specific task at that point in the conversation: namely, the task of 'avoiding giving one's name'. As Sacks's subsequent analysis shows, by 'not hearing', the caller is able to set up a sequential trajectory in which the agent finds less and less opportunity to establish the caller's name without explicitly asking for it. Thereby the caller is able to begin the conversation by avoiding giving a name without actually refusing to do so.

The second idea is that talk can thus be seen as *methodic*. Sacks takes as his starting point one particular, situated episode of talk and asks: is there a way in which we can see this event as an outcome of the use of methods? As Schegloff remarks in his account of Sacks's early work, the kinds of issues to which Sacks recurrently addresses himself can be couched in terms of how conversational moves are methodic answers to given problems. For instance, describing some of the first set of lectures, given in 1964 (the lectures themselves can be found in Sacks 1992, vol. 1):

How to get someone's name without asking for it (give yours), lecture 1.
How to avoid giving your name without refusing to give it (initiate repair), lecture 1.
How to avoid giving help without refusing to give it (treat the circumstance as a joke), lecture 2. ...

How to get help for suicidalness without requesting it (ask 'how does this organisation work?'), lecture 10.
How to talk in a therapy session without revealing yourself (joke), lecture 12. (Schegloff 1992a: xxvii–xxviii)

It is important to emphasize that Sacks's approach in this was not to establish 'recipes, or rules, or definitions of types of actions' (Schegloff 1992a: xviii). He is *not* saying that 'I can't hear you' always and everywhere represents a way of avoiding giving one's name. Rather, his approach, and the approach which CA generally has adopted, is to view utterances as actions which are situated within specific contexts. Thus the methodic character of talk is always addressed to the details of the interactional and sequential context in which it is produced. In this particular instance, the respective activities being engaged in by the caller and the agent are, broadly speaking, those of seeking help about a feeling of suicidalness and of finding a way of providing that help. As Sacks remarks elsewhere, the agent has good organizational reasons for seeking the caller's name, since the Suicide Prevention Center tries to keep records of all its contacts. But the caller may have equally good social reasons for wanting to avoid giving a name, since by that act, he or she becomes organizationally categorized as a 'potential suicide'. It is in this interactional context that the conversational move of doing 'not hearing', in the sequential context following an agent's announcement of their name, becomes analysable as a method for avoiding giving one's name.

This approach differentiates Sacks's perspective from another well-known perspective on the social uses of language, namely speech act theory. Speech act theory originated in the work of John Austin (1962), who argued that all utterances performed actions, rather than simply describing the world in ways that were either true or false (as had been maintained by philosophers of language such as the logical positivists of the Vienna School). Around the time that Sacks was developing his ideas, John Searle, in a famous paper called 'What is a speech act?' (1965), had applied this approach by taking the act of 'promising' and attempting to define the rules and conditions (the 'felicity conditions') that would make an utterance recognizable as a promise. However, Searle's analysis set out to define the act of promising in a *decontextualized* way: for instance, he began by invoking 'a typical speech situation involving a speaker, a hearer, and an utterance by the speaker' (1965: 221). Also, the rules he described were grounded in intuition rather than in the observation of any empirical examples of talk.

But as we have already seen, Sacks begins with *actual* utterances in actual contexts. This concern with real-world data, and with the situated, contexted nature of talk-in-interaction, characterizes all of Sacks's work and is a core feature of the conversation analytic method. Although, as we will see presently, there is also a concern in CA to establish how conversational devices and sequence types exhibit general features and function in essentially similar ways across varying contexts, that concern differentiates itself from the speech act approach by being consistently and carefully grounded in particularized accounts of naturally occurring data.

The third idea that we referred to is one that is equally key to the distinctiveness of CA as a social scientific method. This is that talk-in-interaction can be treated as an object of analysis in its own right, rather than simply as a window through which we can view other social processes or broader sociological variables. This represents a challenge to conventional sociological thinking which sees talk as essentially trivial, except in so far as it is a tool for finding out about larger-scale social phenomena such as class, gender or deviancy, through responses to interview questions, for example. It also challenges the standard perspective in sociolinguistics, which attempts to show a causal relationship in the ways in which linguistic variables are themselves affected by sociological variables (Labov 1972). As we will show in later chapters, there has grown up a significant 'applied' wing in conversation analysis which focuses on demonstrating the key role of talk in broader institutional processes. But even this applied work takes the essential CA starting point that talk-in-interaction is to be seen as its own social process, governed by its own regularities.

Underlying all this is perhaps Sacks's most original idea; namely, that there is 'order at all points' in talk-in-interaction. Sacks pointed out that, for the most part, theories in the social sciences have been based on a distinction between 'what are in the first instance known to be "big issues", and ... those which are terribly mundane, occasional, local, and the like' (Sacks 1984a: 22), where only the former are considered to be proper subjects for social scientific research. More or less explicit here is the view that:

> The search for good problems by reference to known big issues will have large-scale, massive institutions as the apparatus by which order is generated and by a study of which order will be found. If, on the other hand, we figure or guess or decide that whatever humans do, they are just another animal after all, maybe more complicated than others but perhaps not noticeably so, then *whatever humans do can be examined to discover some way they do it. . . . That is, we may alternatively take it that there is order at all points.* (Sacks 1984a: 22; emphasis added)

The upshot of this is that wherever we choose to direct our analytic gaze at the activities of humans, we will find some orderly phenomena, and we will be able to describe the order which informs the production of those phenomena. After all, a commonsense assumption is that conversation itself is a mundane, local event that is more random than ordered. The findings of conversation analysis represent a persistent challenge to that assumption.

It is important to emphasize that although we are citing here from a 1984 (and therefore posthumous) publication, Harvey Sacks actually made these remarks in 1966 (to be exact, in lecture 33 from spring 1966 – see Sacks 1992, vol. 1: 483–8). At almost exactly the same time, the linguist Noam Chomsky was arguing for the opposite view, which has underpinned most subsequent research in structural linguistics, namely that ordinary talk could not be the object of study for linguistics since it is too disordered; it is an essentially degenerate realization of linguistic competence (Chomsky 1965). While this makes some sense within Chomsky's perspective, which is that linguistic competence mostly consists of tacit knowledge of syntactic structures, it is none the less a prime example of the approach that Sacks was arguing against: that the place where order can be found is decided purely on the basis of prior analytic assumptions.

Sacks (1984a) quotes other examples. For instance, the famous linguistic anthropologist Edward Sapir, in his book *Language* (1921), suggests that language is like a motor powerful enough to drive an elevator but for the most part only driving a doorbell. Sacks cites a comment by Max Weinreich (1963: 147): 'The more pressing task for linguistics, it seems to me, is to explain the elevator, not the doorbell; avoiding examples of excessively casual or ceremonial speech . . .' Once again, there is the assumption that 'we know, right off, where language is deep and interesting, [and] that we can know that without an analysis of what it is that it might be doing' (Sacks 1984a: 24). For CA, the notion of order at all points means that nothing in talk-in-interaction should be dismissed as trivial or uninteresting *before* we have subjected it to analysis.

This brief contextualizing discussion has pointed up the key insights which serve as the methodological basis for conversation analysis. We can summarize these now in the form of the following propositions:

- Talk-in-interaction is systematically organized and deeply ordered.
- The production of talk-in-interaction is methodic.
- The analysis of talk-in-interaction should be based on naturally occurring data.
- Analysis should not initially be constrained by prior theoretical assumptions.

So far we have hinted at some of the intellectual background against which these ideas can be understood, by mentioning perspectives such as speech act theory and sociolinguistics, to which CA offers specific challenges. But in order to appreciate more fully the originality of Sacks's thinking, we need to describe the broader disciplinary matrix out of which CA emerged. In the next section we discuss this in terms of the social sciences more generally, focusing especially on the relevance of sociology. This is because, while its analysis of language use in the form of talk gives CA an obvious relevance for branches of linguistics such as sociolinguistics, discourse analysis, or pragmatics (Levinson 1983), the key questions that CA addresses arise more from a sociological than a linguistic basis. Martin Montgomery has put this point very well. Distinguishing between discourse analysis in linguistics (Brown and Yule 1982) and conversation analysis, Montgomery remarks that the former approach tends to be concerned with 'verbal interaction as a manifestation of the linguistic order', whereas 'conversation analysis is more concerned with verbal interaction as instances of the situated social order' (1986: 51). Accordingly, we now turn to this interest in the situated social order.

The sociological background

Sacks worked in a sociology department, and the significance of
sociology might be seen merely as an outcome of that locational
fact. But Sacks clearly viewed himself as engaging in work which
not only addressed fundamental sociological problems, but also
problems within sociology itself. This is evident from the titles of
some of his earliest publications, such as 'Sociological description' (Sacks 1963), or 'An initial investigation of the usability of
conversational data for doing sociology' (Sacks 1972a).

The kinds of sociological issues which Sacks addressed centred
around a particular conception of the kind of enterprise sociology should be. Principally he was concerned to find a way in
which sociology could become a naturalistic, observational science. As we have already hinted, Sacks did not have much time
for the standard methodologies in either linguistics or sociology.
In linguistics at that time the prevailing procedure was to study
invented examples of language for their formal properties, without paying any attention to how language is actually used in
interaction. And while this may be an acceptable procedure if
one is interested in the structures of syntax (Chomsky 1965),
once one becomes interested in *sequences* of talk then intuition
becomes much less reliable. As Sacks put it:

> It happens to be perfectly reasonable for linguistics and philo-
> sophy to proceed by considering: 'Well, let's take a certain locu-
> tion, a sentence. Would anybody say that? If they said it would we
> figure it was grammatical? or a puzzle? or not?' And pretty much
> reasonably educated people feel comfortable with such a proced-
> ure.... One can invent new sentences and feel comfortable with
> them. One cannot invent new sequences of conversation and feel
> comfortable about them. You may be able to take 'a question and
> an answer', but if we have to extend it very far, then the issue of
> whether somebody would really say that, after, say, the fifth utter-
> ance, is one which we could not confidently argue. One doesn't
> have a strong intuition for sequencing in conversation. (1992, vol.
> 2: 5)

We have already outlined the resulting insistence in CA that the
talk to be analysed should be recorded in naturally occurring settings.

For sociology, Sacks's criticism similarly focused on the question of observability. In one of his earliest lectures, he put forward a powerful argument against the prevailing notion in sociology that the phenomena most worthy of analysis were unobservable – for instance, attitudes, class mobility, or the causes of deviance. This view, which Sacks traced back to the influence of the psychologist G. H. Mead (1934), underlies the use of such standard sociological methods as in-depth interviews and survey questionnaires, the aim of which is precisely to enable the analyst to get at the unobservables which, it is assumed, lie behind people's actions and can only be discerned in the aggregate, usually through the use of some form of statistical analysis.

However, as Sacks noted: 'social activities are observable; you can see them all around you, and you can write them down ... If you think you can see it, that means we can build an observational study, and we can build a natural study' (1992, vol. 1: 28).

As this view suggests, Sacks had a much more positive attitude towards the alternative, ethnographic school of sociology which had its roots in the Chicago School (for instance, Whyte 1943; Park 1952; Becker 1953; Hughes 1970). For these sociologists, the prime concern was a close attention to observational detail in their studies of the everyday lives of social groups such as street corner gangs, hobos and marijuana users. Sacks admired this work, but was still critical of it:

> Instead of pushing aside the older ethnographic work ... I would treat it as the only work worth criticizing in sociology, where criticizing is giving some dignity to something. So, for example, the relevance of the works of the Chicago sociologists is that they contain a lot of information about this-and-that. And this-and-that is what the world is made up of. (1992, vol. 1: 27)

Nevertheless, ethnographic work is problematic for three main reasons, all of which are closely interrelated. First, it tends to rely very heavily on information gained through interviews with certain trusted members of the group or setting being studied. As Sacks put it: 'the trouble with their work is that they're using informants; that is, they're asking questions of their subjects. That means that they're studying the categories that Members use ... they are not investigating the categories by attempting to find them in the activities in which they're employed' (1992, vol. 1: 27).

This brings us to the second point, which is that for Sacks both ethnography and survey research have a close reliance on the commonsense knowledge of members of society, but use that commonsense simply as a resource, whereas it should be turned into a *topic* of study. This is a view which he owed to Harold Garfinkel (1967), about whom we say more below. For Sacks, what we as members know is interesting not so much as a resource but as something which needs to be systematically explicated: 'what I want to do is turn that around: to use what "we" know, what any Member knows, to pose us some problems. What activity is being done, for example' (1992, vol. 1: 487).

Related to these problems is a third, which is that in ethnographic research, the details of actual events are not made available to the reader. What is presented is an account of the practices of a setting's members based on information gleaned by the ethnographer from observations and interviews with informants. Thus the reader has to take it on trust that what the ethnographer says happened, actually happened, and happened in the way reported. Sacks, as we began this section by saying, wanted to make sociology into a *naturalistic, observational* science of social life:

> The difference between [ethnography] and what I'm trying to do is, I'm trying to develop a sociology where the reader has as much information as the author, and can reproduce the analysis. If you ever read a biological paper it will say, for example, 'I used such-and-such which I bought at Joe's drugstore.' And they tell you just what they do, and you can pick it up and see whether it holds. You can re-do the observations. Here, I'm showing my materials and others can analyse them as well, and it's much more concrete than the Chicago stuff tended to be. (1992, vol. 1: 27)

Sacks, then, was basing his critique of existing approaches in some way on a particular conception of how natural sciences such as biology go about producing and reporting their findings. Whether or not this model was an accurate one (see, for example, Lynch and Bogen 1994), it shows once again the radicalism and originality of Sacks's thinking. What Sacks sought to show was that we can deal purely observationally with the natural facts of everyday social life, and analyse them in an interesting, non-intuitive and non-trivial manner.

On a more theoretical level, Sacks's view of sociology was

anchored more fundamentally in two contemporary perspectives with which he had a great deal of affinity. One was Goffman's sustained attempt to establish the deep sociological relevance of the 'interaction order' of face-to-face communication (Goffman 1959; 1983). The other was the field of ethnomethodology, which had developed in Garfinkel's studies of practical reasoning and commonsense knowledge in everyday life (Garfinkel 1967). We will look in slightly more detail at each of these influences.

Goffman and the interaction order

In the 1950s, Erving Goffman developed a form of sociology which focused on the presentation of 'self' in the multifarious situations of everyday life (Goffman 1959). At the core of this work was the *ritual* nature of face-to-face interaction. His argument was that we 'perform' our social selves, managing the ways we appear in everyday situations so as to affect, in either overt or tacit ways, how others orient to us. At the same time, a person's self becomes treated as a 'sacred' object, which is shown by the ways we establish boundaries around our physical bodies and possessions, 'territories of the self' (Goffman 1971) which we expect others to respect. The original-ity in Goffman's thinking came from his view that this domain of everyday interpersonal interaction, which was seen as deeply trivial and arbitrary by mainstream sociology, was a site of social order and should be the subject of structural sociological investi-gation.

The influence of this approach can be traced in Sacks's think-ing, for instance in his concern with how people accomplish many of their communicative actions indirectly, which we touched on earlier in discussing the suicide prevention calls. Indeed, Sacks had been a student of Goffman's, and one of his early papers, 'Notes on police assessment of moral character' (Sacks 1972b), was worked up from a graduate essay written for one of Goff-man's classes. However, although Sacks undoubtedly drew from Goffman in his interest in the orderly properties of face-to-face interaction, his approach was ultimately very different from Goffman's.

In his investigations, Goffman was primarily interested in what he called the 'interaction order' (Goffman 1983). Having begun from a central concern with the strategies of self-presentation which individuals use in the various settings of everyday life, he came in his late work to focus more and more on the central importance of language in everyday social interaction. In particular, his last book, published in 1981, was titled *Forms of Talk*, and as the title suggests Goffman had by that stage become influenced not only by the work of ethnographers of communication (Gumperz and Hymes 1972), but also by the growing field of conversation analysis itself (about which he was critical, though Schegloff (1988b) has argued that many of his criticisms were based on misreadings of the CA literature).

But while this slight shift in focus occurred as Goffman's work developed, his interests remained essentially the same: his main aim was to document the ritual procedures which inform the orderly conduct of everyday life. The upshot of this is that when he studied talk he maintained a strict distinction between its 'system' properties and its 'ritual' properties. System properties had to do with features ensuring basic intelligibility, such as orderly turn-taking, whereas ritual properties had to do with such things as the protection of 'face', the ways in which we tend to avoid giving offence to others, politeness and the many other 'ceremonial' aspects of interaction. For Goffman, these were two theoretically distinct modes of the interaction order.

For Sacks, however, there is no meaningful difference between system and ritual aspects of talk-in-interaction. This is aptly demonstrated by a paper called 'Everyone has to lie' (Sacks 1975) in which Sacks shows that the 'polite' answer to a 'How are you?' inquiry, that is, 'Fine', has as much to do with what Goffman called system requirements as it does with ritual requirements. This is because the question itself sets up a particular sequential trajectory. We do not expect someone to respond to 'How are you' with a literal account of their state of health. Indeed Garfinkel (1967) had shown the power of this expectation by asking his students to purposely break it, treating the inquiries of their unknowing acquaintances literally. Predictably, this rapidly led to problems in the relationship between the 'experimenters' and their unwitting 'subjects' (see our discussion of ethnomethodology below). Thus, if someone wanted to 'tell the truth' about how they were, they would need to indicate that special circumstances were being brought into play. Similarly, to respond with anything other than a neutral 'Fine' or 'Okay', such as 'Terrible' or 'Fantastic', would set up its own sequential trajectory, in which the onus would then be on the original inquirer to invite one to expand on the reasons for this. Thus Sacks's interest in the ritual or ceremonial order differed fundamentally from Goffman's, in that it began from the sequential order of talk-in-interaction itself.

Sacks also went beyond Goffman in terms of methodology. Goffman tended to eschew systematic methods of data collection and analysis in favour of a magpie-like selection from whatever materials he could find that usefully illustrated his theoretical point (be they snippets of overheard conversation, extracts from novels or TV shows, or segments from his own fieldwork in settings such as a Shetland Islands community or a mental asylum). Thus, in his work, data is used largely illustratively and the main thrust of the writing is in the direction of the development of his particular theory of interpersonal interaction.

Sacks could also be eclectic in his use of illustrative data (for instance, he often drew from sources such as the writings of philosophers, Freud or the Old Testament). However, the whole thrust of his argument is that theory ought to be data driven, rather than data being used to support theory. Rather than generating a research idea and then going out to find data which supported it, Sacks maintained that research should begin with a process of 'unmotivated looking':

> people often ask me why I choose the particular data I choose. Is it some problem that I have in mind that caused me to pick this corpus or this segment? And I am insistent that I just happened to have it, it became fascinating, and I spent some time at it. Furthermore, it is not that I attack any piece of data I happen to have according to some problems I bring to it. When we start out with a piece of data, the question of what we are going to end up with, what kind of findings it will give, should not be a consideration. We sit down with a piece of data, make a bunch of observations, and see where they will go. (Sacks 1984a: 27)

Ultimately, then, the similarities between Goffman's and Sacks's approaches to studying the orderliness of everyday interaction are less significant than the differences, both theoretically and methodologically.

Ethnomethodology

Contemporaneously with Goffman, Garfinkel was developing the form of sociology which became known as ethnomethodology (Garfinkel 1967). Ethnomethodology similarly proposes that everyday interaction constitutes a legitimate domain of sociological study, but with a somewhat different emphasis. Garfinkel's work stands in clear opposition to the predominant sociological paradigm of that time, functionalism, especially as associated with Talcott Parsons (1937; see Heritage 1984a). Functionalism was interested in constructing explanations for how societies manifest order and stability over time, and how it is that individuals normally avoid blindly pursuing their own appetites and desires and show the kind of other-awareness that Goffman studied in the form of the ritual order. Its explanation was that we internalize societal norms and values through a process of socialization: negative and positive reinforcement exercised through institutions such as the family and the education system. Having internalized these values, we then unconsciously reproduce them in our actions, thereby ensuring that society carries on in an orderly fashion. Beginning from this model, the main issue for functionalism became the explanation of deviance.

Garfinkel argued, first, that Parsons's focus on the internalization of societal norms and values effectively denied the knowledgeability of ordinary members of society. For Garfinkel, members are capable of rationally understanding and accounting for their own actions in society. Indeed, it is precisely in that rational accountability that members come to be treated, and to see themselves, as 'members of society'. This is quite different from the logic of Parsons's perspective, which treats members as 'cultural dopes', to use Garfinkel's phrase. At the same time, functionalism's principal concern with deviance and transgression simply trades on the commonsense knowledge of members of society: rather than looking at how deviant categories are constructed and used in accountable ways by members, functionalism takes the existence of deviance for granted and seeks to locate its 'causes'. Against this, Garfinkel proposed that members' commonsense knowledge should become a *topic* of study, rather than simply a resource (for a detailed discussion, see Heritage 1984a).

Thus the aim of sociology should not be to understand how norms are internalized, such that people end up either reproducing these norms or deviating from them; but rather to describe the methods that people use for *accounting* for their own actions and those of others. These are the 'ethno-methods' which are the subject of ethnomethodological inquiry.

Sacks had a close association with Garfinkel in the early stages of his career, and the two co-authored an important paper (Garfinkel and Sacks 1970). That paper drew many key parallels between the methods of practical reasoning and sense-making within cultural settings and members' mastery of ordinary language resources as the medium for this sense-making. Indeed, Garfinkel had always recognized the importance of language for ethnomethodological study (see, for instance, the discussion by Heritage (1984a) of the originality of Garfinkel's thinking on this). But a crucial contribution was made by Sacks when he developed a systematic method by which the natural use of language could be studied. In fact, it is true to say that Sacks's approach, in its focus on the analysis of naturally occurring talk-in-interaction, represents the most fruitful means of doing ethnomethodological study.

To expand on this a little, one of the problems that ethnomethodology encounters is that of how to gain analytic access to the level of commonsense knowledge which it seeks to study. Since the accounting practices Garfinkel was interested in were, on his own admission, taken for granted by members, 'seen but unnoticed', it was difficult to think of a method by which they could be revealed. The earliest research consisted of 'breaching' experiments in which the taken-for-granted routines of ordinary life were intentionally disrupted in order to observe how people dealt with their sudden lack of certainty (Garfinkel 1956; 1963; 1967). For instance, Garfinkel would instruct his student 'experimenters' to engage others (called 'subjects') in interaction and then to repeatedly request that the subject clarify whatever he or she said. Thus, on being asked 'How are you?', the experimenter would ignore the routine and expected use of this question as being what Goffman might have called a 'ritual' utterance, and respond instead in the following kind of way:

(3)   **[Garfinkel 1967: 44]**
  S: How are you?
  E: How am I in regard to what? My health, my finances, my
    school work, my peace of mind, my . . .
  S: ((Red in the face and suddenly out of control)) Look! I was just
    trying to be polite. Frankly, I don't give a damn how you are.

Garfinkel's aim in designing these experiments was:

> to start with familiar scenes and ask what can be done to make
> trouble. The operations that one would have to perform in order
> to multiply the senseless features of perceived environments; to
> produce and sustain bewilderment, consternation, and confusion;
> to produce the socially structured effects of anxiety, shame, guilt
> and indignation; and to produce disorganized interaction *should
> tell us something about how the structures of everyday activities are
> ordinarily and routinely produced and maintained.* (Garfinkel
> 1967: 38; emphasis added)

The breaching experiments led to many significant theoretical
insights into the nature of intersubjectivity. Although Garfinkel
designed these experiments (of which we have mentioned only
one example) explicitly in order to undermine participants' sense
of mutual understanding and trust in a shared reality, in fact he
found that it was very difficult to accomplish this. Basically, subjects would find some way of accounting for the 'strange' behaviour of the experimenters. They did this principally by treating
the experimenters as rational agents who had actively *chosen* to
behave in this way, and/or who had some underlying *reason* for
so doing. Thus Garfinkel found that members' accounting practices were so powerful that even when an attempt was made to
destroy what was 'taken-for-granted', persons still found rational
ways of sustaining their belief in those taken-for-granted features
of social reality (for a detailed discussion of this point, see Heritage 1984a: 75–102). This served to confirm Garfinkel's central
proposition that:

> a concern for the nature, production and recognition of reason-
> able, realistic and analysable actions is not the monopoly of
> philosophers and professional sociologists. Members of society are
> concerned as a matter of course and necessarily with these matters
> both as features and for the socially managed production of their
> everyday affairs. (Garfinkel 1967: 75)

However, as Garfinkel himself realized, the possibilities of breaching experiments are essentially limited, since they necessarily only tell us about what participants do in the 'special' situation constructed by the breach: they do not show how mutual understandings are constructed and maintained in the unremarkable course of mundane interaction. At the same time, what are really to be sought in ethnomethodology are not so much the methods used to repair 'breakdowns' in the taken for granted, but the commonsense methods used in the very construction and maintenance of accountable actions in the first place. Other early research attempted this by using conventional ethnographic methods such as participant observation and interviewing (Wieder 1974). However, as we outlined above, the main problem here is that the analysis is based on the researcher's own account, generated in fieldnotes after the event, rather than the natural, situated actions of the participants. Hence the analytic account is not only post hoc, but also a reconstructed version of what actually happened in the setting.

By deciding to focus on recorded conversations, therefore, Sacks managed to avoid these methodological pitfalls. The use of recordings provided a means by which members' sense-making, the establishment and maintenance of mutual understanding in interaction, could be observed both in situ and as it were 'in flight'. This method enabled Sacks to pursue his interest in 'ethno-methods' far more successfully than the alternatives, since the methods by which people understand each other in talk are available to observation in the close details of turn-taking itself, for instance through the next-turn proof procedure.

The reasoning behind these methodological concerns stems from Garfinkel's critique of conventional research methods in sociology, a critique which Sacks shared (see Garfinkel and Sacks 1970). Most of sociology, in Garfinkel and Sacks's view, is *ironic*: that is, it claims that members of society do not 'really' know what's going on around them, even though they may think they do, and that it is up to sociologists to find out how social processes 'actually' operate. In short, sociology ironicizes members' knowledge, seeing people as the puppets of social forces which are beyond their comprehension (though not beyond the understanding of sociologists).

Garfinkel was extremely critical of this prevailing trend in sociology, and his critique extended to the research methods which such a view leads to: principally, survey research and quantitative analysis. For him, the way in which findings are generated by a social survey is not objective but essentially and unavoidably an *interpretive* process in which researchers and coders rely on their ordinary members' knowledge in order to fit each unique questionnaire response into the pre-established categories that will form the matrix for the findings (Garfinkel 1967: 18–24). Of course, survey researchers are aware of the role of interpretation; but they refer to this in terms of problems in validity or reliability of findings, and attempt to establish methodological solutions for these problems. For instance, explicit coding instructions may be drawn up in order to avoid ad hoc interpretations of individual cases. For Garfinkel, however, this is to miss the point, because interpretation and commonsense knowledge are necessary and *unavoidable* aspects of the production of social science. As he observed in a telling remark on coding procedures: 'To treat instructions as though ad hoc features in their use were a nuisance, or to treat their presence as grounds for complaint about the incompleteness of instructions, is very much like complaining that if the walls of a building were only gotten out of the way, one could see better what was keeping the roof up' (1967: 22).

In fact, Garfinkel's critique of such approaches expanded into a critique of all attempts to treat sociology as a science which is capable of producing objective findings about society. With this view, Garfinkel placed himself squarely in the hermeneutic or phenomenological camp of social theory, which from the outset of the discipline has challenged the alternative positivist camp's argument that social research can and should be based on a model of objectivity derived from the natural sciences (for an introduction to this debate, see Cuff and Payne 1984).

Sacks diverged from Garfinkel on this latter point, quite openly admitting that what he was trying to do was to construct a natural observational science of social life. In his earliest publication, Sacks had begun by saying: 'I take it that at least some sociologists seek to make a science of the discipline; this is a concern I share, and it is only from the perspective of such a concern that the ensuing discussion seems appropriate' (1963: 2). And in a later lecture, while discussing a particular fragment of data, he made an explicit statement of a form of 'objectivism' in his research aims:

our aim is ... to get into a position to transform, in what I figure is almost a literal, physical sense, our view of what happened here as some interaction that could be treated as the thing we're studying, to interactions being spewed out by a machinery, the machinery being what we're trying to find; where, in order to find it we've got to get a whole bunch of its products. We can come to know that they can really be thought of as products, and that we can really think of a machine spewing them out.... And this would be another way to be interested in the whole thing as some actual sequence, i.e., as an assembled set of parts that could be otherwise fitted together. (Sacks 1992, vol. 2: 169)

In an important sense, then, Sacks was interested in finding the organization of talk-in-interaction *in its own right*, as a 'machinery' independent of individual speakers, which provides the resources drawn on by speakers in constructing their participation in any given interaction. This essentially structuralist view informs the contemporary research aims of conversation analysis, and its implications for the analysis of data and the discussion of findings will be drawn out in the chapters that follow.

Yet while this perspective appears to pay little attention to participants as subjects, and hence to go against the eth-nomethodological concern with explicating methods of sense-making from the members' perspective, this is not the case. As we outlined earlier, CA shares this concern. The reconciliation of Sacks's vision of talk-in-interaction as the product of a 'machine' and his aim to see the order of conversation as a members' concern is found in his central idea that the structural resources used in conversation are simultaneously *context-sensitive* and *context-free* (Sacks, Schegloff and Jefferson 1974). The resources are context-free in the sense that the techniques any set of conversationalists may use to get some interactional work done are not tied to the local circumstances of that specific occasion. Rather, we find that conversational patterns are enormously recursive: the same kinds of techniques are used by different participants in different circumstances. Yet at the same time, the use of those resources is context-sensitive in the sense that, on each specific occasion, *these* participants in particular are designing their talk in the light of what has happened before in *this* conversation, and possibly also in their relationship as a whole, among other contextual specifics. The aim of conversation analysis, as it has developed out of Sacks's work, is to explicate the structural organization of talk-in-interaction at this interface between context-free resources and their context-sensitive applications.

We began this chapter with a preliminary definition of what conversation analysis is; how it views the world of talk-in-interaction and the particular perspective it takes in the analysis of that activity. That definition was rather densely packed, and in expanding on it we subsequently traced the key features of the intellectual history through which the conversation analytic mentality was shaped. That involved a discussion of the path-breaking work of Harvey Sacks, which we contextualized in relation to prevailing assumptions and methodologies in sociology and, to a lesser extent, linguistics.

It is important to conclude this opening chapter by stressing a number of points that may have been obscured by our focus on the singular achievements of Sacks. The first is that while Sacks was an important founding figure, and was during his lifetime the intellectual core of the developing subdiscipline of CA, by its very nature CA transcends the achievements and ideas of one person. To go back briefly to the case of Goffman, his work on the interaction order is widely recognized to have been ultimately idiosyncratic, the product of his particular cast of mind. It is difficult to imagine how other researchers might carry on the work initiated by Goffman, largely because what he produced is a corpus of individually brilliant studies without developing a recognizable method or initiating a cumulative research programme. Sacks, by contrast, succeeded in doing both these things. Although the inception and, to some extent, the widespread adoption of the conversation analytic perspective owed much to his individually brilliant cast of mind, his way of working resulted in the development of a distinctive method which could be employed by others. Indeed, our primary aim in writing this book is to introduce that method to a still wider audience. At the same time, that method allows the production of a cumulative body of findings, and therefore CA can be accurately described as a research programme, whose aim is to describe the methodic bases of orderly communication in talk-in-interaction.

The final point is that although we have outlined the different relevancies that CA has for the wider disciplines of linguistics and sociology, in fact CA is by its very nature *inter*disciplinary. As Schegloff has remarked, 'If it is not a distinctive discipline of its own (which it may well turn out to be), CA is at a point where linguistics and sociology (and several other disciplines, anthropology and psychology among them) meet' (1991: 46). From linguistics CA takes the view that language is a structured system for the production of meaning. But in line with certain subfields of linguistics such as pragmatics, CA views language primarily as a vehicle for communicative interaction. And, in line with recent developments in sociology (Knorr-Cetina and Cicourel 1981; Giddens 1984; Thompson 1984), CA sees both communication and interaction as inherently social processes, deeply involved in the production and maintenance of social institutions of all kinds, from everyday intersubjectivity, to the family, to the nation-state. As the chapters of this book proceed, those interdisciplinary relevancies and relationships will become clearer as they inform our discussions of methodological and applied aspects of CA.

CHAPTER 2

Foundations of Conversation Analysis

At the heart of CA is a concern with the nature of turn-taking in talk-in-interaction: how is it organized, how do participants accomplish orderly (or even apparently disorderly) turn-taking, and what are the systematic resources which are used in this accomplishment? We will refer to this as a concern with the *sequential order* of talk. It is intuitively evident that conversation, and other forms of talk-in-interaction, centrally involve people taking turns at talking. But a key notion in CA is that those turns are not just serially ordered (that is, coming one after the other); they are *sequentially* ordered, which is to say that there are describable ways in which turns are linked together into definite sequences. One aim of CA therefore is to reveal this sequential order.

Conversation analysts treat the transitions between turns during talk-in-interaction as revealing two kinds of things. First of all, the 'next turn' is the place where speakers display their understanding of the prior turn's possible completion. That is, it displays the results of an analysis that the next speaker has performed on the type of utterance the prior speaker has produced. Recall our discussion in the previous chapter about the importance of the next-turn proof procedure as a means of gaining an analytic foothold in the order of talk from the participants' perspective. Another aspect of this is that the relationship between turns reveals how the participants themselves actively analyse the ongoing production of talk in order to negotiate their own, situated participation in it. Moreover, a second important dimension revealed in speakers' next turns is their analysis and understanding of the prior turn's *content* – in other words, the action it has been designed to do.

For this reason, CA has an equally important intere͟
we will call the *inferential order* of talk: the kinds of cultura͟
interpretive resources participants rely on in order to understan͟
one another in appropriate ways. It is here that the continuing
influence of ethnomethodology, with its emphasis on methods of
practical reasoning about social affairs, can still be located. (This
area is of central concern in chapters 7 and 8.) In short, CA is not
only concerned with how turn-taking is accomplished, but also
with what participants take it they are actually doing in their talk.

The interplay between these two concerns – the sequential
order of talk-in-interaction and its normative and inferential
properties – runs throughout conversation analytic research, and
our aim in this chapter is to illustrate that through a discussion of
key analytic concepts and findings. We will focus on three areas
that are of general relevance: the rules of turn-taking; the management of overlapping talk; and the organization of conversational repair. We begin, however, with a preliminary discussion
of the interplay between sequential and inferential concerns in
the case of one particular type of conversational sequence: the
'adjacency pair'.

Conversational sequences: adjacency pairs and 'preference'

One of the most noticeable things about conversation is that certain classes of utterances conventionally come in pairs. For
instance, questions and answers; greetings and return greetings;
or invitations and acceptances/declinations. The properties of
these 'paired action sequences' interested Sacks throughout his
career. In the earliest lectures Sacks was beginning to examine
the ways in which what he called 'tying rules' operate to link
paired actions together. In the later lectures, especially those for
spring 1972 (Sacks 1992, vol. 2: 521–70), Sacks developed an
extraordinarily detailed formal account of what, by that stage, he
was calling adjacency pairs. Basically, these are pairs of utterances which are *ordered*, that is, there is a recognizable difference between first parts and second parts of the pair; and in
which given first pair parts require particular second parts (or a
particular range of seconds). In other words, an invitation is the
first part of the 'invitation–response' adjacency pair, and we

recognize that invitations should be followed by a specific range of responses: mainly acceptances or declinations. Invitations should not be followed by greetings, for instance.

These sequences are called adjacency pairs because, ideally, the two parts should be produced next to each other. The basic rule for adjacency pairs was formulated in this way in an early publication by Schegloff and Sacks: 'given the recognisable production of a first pair part, on its first possible completion its speaker should stop and a next speaker should start and produce a second pair part from the pair type the first is recognisably a member of' (1973: 295). We return in the next section to the specific uses of terms like 'rule' and 'first possible completion' in CA. For the present, it is important to note that this is of course merely an ideal characterization. The parts of adjacency pairs do not need to be strictly adjacent at all. There are systematic insertions that can legitimately come between first and second pair parts. The point, however, is that some classes of utterances are conventionally paired such that, on the production of a first pair part, the second part becomes *relevant* and remains so even if it is not produced in the next serial turn. This brings in the key point that there is a difference between the serial nature of talk-in-interaction and its sequential properties. The next turn in an adjacency pair *sequence* is a relevant second pair part. But that need not be the next turn in the *series* of turns making up some particular conversation.

For instance, the following is a simple example of an insertion sequence:

(1)   **[Levinson 1983: 304]**
    1 A: Can I have a bottle of Mich?   **Q1**
    2 B: Are you over twenty-one?   Ins 1
    3 A: No.   Ins 2
    4 B: No.   **A1**

Line 1 represents the first part of a question–answer adjacency pair. When it is complete, the speaker stops, and the next speaker starts in line 2. However, what B produces is not the second part of the pair but the first part of another pair: a question–answer pair produced as an insertion sequence. The reason it is an insertion is because the question in line 2 does not ignore or propose not to answer the question in line 1. Rather, it serves to defer the answer until further relevant information (in this case, whether speaker A is old enough to buy beer) has been obtained. As we see, speaker A orients to that deferral by answering the inserted question in line 3, rather than, for example, asking his initial question again or complaining that it has not been answered. Once the insertion sequence is completed, B shows that he is still orienting to the relevance of the original adjacency pair by moving on in line 4 to provide the relevant second part.

This example illustrates a further aspect of paired action sequences. Note that we referred to the participants 'orienting to' the relevance of adjacency pairs and insertion sequences. What this means is that they display to one another their understandings of what each utterance is aiming to accomplish. Thus the adjacency pair concept is not simply to do with the bare fact that some utterances come in pairs. Rather, adjacency pairs have a fundamental significance for one of the most basic issues in CA: the question of how mutual understanding is accomplished and displayed in talk. As Schegloff and Sacks put it:

> What two utterances, produced by different speakers, can do that one utterance cannot do is: by an adjacently positioned second, a speaker can show that he understood what a prior aimed at, and that he is willing to go along with that. Also, by virtue of the occurrence of an adjacently produced second, the doer of a first can see that what he intended was indeed understood, and that it was or was not accepted. Also, of course, a second can assert his failure to understand, or disagreement, and inspection of a second by a first can allow the first speaker to see that while the second thought he understood, indeed he misunderstood. (1973: 296)

Participants, then, can use the adjacency pair mechanism to display to one another, and hence to the analyst also, their ongoing understanding and sense-making of one another's talk.

These observations throw up a complex set of issues around how conversation analysts approach the nature of turn-taking, intersubjectivity and the importance of repair and correction in the management of talk-in-interaction. In later sections of this chapter we discuss these issues at greater length. For the present, however, we will proceed to say some further things about adjacency pairs themselves and other kinds of inferential work that can be involved in their production.

It is important to emphasize that the adjacency pair concept is not intended to capture some empirical generalization, such as that in 85 per cent of cases first parts are followed by second parts (Heritage 1984a: 246–7). Rather, what is to be stressed is the *normative* character of adjacency pairs. That is to say, whatever utterance follows a first pair part will be monitored by the first speaker for whether, and how, it works as a relevant second part. Inferences can be drawn about the non-appearance of a second pair part: for instance, not returning a greeting may lead to the inference that the first greeter is being snubbed.

Thus, for sequences such as adjacency pairs, the robustness of the sequence can often be seen precisely in those cases where what is normatively expected to occur does not (for instance, a question does not get an answer). This is described under the heading of *conditional relevance* (Schegloff 1968). What this means is that given the initial condition of a first pair part being uttered, the second part of that pair is then relevant; consequently, the absence of such a second part is a 'noticeable absence', and the speaker of the first part may infer a reason for that absence.

An example of noticeable absence in a question–answer sequence is the following:

```
(2)   [TW:M:38]
      1     Child:    Have to cut these Mummy. (1.3) Won't we
      2               Mummy.
      3               (1.5)
      4→    Child:    Won't we.
      5     Mother:   Yes.
```

The child asks the mother to confirm her observation that they will 'Have to cut these', then, getting no response in the 1.5-second pause in line 3, makes an issue out of that absence of an answer by repeating the question (line 4). After this repeat try, the mother answers.

Another example comes from an attempted greeting sequence:

```
(3)   [IH:FN]
      (Two colleagues pass in the corridor)
      1     A:    ⟦Hello.
      2     B:    ⟦((almost inaudible)) Hi
      3           (Pause: B continues walking)
      4→    A:    ((shouts)) HEllo!
```

A initiates a greeting in line 1; however, it turns out that B also produces a first greeting at exactly the same time (the simultaneity is represented by the double square brackets: see chapter 3 for a detailed discussion of transcription conventions). It seems that B's simultaneous, but almost inaudible, greeting was not heard by A. After a pause, A makes quite a big issue out of what she perceives as an absence by shouting her second attempt to initiate greetings.

Adjacency pairs thus constitute a powerful normative framework for the assessment of interlocutors' actions and motives by producers of first parts. This shows that talk-in-interaction is not just a matter of taking turns but is a matter of accomplishing *actions*. Within this framework, failure (or perceived failure) to take a turn in the appropriate place can itself be interpreted as accomplishing some type of action. As Sacks (1992) remarked, one reason why talk-in-interaction is such a good place for observing members' methods of sense-making is because it systematically requires hearers to attend to what speakers are saying, and to come to and display some understanding of it. As we show below, close monitoring is needed to identify when an appropriate juncture to take a turn occurs; by the same token, failure to take a turn when one is 'required' to can be treated as an accountable action.

'Preference'

Another inferential aspect of adjacency pair sequences stems from the fact that certain first pair parts make alternative actions relevant in second position. Examples include offers, which can be accepted or refused; assessments, which can be agreed with or disagreed with; and requests, which can be granted or declined. Research has shown that these alternatives are non-equivalent. In other words, acceptances, agreements or grantings are produced in systematically different ways than their negative alternatives. These design differences are described in terms of a 'preference' organization. The format for agreements is labelled the 'preferred' action turn shape and the disagreement format is called the 'dispreferred' action turn shape (Pomerantz 1984a: 64).

The concept of preference as it is used in CA is not intended to refer to the psychological motives of individuals, but rather to

structural features of the design of turns associated with particular activities, by which participants can draw conventionalized
inferences about the kinds of action a turn is performing. One
thing Sacks (1987) observed is that initial actions can be designed
to invite a particular kind of response. For instance, the phrase
'isn't it?' might be appended to an assessment, thereby inviting
the recipient's agreement. In such cases, as in the following two
extracts, the default response gets produced straight away (without any gap) and without any mitigation:

(4) **[JS:II:28]**
```
1     Jo:    T's- it's a beautiful day out isn't it?
2→    Lee:   Yeh it's just gorgeous.
```

(5) **[VIYMC:1:2]**
```
1     Pat:   It's a really clear lake isn't it?
2→    Les:   It's wonderful.
```

By contrast, turns that in some way depart from what seems to
be expected incorporate a variety of 'dispreference markers'
(Pomerantz 1984a). One of the most significant ways speakers
have of indicating the dispreferred status of a turn is by starting
the turn with markers such as 'Well' or 'Um':

(6) **[Sacks 1987]**
```
1     A:    You coming down early?
2→    B:    Well, I got a lot of things to do before getting
3           cleared up tomorrow. I w- probably won't be too
4           early.
```

As Sacks (1987) observes, A's first turn here appears to 'prefer' a
'Yes' answer. Note, for instance, that the opposite expectation
would be conveyed by 'You're not coming down early are you?'
However, B evidently does not want to go along with the
assumption implicit in A's turn. He constructs his response so
that it exhibits two principal features of dispreferred turn shapes.
First, the response is 'formed up so that the disagreement is as
weak as possible' (Sacks 1987: 58). Notice in particular line 3,
where 'I w-', which looks like a start on 'I won't be too early', is
changed so that it takes the weaker form 'probably won't be too
early'. Secondly, the actual disagreement is not produced early in
the turn, like the agreements in extracts (4) and (5), but is held
off until B has not only produced a 'Well', but also has presented
an *account* for why he won't be early (lines 2–3).

Thus preferred actions are characteristically performed straightforwardly and without delay, while dispreferred actions are delayed, qualified and accounted for. As we mentioned above, the concept refers to these structural features of turn design and not to individual motivations or psychological dispositions. The reasoning behind this is not to claim that such motivations play no part in adjacency pairs such as invitations and acceptances/declinations. Rather, it is to emphasize that the alternative designs of second pair parts represent institutionalized ways of speaking by which specific actions get accomplished. After all, we know that it is perfectly possible to decline an invitation in the 'polite' manner, using a dispreferred turn format, even though we privately have no intention ever of accepting an invitation from that person.

Schegloff describes two complementary ways in which the concept of preference is used in CA, and indicates some of the relevancies of the concept in a broader sense. One approach is represented by the work of Sacks, outlined above, and focuses on how first parts can be designed to prefer certain seconds. In this approach, preference has to do with the structure of sequences, in the sense that:

> Whether a question [for instance] prefers a 'yes' or a 'no' response is a matter of its speaker's construction of it ... the preference is built into the sequence, and is not a matter of the respondent's construction of the response. If the question is built to prefer 'yes', then 'no' is a dispreferred response, even if delivered without delay and in turn-initial position, and vice versa. (Schegloff 1988c: 453)

By contrast, in much of the work by Pomerantz (1984a), the issue is thought of in terms of how *second* parts are designed. Thus:

> Speakers display the kind of action they are doing, and the kind of stance they take toward what they are doing, by their deployment of [dispreferred turn-shapes] ... They do the response they do 'as a preferred' or 'as a dispreferred', rather than doing 'the preferred or dispreferred response'. (Schegloff 1988c: 453)

These two approaches are complementary in the sense that they both tell us something about the inferential properties of sequences. For instance, speakers may design first parts in particular ways in order to get certain social actions done. 'You coming down early?' versus 'You're not coming early, are you?' is an example in which the speaker can constrain the inferences that the recipient may make as to his or her actual (vernacular) preference. Similarly, certain kinds of first parts conventionally 'prefer' different second parts in different contexts. An example Schegloff provides is that of offers. We might assert that, as actions, offers prefer acceptances and disprefer refusals. But 'some offers may well prefer declines, or prefer them at first; initial offers of second helpings of dessert, for instance' (Schegloff 1988c: 454).

Yet at the same time, 'in determining what the preference structure of some sequence type is, one resource is surely the practices of responding which are observably employed by recipients of its first part' (ibid.). And, of course, speakers of second parts can use the dispreference markers strategically as a way of 'getting out' of some undesired situation. This is especially so in the light of research by Davidson (1984) which has shown that dispreferred turn shapes can be used by a first speaker as a basis for revising the question, invitation or whatever prior to the actual disagreement being spoken.

Preference is thus a powerful inferential device in talk-in-interaction. Its presence can also tell us something about the structure of social relationships. For instance, it seems that a general 'preference for agreement' operates in everyday interaction. That is, speakers use the preferred turn format to do agreements, acceptances and the like, while disagreements take the dispreferred turn shape. There is thus a sense in which preference structures play an important role in the maintenance of social solidarity. This is even so in the one major exception to this rule: responses to self-deprecations (Pomerantz 1978). Here, actually agreeing with the prior turn would be tantamount to endorsing the speaker's self-criticism. Thus self-deprecations prefer disagreement; correspondingly, a speaker who wishes to agree with the self-deprecation tends to do so using a dispreferred turn format. From a slightly different angle, researchers looking at argument and conflict in interaction have illustrated that, in arguments, ordinary preference structures are removed (Goodwin 1990) or even reversed: that is, disagreements take preferred forms while agreements are produced as dispreferred (Kotthoff 1993).

These points on adjacency pairs and preference introduce us to the sequential and inferential properties of talk seen from a conversation analytic perspective. In the following sections we continue to explore the basic findings of CA along these lines, beginning with a general account of the core issue of turn-taking.

The organization of turn-taking

In 1974, Sacks, Schegloff and Jefferson published 'A simplest systematics for the organisation of turn-taking for conversation' (1974). This paper has become a foundational study in conversation analysis. In it, the authors outline a model for describing how speakers manage turn-taking in mundane conversation. It is important to note the phrase 'mundane conversation' here, because for CA the word 'mundane' does not refer in its colloquial sense to any notion that conversation is a lower, less serious or less consequential form of talk-in-interaction than any other. The term is used in a technical sense to describe a particular form of talk in which what people say, how they say it and the length of the turn in which they say it – in other words, turn *form*, turn *content* and turn *length* – are free to vary. The paper also outlines a method for distinguishing analytically between different forms of talk-in-interaction, of which everyday casual conversations are only one sort; also to be included are more formalized or ceremonial forms ranging from loosely structured interviews between doctors and their patients, to high ceremonies such as weddings. In chapter 6, we address the ways in which, in these other forms of talk, broadly described as 'institutional', various constraints can be observed on one or more of the three parameters of turn form, turn content and turn length.

The turn-taking model begins from the idea that turns in conversation are resources which, like goods in an economy, are distributed in systematic ways among speakers. The authors note three very basic facts about conversation: (1) turn-taking occurs; (2) one speaker tends to talk at a time; and (3) turns are taken with as little gap or overlap between them as possible. Obviously, this is not to say that there is never more than one speaker talking at a time, or that gaps and overlaps do not occur. Rather, the point is that the ideal is for as much interspeaker coordination as possible. But that is not just an abstract ideal. In empirical materials we find that, overwhelmingly, speaker change occurs with minimal gap and overlap, indicating that participants themselves orient to the ideal for coordination. More recent research has raised the possibility that in interactions involving more than two participants, or where the participants are in very close or longstanding relationships, this ideal may be relaxed, leading to a much greater degree of gap and especially overlap (for instance, Coates 1995). However, the increased occurrence of these phenomena in particular conversations does not mean that Sacks, Schegloff and Jefferson's account is weakened or invalidated. Indeed, as we show below, when the details of overlapping talk are examined closely enough, participants can still be found to be orienting to the basic practices of turn-taking that the model outlines.

The turn-taking model has two components: a 'turn construction' component and a 'turn distribution' component. Turns at talk can be seen as constructed out of units (called turn-construction units), which broadly correspond to linguistic categories such as sentences, clauses, single words (for instance, 'Hey!' or 'What?') or phrases. It is important to realize that it is not part of the conversation analyst's aim to define, in some abstract way, what a turn-construction unit is, as a linguist for instance may want to define what a sentence is. Conversation analysts cannot take a prescriptive stance on this question, because what a turn-construction unit consists of in any situated stretch of talk is a *members'* problem. That is, such a unit is essentially anything out of which a legitimate turn has recognizably – for the participants – been built.

This suggests two key features of turn-construction units. First, they have the property of 'projectability'. That is, it is possible for participants to project, in the course of a turn-construction unit, what sort of unit it is and at what point it is likely to end. This leads to the second feature, which is that turn-construction units bring into play 'transition-relevance places' at their boundaries. In other words, at the end of each unit there is the possibility for legitimate transition between speakers. These two properties can be illustrated with the following extract:

(7)   [SBL:1:1:10:15]
      1 Rose: Why don't you come and see me some⌈times
      2 Bea: ⌊I would
      3   like to
      4 Rose: I would like you to

The second speaker here is able to recognize Rose's utterance, 'Why don't you come and see me sometimes', as a form of invitation, and to respond to it with an acceptance before it has actually finished (line 2). This is indicated in the transcript by the large square bracket which shows that Bea's turn 'I would like to' overlaps Rose's talk in the middle of 'sometimes'.

One point to note is that although Bea's projection of the first turn's transition-relevance place – that is, after 'sometimes' – turns out to be accurate (as shown in Rose's following turn, 'I would like you to'), the turn could have taken a different shape. For instance, Rose could have been about to say 'Why don't you come and see me *sometime this week*', which would have made the invitation much more specific, and Bea may then have had to give a different response. By starting to talk when she does, therefore, Bea not only projects the end of a particular turn-construction unit, but also displays an understanding of what kind of invitation that unit represents. Recall, on this point, our remarks in the previous chapter about the next-turn proof procedure as a means of gaining analytic access to participants' understandings of each other's talk.

But what would have happened if Rose *had* been about to append something further, such as 'this week', to her invitation? This leads us to the second part of the turn-taking model: the mechanism for distributing turns between participants. Sacks, Schegloff and Jefferson (1974) propose a simple set of rules which describe how turns come to be allocated at transition-relevance places. There are two main rules, with the first one being subdivided into three. At the initial transition-relevance place of a turn:

Rule 1 (a) If the current speaker has identified, or selected, a particular next speaker, then that speaker should take a turn at that place.
(b) If no such selection has been made, then any next speaker may (but need not) self-select at that point. If self-selection occurs, then first speaker has the right to the turn.
(c) If no next speaker has been selected, then alternatively the current speaker may, but need not, continue talking with another turn-constructional unit, unless another speaker has self-selected, in which case that speaker gains the right to the turn.

Rule 2   Whichever option has operated, then rules 1a–c come into play
          again for the next transition-relevance place.

This set of rules is simple, but deceptively so, since it is able to
account for the vast range of turn-taking practices in conversations involving any number of participants, in any set of relationships, speaking in whatever context and with whatever topics in
play. In a series of early papers, conversation analysts explored
the robustness as well as the interactional implications of this
rule set (Jefferson 1973; Schegloff and Sacks 1973; Schegloff, Jefferson and Sacks 1977; Schegloff 1982; see also Schegloff 1992b).
The main point that these papers sought to demonstrate was that
the rule set operates as an *oriented-to* set of normative practices
which members use to accomplish orderly turn-taking.

The fact that it is oriented to, and thus normative, is crucial
here. It is not being proposed that these rules are in some sense
external to any concrete occasion of talk, or that they furnish
law-like constraints on participants. Rather, the rules are
intended as descriptions of the practices which participants display an orientation to in actual, local occasions of turn-taking.
Although they are different from the more prescriptive rules of
grammar, as with those rules it is not necessary for speakers to
'know' these rules in any discursive sense. It is more accurate to
say that they are instantiated and therefore reproduced on each
concrete occasion of talk-in-interaction.

In this sense, perhaps the word 'rules' is misleading. This is discussed by Schegloff (1992b), and also in two papers by Button
(1990; Button and Sharrock 1995). Schegloff is responding to an
article by Searle which had criticized CA on the basis that the
rules described in Sacks, Schegloff and Jefferson (1974) could not
be rules at all since they are not causal: 'The rule for turn-taking
... doesn't even have the appearance of being a rule since it
doesn't specify the relevant sort of intentional content that plays
a causal role in the production of the behaviour' (Searle 1986:
18). In other words, the rules merely describe observed regularities, and do not provide for what is *constitutive* of the production
of conversation. Schegloff accepts that the word 'rule' may be
problematic, and instead says: 'I am willing to adopt for now an
alternate term, such as "practice" or "usage".' But he goes on to
insist: 'There is still an interrelated set of these, whatever we call
them; they are still followable, followed, practiced, employed –

oriented to by the participants, and not merely, as [Searle] sug-gest[s], "extensionally equivalent descriptions of behaviour"'
(1992b: 120).

Button also argues that Searle's interpretation misconstrues
the nature of the turn-taking rule set, because those rules are not
in the first place intended to be causal. Rather:

> They are rules that *in their conduct people display an orientation
> to*. That is, the relevance of the rules for a person's conduct is dis-
> played and preserved *in* their conduct.... [T]he rule-set which is
> posited in [Sacks, Schegloff and Jefferson 1974] does not lie
> behind the actions of constructing a turn, allocating a turn, and
> coordinating speaker transfer and thereby causing those things to
> happen. We do not *get* a turn *because* of the rules. Rather, the way
> in which a turn is taken displays an orientation to the rule. A rule
> is followed as part of accomplishing the action. The sense of rule
> here is, then, part of the logical grammar of the action. There is
> not an internalised rule that causes the action. The rule does not
> *precede* the action. Rather, the rule is discoverable *in* the action.
> (Button 1990: 79; original emphasis)

This is an essentially ethnomethodological conception of rules.
As Button points out, Garfinkel had once stated that:

> A leading policy [of ethnomethodology] is to refuse serious con-
> sideration to the prevailing proposal that ... rational properties of
> practical activities be assessed, recognized, categorized, described
> by using a rule or a standard obtained *outside the actual settings
> within which such properties are recognized, used, produced and
> talked about by settings' members*. (Garfinkel 1967: 3; emphasis
> added)

The aim, in other words, is not to develop a prescriptive set of
rules which are supposed to lie behind action, but to describe and
analyse the situated practices of rule use in actual contexts of
interaction.

There are a number of types of evidence which demonstrate
that participants actively orient to the rule set described by
Sacks, Schegloff and Jefferson (1974), and we will come to these
presently. First, let us return to our hypothetical question about
extract (7): what if Rose had not actually been about to finish her
turn at the point when Bea projected its completion? Would
Bea's turn then have been a 'violation' of the rules?

On one level, it should be clear that the answer is no. Bea projected a transition-relevance place at the end of what was a *possibly* complete turn-construction unit by Rose: the question 'Why don't you come and see me sometimes?' As we have said, neither the rule set nor CA itself goes about prescribing and predicting what turn-construction units can legitimately consist of. This is an issue for the participants in conversation, not the conversation analyst. So Bea acted entirely within the rules – or, to be more accurate, her behaviour shows her orienting to the rules: in particular, rule 1b as outlined above.

Even if her projection of a transition-relevance place had turned out to be inaccurate, that would not matter in terms of the rules for turn-taking, since as Schegloff (1992b) points out, participants orient to *possible* transition-relevance places, not to 'actual' ones. There are good organizational reasons for this. As we have said, the ideal in conversation is for one speaker to talk at a time with as little gap and overlap as possible between turns. This means that speakers need to coordinate their bid for a turn as closely as possible with the completion of a current speaker's turn-construction unit. If they were to wait for the speaker to actually stop speaking, that would mean they might lose the opportunity of a turn to someone else, or else the current speaker might carry on with another unit. For this reason it is the *possibility* of completion, rather than its actual occurrence, that is the most relevant factor in managing turn-taking. If this were not the case, as Schegloff remarks, then we would expect to see gaps of silence between turns as next speakers made sure that the current speaker had actually finished. This is not what we tend to find in empirical materials.

However, on another level, there is in fact no answer, in the abstract, to the question of whether Bea's turn would have been considered a violation of turn-taking rules, because this would be an issue that was worked out by the participants themselves, on that occasion of talk. In other words, it would have been up to Rose, as the continuing speaker, to indicate to Bea that her turn was in some way 'interruptive' of Rose's unfinished talk. Of course, this kind of thing frequently happens, as illustrated by the following extract, which is taken from a discussion on a talk radio show about the problem of dog excrement on pavements:

(8)   [H:2.2.89:4:1–2]

```
1  Host:     Well did you- did you then explain that, you
2            understood that, you know dogs have the call of
3            nature just as er as people do, and they don't
4            have the same kind of control and so
5            the┌refore, s- so
6  Caller:       └No, but dogs can be tr┌ained
7  Host:                                 └I haven't finished,
8            so therefore the owner ... being there has the
9            responsibility ...
```

In line 7, the host treats the caller's utterance as an interruption, by saying 'I haven't finished', and then carrying on with his point about dog owners being responsible. Thus he treats her as having violated turn-taking rules by not orienting to the completion of his turn.

It may be, though, that the caller does orient to a possible completion point in the host's turn: for instance, after 'dogs have the call of nature just as er as people do, and they don't have the same kind of control', at which point she comes in with her argument: 'No, but dogs can be trained'. However, there turns out to be some warrant for the host's treating this turn as violative, since before the caller actually starts talking he has begun on a next turn-construction unit: 'and so therefore ...' (lines 4–5). So what we find in this extract is both speakers orienting to different aspects of the rule set. The caller orients to rule 1b, that at a (possible) transition-relevance place a next speaker may self-select; while the host orients to 1c, that at a (possible) transition-relevance place the current speaker may continue talking, unless another has self-selected. Here, although the caller has self-selected, the host treats himself as the first starter on the next unit, and hence as having rights to the turn.

Clearly, then, the issue of how the rules operate in actual instances of talk-in-interaction is down to the participants. It is in this sense that our preceding comments about the rules being oriented to by members is to be understood. In fact, a great deal of work on apparent violations of the rule set demonstrates how those apparent violations are actually robust illustrations of how closely members do orient to the rules. We will discuss two areas of this work: overlap and repair.

Orienting to turn-taking rules: overlapping talk

On the face of it, overlapping talk may be considered evidence of an incoming speaker's failure to take notice of whether the current speaker has or has not finished. However, conversation analysts (in particular, Jefferson 1983; 1986) have shown that most instances of overlap occur in the environment of possible transition-relevance places. While it may seem that overlapping talk is disorderly, Jefferson's work has emphasized that both the onset and the termination of overlap are indeed extremely orderly. In fact, the occurrence of overlap is one prime way in which we can observe participants orienting to the rules of turn-taking that Sacks, Schegloff and Jefferson outlined.

Consider the following extract, which comes from the beginning of a telephone conversation.

```
(9)    [NB:II:2:1–2]
              ((Ring))
     1  N:   Hello:,
     2  E:   .hh HI::.
     3       (.)
     4  N:   Oh: hi:::='ow a:re you Edna:,
     5  E:   FI:NE yer LINE'S BEEN BUSY.
     6  N:   Yea:h (.) my u-fuhh! h- .hhhh my fa:ther's wife
     7       ca:lled me,h .hhh So when she ca:lls me::, h I
     8       always talk fer a lo:ng ti:me cuz she c'n afford it
     9       en I ca:n't.hhh hhhh  huh
    10  E:                    ↑OH: ::: : my go:sh=Ah ↑th ought=
    11  N:                  ((falsetto))    ↑AOO:::::hh!
    12  E:   =my phone wuz outta order:
    13       (0.2)
    14  N:   n :No::?
    15  E:    I called my sister en I get this busy en then I'd
    16       hang up en I'd lift it up again id be: busy.
    17       (0.9)
    18  E:   .hh How you doin'.
    19  N:   .t hhh Pretty good I gutta rai:se.h .hh hh
    20  E:                                        Goo:u d.
    21  N:                                            Yeh
    22       two dollars a week.h
    23       (.)
    24  E:   Oh wo:w.
```

There are a number of overlaps here; they are indicated using the standard convention of a left-hand square bracket (for other conventions used here see the transcription glossary, pp. vi–vii above, and chapter 3). We can describe each of them as orderly and as displaying the participants' orientation to possible transition-relevance places as the points where they may start a turn. For instance, in line 10, what Edna's extended 'OH:::::' overlaps is a quiet laugh, 'hhh hhhh huh', which Nancy fits on to the end of her turn: 'So when she ca:lls me::, h I always talk fer a lo:ng ti:me cuz she c'n afford it en I ca:n't'. Thus 'OH' starts at a legitimate transition-relevance place, even though that start-up results in overlap. Another example is at line 21. Here, what Nancy's talk overlaps is the last phoneme of a recognizable turn-construction unit, 'Goo:ud', which Edna has produced in response to Nancy's announcement 'I gutta rai:se'.

Other instances appear more complex, but can still be accounted for as orderly. In line 11, what we have transcribed as 'AOO:::::hh!' by Nancy is in fact a high-pitched laugh, which seems to be produced in overlap with – but *before* the recognizable completion of – Edna's remark that she thought her phone was out of order (since she had tried numerous times to get through and failed). However, looking more closely at the sequential context, we find that Nancy begins to laugh at a possible transition-relevance place. In the prior turn, Nancy had made a joke about talking on the phone for a long time when her father's wife calls, 'cuz she c'n afford it en I ca:n't'. She then begins quietly to laugh (indicated by the rows of h's). Edna's turn is begun with a loud and high-pitched 'OH::::: my go:sh', to which Nancy almost immediately responds with her similarly high-pitched 'AOO:::::hh!' It is quite possible that Nancy at this point treats Edna as responding to her joke, and starts to laugh by reference to 'OH::::: my gosh' as a recognizable, and potentially complete, joke response.

Now it turns out, as we see, that Edna carries on with her turn: 'OH::::: my go:sh=Ah thought my phone wuz outta order:'. Yet the overlap caused by Nancy can be seen as the product of her orienting to the first possible completion point in that turn. In this way, even apparently 'disorderly' talk can be seen as the product of participants' orientations to the rule set.

In a large-scale study of overlap in conversation, Jefferson (1983; see also 1986) found that enormous amounts of overlapping talk could be accounted for in this sort of way. She identified three major categories of overlap onset: (1) transitional onset (when a next speaker orients to a possible transition-relevance place); (2) recognitional onset (when the next speaker recognizes what current speaker is saying and can project its completion, even if that is before the end of a turn-construction unit); and (3) progressional onset (when there is some disfluency in the current turn and a next speaker suggests a completion in order to move the conversation forward). These categories can be used to account for the orderly production of overlapping talk, even when it is apparently interruptive.

For instance, to return to extract (8):

```
1  Host:     Well did you- did you then explain that, you
2            understood that, you know dogs have the call of
3            nature just as er as people do, and they don't
4            have the same kind of control and so
5            therefore, s- so
6  Caller:        No, but dogs can be trained
7  Host:                               I haven't finished,
8            so therefore the owner ... being there has the
9            responsibility ...
```

The caller's overlapping turn in line 6 can be described as an instance of the first category, transitional onset. As we remarked earlier, although the host *treats* this as an interruption, it is equally possible that the caller has identified and oriented to a possible completion point, a transition-relevance place, in the current turn. Jefferson comments as follows about transitional overlap onset:

> at the point of overlap onset the recipient/now-starting next speaker is doing something perfectly proper, perfectly within his rights and obligations as a recipient/next speaker. He is not doing what we commonly understand to be 'interrupting' – roughly, starting up 'in the midst of' another's turn at talk, not letting the other finish. On the other hand, the current speaker is also doing something perfectly proper. He is producing a single turn at talk which happens to have multiple components in it. (1983: 6)

Our extract shows something further: namely that while transitional onset may be a perfectly orderly place for overlap to occur, it may also systematically be open to being treated as 'interruptive' by the current speaker. We return to the issue of interruption as part of our discussion in chapter 4. For now, the point is that overlapping and apparently interruptive talk, far from being a violation of the rules for turn-taking, actually displays how closely participants orient to the rules; indeed, it can be an outcome of such close orientation.

Repair

Related to this discussion of overlap is the broader area of 'repair'. This is a generic term which is used in CA to cover a wide range of phenomena, from seeming errors in turn-taking such as those involved in much overlapping talk, to any of the forms of what we commonly would call 'correction' – that is, substantive faults in the contents of what someone has said. The term repair is used in the first sense because one way of seeing what is going on is in terms of a 'repair of the turn-taking system'. In the second sense, the term repair is used in preference to alternatives such as correction, because as Schegloff, Jefferson and Sacks (1977) point out, not all conversational repair actually involves any factual error on the speaker's part. We return to this point below.

The area of repair has generated a large amount of work in CA (Jefferson 1972; 1987; Schegloff 1979a; 1987a; 1992c; Schegloff, Jefferson and Sacks 1977). As with overlap, one of the thrusts of this work has been to show how repair illustrates participants' orientations to the basic turn-taking rules. There are two main ways in which this is done. First, as Sacks, Schegloff and Jefferson noted, the turn-taking system itself incorporates its own means of repairing faults. That is, in cases of overlapping talk there is a violation of the 'one speaker at a time' ideal. But this is repaired by a practice that is itself 'a transformation of a central feature of the turn-taking system' (1974: 724): namely, one speaker tends to stop speaking before the completion of a first turn-construction unit. Following are some examples of this.

```
(10)  [SBL:2:2:3:38]
      1     Zoe:    an' he sorta scares me
      2     Amy:    Have you seen 'im?
      3     Zoe:    .hhh We:ll I- I've met 'im,
      4→    Amy:    .hhhhh Well uh actually:⎡when she's-
      5→    Zoe:                            ⎣An' the way the:y
      6             pla:y. Oh:-
      7             (.)
      8     Amy:    Serious huh?
      9     Zoe:    .h Yah,
```

(11) [TRIO:2:III:1]

```
 1      Marjorie:  We:ll? She doesn't kno:w. ((laughs))
 3      Loretta:   Ohh my Go:d,
 4→     Marjorie:  hhhhh Well it ⌈was an-
 5→     Loretta:              ⌊Are you watching Daktari:?
 6                 (0.2)
 7      Marjorie:  nNo:,
 8                 (.)
 9      Loretta:   Oh my go:sh Officer Henry is (.) uh locked in
10                 the ca:ge wi- (0.3) with a lion.
```

(12) [SBL:2:2:3:42–3]

```
 1      Amy:   So: uh, she said don't worry about i:t
 2             an:d so an' I jus' thought .hh the nex' ti::me
 4→            uh that ⌈I have-
 5→     Zoe:         ⌊No:w uh see Pat anno:ys my Frank. hh
 6             (0.3)
 7      Amy:   Ye:ah.
 8             (0.2)
 9      Zoe:   Uh he:'s told me that.
```

In each of these three extracts, as seems generally to be the
case, the current speaker abandons their turn very shortly after
the onset of overlap (line 4 in each of the extracts). In the first
two cases, there are different aspects of the turn-taking system
that are being oriented to by these speakers as they drop out. In
extract (10), Zoe and Amy are talking about a couple they know
who play recreational bridge in a particularly aggressive manner.
Zoe's turn in line 5 seems to be a continuation of her previous
utterance (line 3), marked here by the use of 'and': that is, 'I've
met 'im ... An' the way the:y pla:y ...' In between these components, Amy has taken the opportunity to start a turn of her own
(line 4), which she abandons two words into the overlap, without
having come to the end of a recognizable turn-construction unit.

Extract (11) is taken from a return telephone call in which the
caller, Marjorie, is calling back to report on a conversation she
has just had with a mutual acquaintance. Apparently, as she
answers the phone, Loretta is watching *Daktari* (a popular sixties
show) on TV. So while Marjorie takes Loretta's 'Ohh my Go:d'
(line 2) to be a response to her own initial announcement that
the third party 'doesn't kno:w', and continues to talk by reference to that, in fact this is Loretta's reaction to something that is
happening in the TV show ('Officer Henry is (.) uh locked in
the ca:ge wi- (0.3) with a lion' – lines 9–10). Again, although the
two speakers' talk here is disjunctive, Marjorie repairs that

disjunction by abandoning her turn two words into the overlap (line 4), giving the floor to Loretta.

Extract (12), however, seems to be much more clearly 'interruptive'. Taken from later in the same call as extract (10), here Amy and Zoe are talking about another couple they play bridge with. At the point Zoe overlaps Amy with her remark that 'Pat anno:ys my Frank' (line 5), it is not at all clear what Amy is going on to say about 'the nex' ti::me uh that I have . . .' So this is not a case of recognitional or transitional overlap, to go back to Jefferson's (1983) categories. Neither has there been any immediately prior disjunction in the speakers' topics, as in extract (11); nor is Zoe's utterance a continuation of a previous turn, as in (10). Rather, what it seems she is doing is 'interrupting' in order to empathize with Amy's complaints about 'Pat', who, as she says, also annoys her husband Frank. (On the different types of interruption, see Goldberg 1990.)

One form of repair, then, is a procedural type in which participants orient to various aspects of their ongoing talk in order to manage turn-taking problems. The point Sacks, Schegloff and Jefferson (1974) stress is that in their management of these problems, participants display their continuing orientation to the turn-taking rule set.

The organization of repair

In Schegloff, Jefferson and Sacks's seminal paper (1977) they describe a broader organization of repair in conversation, and in this section we move on to that issue. Before we begin, however, it is important to return to a point mentioned earlier.

There is a wide variety of problems in conversation: incorrect word selection, slips of the tongue, mis-hearings, misunderstandings and so on. However, the analytic strategy adopted by Schegloff, Jefferson and Sacks (1977) was to identify and describe the general properties of an organization for repair which allows participants to deal with the whole *range* of trouble sources. It is for this reason that the term 'repair' is preferred to, say, 'correction', or any other term that refers to a specific kind of trouble source. Moreover, terms such as 'correction' suggest that people only need to engage in repair when something has clearly gone wrong;

however, there are instances of repair even when there is no error or mistake in the conversation: for example, in the following extract a speaker executes repair on a word which is not actually incorrect. (This extract comes from a corpus of calls to the British Airways Flight Information service; see chapter 9 for discussion of the research project for which this corpus was collected.)

(13)   **[BA data 59 T3:SB:F:M]**
```
 1   C:   w-wu-what does that mean in
 2        layme(h)n's te(h)rms ⌈huhh
 3   A:                        ⌊oHh sorry um
 4        that's fiftee-(H)hh fourteen forty five
 5        is quarter to three.
```

In response to an enquiry about the arrival time of a flight, the British Airways agent (A) has replied using the twenty-four hour clock. The caller (C) then seeks a clarification of the arrival time with the utterance 'what does that mean in layme(h)n's te(h)rms'. But before he produces this request, there are two incomplete attempts to say a word beginning with 'w' and 'wu-'. From the initial sounds it is not possible to make out what the word was intended to be; but the subsequent production of the word 'what', beginning with the same 'wh' sound as the aborted items, suggests that here the speaker has simply had three attempts at producing the same word. In which case, we see an instance of repair on an item which does not seem to be in any way incorrect. (Indeed, this may be an instance of incrementally organized self-repair: Schegloff (1979a) notes that efforts to produce a word tend to culminate in a successful third attempt.)

Furthermore, even a repair which involves the replacement of one word or phrase by another may not reflect an error. Rather, the substitution of a lexical item by another may be informed by the speaker's orientation to the specific recipient of a turn (Sacks and Schegloff 1979), or may be produced with respect to specific inferential tasks (Sacks 1979). That is, repair operations may be motivated by interactional and interpersonal considerations.

Repair may also be related to sequential aspects of conversation. Schegloff (1979a) notes that utterances that initiate new topics seem particularly vulnerable to repair. Moreover, the repair tends to occur at the word that introduces the new topic.

(14) [From Schegloff 1979a: 270]
```
1     B:   That's too bad
2     A:   hhhh!
3          (0.5)
4→    B:   (I 'unno) .hh Hey do you see V- (0.3) fat ol' Vivian
5          anymore?
```

Here B's 'That's too bad' stands as a closing remark on a current topic. As the conversation moves to a new topic, A's relationship with Vivian, there is an instance of self-repair on the first attempt to produce the name 'Vivian'.

Repair types

The repair system described by Schegloff, Jefferson and Sacks (1977) is a resource which may be invoked to address a wide variety of conversational events, as well as providing methods by which to identify errors and execute corrections. It embodies a distinction between the initiation of repair (marking something as a source of trouble), and the actual repair itself. There is also the distinction between repair initiated by self (the speaker who produced the trouble source), and repair initiated by other. Consequently, there are four varieties of repair:

- *Self-initiated self-repair* Repair is both initiated and carried out by the speaker of the trouble source.
- *Other-initiated self-repair* Repair is carried out by the speaker of the trouble source but initiated by the recipient.
- *Self-initiated other-repair* The speaker of a trouble source may try and get the recipient to repair the trouble – for instance if a name is proving troublesome to remember.
- *Other-initiated other-repair* The recipient of a trouble-source turn both initiates and carries out the repair. This is closest to what is conventionally understood as 'correction'.

Let us briefly illustrate each of these types by reference to empirical data. First, self-initiated self-repair.

(15) [Heritage I:II:1]
```
1     I:   Is it flu: you've got?
2→    N:   No I don't think- I refuse to have all the:se things
```

Here speaker N starts to produce an answer to the question ('No
I don't think-') and then terminates that in mid-production in
order instead to assert 'I refuse to have all the:se things'. Extract
(16), from the British Airways corpus, provides an example of
self-initiated self-repair on an incorrect word selection (C's cut-
off 'ga(t)-').

(16) **[BA data 5 T1:SA:F:F]**
    1   A: er heathrow or gatwi⌈:ck,
    2→ C: ⌊oh sorry er: from ga(t)-
    3   er heathrow.

Extract (17) is an example of other-initiated self-repair.

(17) **[GTS:5:3]**
    1   Ken: Is Al here today?
    2   Dan: Yeah.
    3   (2.0)
    4→ Roger: he is? hh eh heh
    5   Dan: Well he was.

Roger's turn 'he is? hh eh heh' is an example of what is called a
next-turn repair initiator (NTRI). Other NTRIs may be words
like 'what?' or 'huh?', or even non-verbal gestures, such as a
quizzical look. NTRIs perform several tasks in interaction. Consider the following extracts, in which NTRIs take the form of
partial repeats of the prior turn.

(18) **[GTS:III42(r)ST]**
    1   A: Hey (.) the first ti:me they stopped me from selling
    2   cigarettes was this morning.
    3   (1.0)
    4→ B: From selling cigarettes?
    5   A: Or buying cigarettes.

(19) **[GTS:II:2:54]**
    1   K: 'E likes that waider over there,
    2→ A: Wait-er?
    3   K: Waitress, sorry,
    4   A: 'Ats bedder,

In both cases, it transpires that the first speaker has made a 'slip
of the tongue'. However, the co-participants do not simply prof-
fer the correct word. Nor do they explicitly announce that a mistake has been made. They provide a partial repeat of the prior

turn and thereby recycle the trouble source. On an inspection of this turn the first speaker can infer that there was a problem connected to their earlier utterance, and the partial repeat of the earlier turn identifies for them the precise source of the trouble. Furthermore, as a trouble source has been identified but not repaired, speakers can analyse the NTRI as establishing the relevance of self-repair (see the next section on the 'preference for self-repair').

Extract (20) illustrates self-initiated other-repair. The first speaker's reference to his trouble remembering someone's name initiates the second speaker's repair.

```
(20)  [BC:Green:88]
      1  B:   He had dis uh Mistuh W-m whatever k- I can't
      2       think of his first name, Watts on, the one that
      3       wrote ⌈that piece
      4  A:          ⌊Dan Watts.
```

Finally , we may consider other-initiated other-repair. In both the following extracts there is an explicit correction which is then acknowledged and accepted in the subsequent turn.

```
(21)  [GJ:FN]
      1  Milly:  and then they said something about Kruschev has
      2          leukemia so I thought oh it's all a big put on.
      3→ Jean:   Breshnev.
      4  Milly:  Breshnev has leukemia. So I don't know what to
      5          think.
```

```
(22)  [BA data 36 T2:SA:F:M]
      1  C:   erm I'm just checking is that (.)
      2       right you know (0.5) I d- I don't know
      3       his flight number and ⌈I'm not sure
      4  A:                          ⌊(whi-)
      5  C:   whether he's coming in to channel four
      6       eh:
      7       (.)
      8→ A:   terminal four
      9  C:   yeah
```

Other-initiated other-repair typically assigns the trouble source expressly to the prior turn. Moreover, it is a repair type which simultaneously locates and resolves the trouble, in the form of an explicit correction. It is thus a repair type which attends more overtly to speaker 'error' than the other-initiated self-repairs in extracts (18) and (19).

Repair positions

In this section we will describe the sequential positioning of repair in relation to the trouble source or repairable item. The first two places where repair can occur are within, or immediately after, the turn-construction unit containing the trouble source. These are both described as 'first position' repairs.

(23)   **[BA data 2 T1:SA:F:F]**
    1   A: .h >Well< >yu've< actually wro(t)- rung the wrong
    2   number

In this extract the trouble source is an incorrect word which is abandoned mid-way through its production and replaced with the correct item ('wro' to 'rung').

   The second place in which repair can be done occurs immediately at the next transition-relevance place after the trouble source. In the following extract the trouble source is 'another address', and this is repaired with 'another telephone number' precisely at the next available transition space after the turn-construction unit containing the error.

(24)   **[Heritage I:Call 6:1]**
    1   Mrs. H: Uh:m I: wanted to know if it were at all
    2   possible to make an appointment,h .hh uh:::
    3   with Mister Andrews.=
    4   E: =.t Oh dear uh::m .hhh yes ih-it's his father
    5   talki:ng?
    6   Mrs. H: Ah ha:h?=
    7   E: =Uh::m:, (.) .t in fact he now has his clinic
    8→   at another addr:ess.=Another, another telephone
    9   number I'm sorry:,

   Second position repair can also be initiated and executed in the turn following the turn containing the trouble source: that is, in a next speaker's subsequent turn.

(25)   **[Heritage:II:I:call 3:1]**
    1   S: Mister Samson's house? c'n ⌈I help you?⌉
    2   I: ⌊H e l l o:⌋
    3   I: Mister Samson?
    4→ S: It's not M'st Samson it's his assist'n can I help you.

The final repair space we will discuss occurs in what is called third position – that is, the speaker's turn *after* the recipient's response (Schegloff 1992c). This can be represented schematically as:

1st position: trouble source
2nd position: NTRI
3rd position: repair

(It is important to note that this is not necessarily third *turn* repair: that is, third position repair can occur, for example, after an insertion sequence, but still be directed to the turn prior to that sequence.) The following extract illustrates a third position repair occurring in the third turn.

```
(26)  [Heritage:II:I:call 3:1]
      1  I:   n:No. She wouldn'go: the fu:ll ti:me with        1st Pos
      2       one: puppy would she
      3       (1.2)
      4  S:   Wh'tchu me:an by tha:t.                          2nd Pos
      5  I:   Well you see she's a wee:k early:.               3rd Pos
      6  S:                             Oh I see:
```

Schegloff (1992c) has argued that the majority of troubles are identified and dealt with within these structural repair positions. However, there are some problems which require a 'fourth position' repair. He cites the following case as an instance.

```
(27)  [Schegloff 1992c: 1321]
      1  M:   Loes, do you have a calendar,                   1st Pos
      2  L:   Yeah ((reaches for her desk calendar))          2nd Pos
      3  M:   Do you have one that hangs on the wall?         3rd Pos
      4  L:   Oh you want one.                                4th Pos
      5  M:   Yeah
```

In this case the utterance 'Loes, do you have a calendar,' is the trouble source because of its ambiguity: it could be interpreted as a request for a calendar to keep, or a request to see a calendar to check some specific information. The recipient makes the latter interpretation, displayed by her movement towards a desk calendar. M's subsequent third position utterance 'Do you have one that hangs on the wall?' establishes that he wants a calendar to keep. The trouble source is acknowledged and resolved in the fourth position.

It is noticeable that all of the positions in which repair tends to occur are in close proximity to the trouble source. One reason for this has to do with structural requirements: a system that required speakers to 'backtrack' or recall a trouble source from several turns before would be prone to immense organizational problems. Moreover, trouble sources which are not addressed close to their occurrence can quickly lead to significant problems in an exchange. Schegloff (1992c) provides an example of a call to a talk radio show in which the host and caller fail to identify and deal with a misunderstanding about what each is referring to. Without realizing, they both continue to talk about different events. The resulting confusion soon leads to disagreement, which then escalates to hostility, and Schegloff observes that by the end of the call both parties are practically shouting at each other. In this sense, one important function of the repair system as we have outlined it here is the maintenance of mutual orientation to common topics and fields of reference in talk-in-interaction. Thus Schegloff argues that the organization of repair is closely bound up with the question of interpersonal alignment, or intersubjectivity, in social life.

The preference for self-repair

In this section we will consider evidence which indicates that the repair system exhibits a preference for self-repair over other-repair. It is important to remember that when conversation analysts refer to 'preference' or 'preferred' turns they are not invoking an individual's inclinations or positive attitudes towards a course of behaviour or a way of speaking. As we discussed earlier, 'preference' is used to mark systematic variations in the ways that alternative types of turns are produced.

The evidence for a preference for self-repair is twofold. First, the structural features of the repair system are 'skewed' in favour of self-repair. For example, consider the four structural locations in which the vast majority of repairs are executed: within the same turn-construction unit; at the next possible turn transition place; in the other speaker's next turn; and in the turn which is sequentially (rather than serially) third from the turn containing the trouble source. The first two opportunities to execute repair occur in the turn of the speaker who produced the original trouble source. Indeed, three out of four repair locations are in the trouble producer's turns.

The second source of evidence comes from analysis of inter-action during repair sequences. There are various ways in which turns are designed to facilitate self-repair, or display the speaker's sensitivity to the appropriateness of self-repair and the (possible) impropriety of other-repair.

Consider the following extract from a call to the British Air-ways flight information service. The agent is providing a caller with a telephone number.

(28) **[T1:SA:F:M]**
```
1  A:  the time for you, ⌈.h
2  C                     ⌊yes
3  A:  i:s: oh one seven five night
4      (.)
5  A  ⌈⌈seven  five  ni:ne,⌉          ((Smiley voice))
6  C: ⌊⌊seven five what. (.)⌋ yes
7  A:  one eight one eight,
8  C:  one eight one eight
```

Here the British Airways agent makes a clear error, saying 'night' instead of 'nine' (line 3). The error is recognized by both parties. The agent begins to repeat the last three digits of the telephone number, and does so in a 'smiley' voice which displays her realiza-tion of the mistake, and also its humorous dimension. At the same time, the caller begins to repeat the same last three numbers, and they both progress towards the repairable item in overlap. How-ever, whereas the agent produces the correct last number, 'nine', the caller instead ends with the word 'what', thereby initiating the relevance of repair and identifying the trouble source as the word produced after the numbers 'seven' and 'five'. Thus the caller dis-plays that he recognizes a problem but produces a turn designed to initiate the agent's self-repair, which is produced in overlap with the agent's actual self-repair of the trouble source.

But what happens when an attempt to initiate self-repair fails and the other party has to produce an explicit correction? In the following extract, the caller incorrectly articulates the silent 'x' in Bordeaux. In the subsequent turn the agent produces and emphasizes the correct pronunciation. However, although this mistake is corrected by the agent, it is observable that the repair is not executed immediately after the production of the error.

(29) [T3:SB:F:M]
(The transcription has been modified to highlight the relevant differences
in the pronunciation of the word 'Bordeaux'.)
1 A: flight information can help yo⌈u:?
2 C: ⌊yes could you
3   give me an ETA please on BA
4   three six five from bordecks?
5   (0.4)
6 A: three six five from bordoh? (.) yeah

In this case, the caller displays no recognition that he has mis-
pronounced a word, and the agent has to execute the repair by
providing the correct pronunciation. Explicit other-repair in this
manner can be a sensitive issue: to correct another person is to
draw attention to and topicalize an error or 'lapse in performance'
on their part. This could be interpreted as a slight, a 'put-down' or
might even be cited as evidence of deliberate rudeness, which in
turn may undermine the harmony or accord of the exchange.
Other-repair, then, has potential implications for the coordination
of the interpersonal relations of the relevant parties.

It is noticeable, however, that the agent's correction is not produced bluntly, but mitigated in two ways that are similar to the dispreference markers we discussed earlier in the context of
adjacency pairs. First, the agent pauses after the production of the
trouble source (line 5). In this pause, she may be giving the caller
the opportunity to recognize his mistake and to execute self-repair.
This displays the agent's orientation to the preference for self-
repair over other-repair. Secondly, the repair turn is constructed in
the form of a repeat of the flight details transformed by the use of
upward intonation into a question-seeking clarification from the
caller. This acts to modulate or soften the caller's mistake, thereby
minimizing the chance that the corrected party might feel that they
have been made to look foolish or ignorant (see Jefferson 1987).

There are various further ways in which other-repairs are produced to scale down the extent of the error and preserve interpersonal harmony between the parties. For example, small jokes
may accompany other-repair; alternatively, utterances such as 'I
think you mean ...' may be employed as uncertainty markers,
thereby downplaying the scale or force of the correction:

(30) [JS:II:219–20]
1   Ben: Lissena pigeons
2   Ellen: ⌈Coo-coo:::coo:::
3→   Bill: ⌊Quail, I think

In the following extract the caller has requested information about a flight but has used an identification number which is unfamiliar to the BA agent, who then spends fifteen seconds checking her computer database to try to locate the relevant flight. When she corrects the caller's error she does not do so explicitly, but uses 'I think you might mean' to characterize her proffered alternative as a candidate correct flight number:

(31) [T1:SB:F:M]

```
  1    A:   YEs: hello there
  2    C:                  (ah)hhhh good (0.3) er: the BA
  3         five eight four from Turin. love.
  4    A:   five eight fou:r hold on please?
  5         (15)
  6         er we don't have five eight four sir
  7→        I think you might mean the five seven nine
```

We could discuss many other aspects of repair and how it is organized and used in the course of talk-in-interaction. However, our aim has not been to provide an exhaustive review: rather, we have sought to outline the way in which repair procedures are implicated in the management of turn-taking, and how they impinge on the shape and subsequent trajectory of utterances (for further discussion, see Schegloff 1979a). Neither have we done more than sketch the extent to which interpersonal alignment may be an outcome of repair work (for further discussion on this, see especially Schegloff 1992c). The emphasis of this chapter has been on providing a general flavour of the kinds of findings which the conversation analytic method enables us to make about the structures of repair and other aspects of talk-in-interaction. However, this book is not intended to be merely an account of the collected findings of previous work, but is primarily an introduction to, and illustration of, the craft of empirical research. With this in mind, it is now time to turn away from the description of existing studies to some of the more practical aspects of data transcription and analysis.

PART II

Practices

CHAPTER 3

Data and Transcription Techniques

Conversation analysis places a great deal of emphasis on the use of extracts from transcriptions of tape-recorded, naturally occurring interactions in its research. This chapter is designed to be both a theoretical and a practical introduction to the style of transcription employed in CA. The focus is on the practice or craft of transcription as well as on the methodological and theoretical bases of the transcription system. This is because, as we emphasize, not only the analytic use, but also the actual practice of transcription is a fundamental part of doing CA.

The transcription of data is a procedure at the core of analysis, in two important respects. First, transcription is a necessary initial step in making possible the analysis of recorded interaction in the way that CA requires. Secondly, the practice of transcription and production of a transcript represents a distinctive stage in the process of data analysis itself.

It is important to stress that, for CA, transcripts are *not* thought of as 'the data'. The data consist of tape recordings of naturally occurring interactions. These may be audio or video tapes – although clearly, when the people who are being recorded have visual access to one another an audio-only tape will necessarily miss out what could be very salient features involved in the management of interaction, such as gaze direction (Goodwin 1981) and hand gestures (Schegloff 1984). In the early years of CA (and still to a large extent today), researchers tended to restrict their attention to recordings of telephone conversations, precisely because this allowed them to focus purely on the organization of talk in the absence of such factors (Hopper 1992). Since then, video recordings have been more widely used, but CA's explicit focus on the organization of *talk*-in-interaction means that gesture, body movement and facial expression are not studied in their own right, as may be the case in the field of inter-actional kinesics (Kendon 1990), but rather in exploring the rela-tionships between speech and body movement. However, it is possible, within CA, to analyse audio-only recordings even when the participants have visual access to one another. For instance, Marjorie Goodwin's (1990) detailed study of the management of disputes among children at play on the street offers a compelling analysis of the role of talk in the social organization of the chil-dren's groups using as its data only an audio record supple-mented by ethnographic fieldnotes.

Given this conception of the data, the aim in CA is not simply to transcribe the talk and then discard the tape in favour of the transcript. As Hopper (1989a) observes, the latter is often the practice in social psychology where only the transcripts are analysed in terms of the categories of action which interest the researcher. Conversation analysts, by contrast, do not analyse transcripts alone: rather, they aim to analyse the data (the recorded interaction) using the transcript as a convenient tool of reference. The transcript is seen as a 'representation' of the data; while the tape itself is viewed as a 'reproduction' of a determi-nate social event.

Of course, the tape is only one form of reproduction; and whether it is an audiotape or a videotape, it does not reproduce everything that went on in the vicinity of the recording device during the time it was switched on. (Indeed, we find it difficult to conceive of any way in which such an abstract 'everything' could possibly be recorded.) But conversation analysts take a pragmatic view on this issue. As Sacks once put it, describing why he initially became interested in working with tape-recorded conversations:

> Such materials had a single virtue, that I could replay them. I could transcribe them somewhat and study them extendedly – however long it might take. The tape-recorded materials consti-tuted a 'good enough' record of what had happened. Other things, to be sure, happened, but at least what was on the tape had hap-pened. (Sacks 1984a: 26)

Wherever possible, then, the transcript is used in conjunction with the tape during analysis. As both Hopper (1989a) and Psathas and Anderson (1990) point out in their descriptions of CA transcription procedures, *repeated listening* to the original recording is central to the CA technique. This allows the analyst to gain an intimate acquaintance with the recording at the necessary level of detail. For this reason, and because analysis is not performed on the transcript alone, it is not standard practice in CA to have transcription done by secretaries or professional transcribers. Rather, transcription is done by the analyst. Transcription thereby becomes an integral part of analysis, since in repeatedly listening to the tape one begins to hear and to focus on phenomena that may subsequently form part of an analytic account.

The process of transcribing a data tape is not simply one of writing down the words that people exchanged. Rather, it is a process of writing down in as close detail as possible such features of the recorded interaction as the precise beginning and end points of turns, the duration of pauses, audible sounds which are not words (such as breathiness and laughter), or which are 'ambiguous' vocalizations, and marking the stresses, extensions and truncations that are found in individual words and syllables. Because CA is concerned with how people manage and accomplish the sequential order of talk-in-interaction, transcription is, first of all, an attempt to capture talk as it actually occurs, in all its apparent messiness. As a result, CA transcripts can often appear formidably complex to the untrained eye.

It is possible, however, to learn relatively quickly how to read transcripts of conversation. This is because CA has developed a distinctive style of transcription, involving a comprehensive range of standardized conventions, unlike many other approaches which use recorded talk as their data (see Hopper 1989a; Ochs 1979). This system, developed principally by Gail Jefferson, is in general use by conversation analysts working in many different countries on widely varying forms of recorded interaction. One of the aims of this chapter is to provide the resources by which it is possible to become familiar with conversation analytic transcription conventions.

Approaching transcription: some preliminary issues

Clearly, there are innumerable phenomena in any given stretch of talk which could be transcribed to varying levels of detail. No transcription system exists which is able, or even lays claim to being able, to capture all the possible features of talk that may be observable. As Kendon puts it: 'It is a mistake to think that there can be a truly neutral transcription system, which, if only we had it, we could then use to produce transcriptions suitable for any kind of investigation ... Transcriptions, thus, embody hypotheses' (1982: 478). Similarly, Ochs describes transcription as 'a selective process reflecting theoretical goals and definitions' (1979: 44). This is no less true of CA transcriptions. A CA transcript embodies in its format and in the phenomena it marks out the analytic concerns which conversation analysts bring to the data. These concerns are of two types:

- *Dynamics of turn-taking* On this level, transcripts seek to capture the details of the beginnings and endings of turns taken in talk-in-interaction, including precise details of overlap, gaps and pauses, and audible breathing.
- *Characteristics of speech delivery* Here, transcripts mark noticeable features of stress, enunciation, intonation and pitch.

At the most basic level, the central concern with turn-taking is embodied in the very layout of CA transcripts, in which talk is represented in the form of utterances following one another down the page. Conversation analysts are also concerned to transcribe as precisely as possible all of the sounds that are uttered by participants, whether or not these are conventionally recognizable words. This is because CA assumes that any sound may have interactional import and communicative meaning. Hence there are conventions for transcribing such things as audible breathing, because an audible in-breath is often a signal that its producer is about to speak, and so that sound can be consequential for the management of turn transition.

Two particular aspects of speech delivery that are of great importance for doing conversation analytic work are: (1) when spoken syllables are *stretched*; and (2) basic features of *intonation*. Both aspects can be closely related to issues of turn-taking. For instance, stretching a sound at the possible boundary of a turn, or possible transition-relevance place, can be a way of 'holding the floor' or preventing another speaker from starting a turn at that point. And different intonation contours used at the boundaries of turn-construction units such as clauses can indicate whether the speaker may be intending to continue, or, if the intonation is markedly falling, possibly coming to the end of a full turn.

The way these characteristics of speech delivery are marked tends to be relatively gross when compared, say, to transcripts produced by professional phoneticians who have their own sets of technical symbols for representing such phenomena. Indeed, phoneticians such as Kelly and Local, who are basically sympathetic to CA, have questioned the utility of these aspects of CA transcription. They remark that for the details of turn-taking, for example gaps and pauses, overlaps and audible breathing activity, CA transcription is: 'consistent and systematic. At other places, however – in reflecting features of tempo, pitch, loudness, vowel quality and voice quality, for example – the transcriptions [seem] inconsistent and arbitrary' (1989: 204)

Kelly and Local suggest that t̲ʰ̲   gained analytically from pavin̲   etic phenomena. H   analyst and the rea   techniques; whereas   istics in CA transcrip   much of the actual so   till making them acc   rs' (Sacks, Schegloff   Before   need to introduce t   conversation analyst   ibing the basic conve   then we will illustrate   ecorded telephone co

...ᴠ̲ᴀ̲ᴛɪons

The first necessary step in doing transcription is to understand the transcription conventions that CA uses, and to have a sense of which features of talk to concentrate on when listening to tape recordings. It is often said that CA transcription procedures are designed to make for more and more 'accurate' transcripts of naturally occurring talk (for instance, Graddol, Cheshire and

Swann 1994: 181). However, this is only partly true. The principal features of talk represented in CA transcripts are almost all involved with particular *analytic* issues: issues to do with analysing the local production of order in naturally occurring talk-in-interaction. The features that should be listened for during transcription, as we have already noted, fall into two broad categories: those to do with turn-taking and those to do with what we loosely call 'speech delivery'. In this section, we introduce the principal conventions used to transcribe these features.

Turn-taking and overlap

Most research in CA is based on the 'simplest systematics' model outlined in Sacks, Schegloff and Jefferson (1974). That ideal model of conversational turn-taking stressed the exchange of turns with minimal gap and overlap between them. Of course, in actual conversations both gaps and overlaps are frequent; and so they must be marked even if only for representational adequacy. However, overlaps in particular are bound up with the management of turn-taking and the observable achievement of mutual understanding in talk-in-interaction. As we saw in the previous chapter, Jefferson (1986) has shown that, on close inspection, much overlapping talk which appears interruptive is in fact closely coordinated with the occurrence of transition-relevance places.

Overlap onset is marked in transcripts by the use of left-hand square brackets:

```
(1)   [SBL:1:1:11:5]
      1     B:   Uh huh and I'm so:rry I didn' get Mar:gret I
      2          really['ve been wan'ing to.
      3→   D:        [W'll I think she mu:st've stayed out'v
      4          to:wn
      5          (0.2)
      6     B:   I thi[nk so too.
      7→   D:        [in Fre:sno sh- see she'n Pe::g (0.7)
      8          dro:ve over to 'er sister's 'oo lives in Fresno::.
```

As we see with this extract, the aim is to be as precise as possible about marking the point at which overlap begins: even when, as in lines 6 and 7, that is in the middle of a word. By marking the

precise points of onset in overlapping talk, very close calibrations
in the understandings that speakers display of each other's talk
become available for analysis.

Other forms of overlap may also be marked. For instance,
speakers may start a turn simultaneously. This is marked by the
use of a double left-hand bracket:

(2) **[Heritage:I:II:3]**
```
1      I:    Well .h I a-always feel it's best to get it
2            all over at ⌈the same time y⌉ou know.
3      N:              ⌊Well        ye::s.⌋
4      N:    Ye:s.
5→     I:    ⌈⌈It's uh:
6→     N:    ⌊⌊And and who did you go to.
```

While it is not always strictly necessary to mark the end of a
stretch of overlapping talk, studies such as Schegloff's (1987a)
account of 'recycled turn-beginnings' show how, by focusing on
the point at which overlap ends, important aspects of the ongoing
management of conversation can thereby be revealed. When the
end of overlap is marked, that is done by a single right-hand
square bracket:

(3) **[Schegloff 1987a: 75]**
```
1      R:    in fact they must have grown a culture, you
2            know, they must've- I mean how long- he's
3            been in hospital for a few days right?
4            Takes a⌈bout a week to grow a culture⌉
5→     K:           ⌊I  don't  think  they  grow  a⌋ I don't
6            think they grow a culture to do a biopsy.
```

It is noticeable here that K, finding himself beginning to speak in
overlap with R's continuation of his turn about growing a culture
for a biopsy, does not drop out of the competition for the floor
but keeps going until R comes to a next recognizable completion
point. At that stage, however, rather than simply carrying on
talking, K, with remarkable precision, restarts his turn, thereby
displaying how speakers can coordinate turn transitions with
transition-relevance places even when a first attempt to do so has
failed.

Utterances may also sound 'latched' together: they may occur
right next to each other with absolutely no gap, but also no overlap, between them. This is marked by equals signs, thus:

(4)   [NB:IV:10]
```
1  E:   Is the swimming pool enclosed with the
2       gla:ss bit?=
3  N:   =No::, it's uh: ou:ts- (.) eh no outside
```

Equals signs are also used to deal with a problem inherent in the attempt to represent naturally occurring talk on the page: the fact that page lines are strictly limited in length, whereas conversational turns are not. This means that a single utterance may need to be broken up, if, for instance, another speaker says something during its course. In such a case, the two parts of the longer turn are connected by equals signs, with the embedded utterance transcribed on a line between:

(5)   [NB:IV:14]
```
1  N:   But eh- it's- it's terrible to keep people
2       ali:ve and you ⌜know and just let them=
3  E:                ⌞Right.
4  N:   =suffer day in and day out,
```

In a similar sense, a protracted spate of simultaneous talk may require a combination of left and right brackets and equals signs, if the spate extends across a number of lines on the page:

(6)   [NB:IV:14]
```
1  E:   Well, we don't know what it's all about
2       I g-I- ((sniff)) Don't get yourself=
3  N:   =⌜Oh I'm not. I just- you know I wish⌝
4  E:    ⌞Honey you've got to get a hold of your- I know⌟=
5  N:   =I'd- I'd kind of liked to gone out there but
6       I was afraid of the fog
```

It is also worth noting that an early device for transcribing the onset of overlap was the double slash (//). This is no longer widely used in transcription. Occasionally, though, it will be used to mark the point of overlap onset when a single line from a longer data extract is being discussed in the text. The longer extract might be the following:

(7)   [SBL:2:1]
```
1  B:   I still haven't my dishes done, I'm
2       right in the middle of doing them, but
3       I stopped ⌜to call you.
4  J:             ⌞Well I worked on my- medicine
5       cabinet again, I'm so mad at that painter,
```

Then B's turn might be cited in this way: 'I still haven't my dishes done, I'm right in the middle of doing them, but I stopped//to call you.'

Gaps and pauses

From the beginning, conversation analysts have timed intervals in the stream of talk relatively precisely, in tenths of a second. Again, this is not just a matter of accuracy. Work on dispreferred responses (Davidson 1984; Pomerantz 1984a) has demonstrated that pauses even as short as two or three tenths of a second can have some interactional, and therefore analytic, significance. Slightly later, Jefferson (1989) produced an extensive exploration of the interactional significance that is attached to silences of one second in length during conversation. It is clear that using a catch-all device such as writing 'pause' in transcripts would not have enabled many of the finer analytic points contained in these papers to be made.

Timings of pauses, then, are important features of transcripts. The timings, which are usually done with a stopwatch, are inserted in the transcript at the precise point of their occurrence in the recording. They may occur within a turn:

(8)   [SBL:2:7:20]
     1   A: I- if you want to uh(b) (1.1) maybe get up a game ...

Or they may occur between turns:

(9)   [SBL:2:7:20] (continuation of (8))
     1   A: I- if you w ant to uh(b) (1.1) maybe get up a game
     2   some morning while you're out the:re,=why that's
     3   always fu:n,
     4   B: Mm hm.
     5→   (0.5)
     6   A: So let me kno:w.

Pauses that are detectable, but run for less than 0.2 of a second, are indicated by a period within parentheses:

(10) **[SBL:2:7:20]** (Continuation of (9))
    6   A: So let me kno:w.
    7→   (.)
    8   B: Yah will do:.

Breathiness

Breathiness which is audible to the transcriptionist is marked by 'h' for exhalation and '.h' for inhalation. As we have already remarked, this feature of recordings is transcribed because (among other reasons) audible in-breaths may be involved with the management of turn-taking, in as much as an open-mouthed in-breath may mark a participant's attempt to start a turn. Notice how in the following extract, speaker E draws in a long breath at line 3, which overlaps substantially with P's invitation. This in-breath signals her attempt to take the floor and respond to the invitation; although the reasons for it may be analytically complex. One relevant factor is that P's invitation has multiple possible completion points ('you wanna go to the store/ er anything/ over at the Market Basket/ er anything?'), so that E's in-breath may be because she has decided on her response but is waiting for the invitation to come to an end (see Davidson 1984). As soon as the final 'er anything?' has been produced, she stops her in-breath and begins to speak:

(11) **[NB:52:2:66]**
    1   P: Oh I mean uh: you wanna go to the store er anything
    2   over at the Market ⌈Basket   er   anything?⌉
    3   E: ⌊.hhhhhhhhhhhhhhhhhhhⁱh Well honey …

In transcripts, the longer the breath, roughly, the longer the line of 'h' or '.h' provided in the transcript:

(12) **[HG:28]**
    1→   N: .hhh
    2   (0.5)
    3   N: A::nywa::y,
    4   (.)
    5→   H: eh-eh .hhhhhhh Uh::m,

The lengths of these breaths are not timed in any strict sense. Rather, the length of a breath is assessed impressionistically, relative to the general tempo of the surrounding talk (although more precise measurement is possible, of course, when the entire breath takes place within overlap, as happens in line 3 of extract (11) above).

Transcripts also mark plosive aspiration within a word: this happens, for instance, when someone speaks 'through' laughter (that is, laughs while enunciating a word or phrase). This is indicated by placing the 'h' in parentheses. However, due to the nature of the phenomenon, this can be very hard to do, and the transcriptionist may need to listen to the same word or group of words many times before he or she can achieve a satisfactory textual rendering of the sounds that occur on the tape:

(13) [EB:1]
```
1  S:   I hope by next semester it'll be a bi(h)t
2       b(h)edd(h)er heh heh heh heh .hh
```

(14) [H:2.2.89:4:3]
```
1    H:  Yes but you ca:n't actually:, take anybody to
2        la::w, .h jus:t on:, an accusation.
3        (1.1)
4    C:  .p .hhh (.) No I kno:w I'm not just making
5        accusations I've got proof of my own
6→       ey(h)(huh huh hih)es! .hhhh
```

Laughter

In a series of papers on laughter, Jefferson (1979; 1985; Jefferson, Sacks and Schegloff 1987) showed that laughter, as it occurs in talk-in-interaction, is a finely coordinated interactional phenomenon. This in turn meant that laughter, which may previously have been represented descriptively by the transcriber simply writing '(laughs)', now should be transcribed as literally as possible in the form of onomatopoeic renditions of *laugh particles*: 'ha ha', 'heh heh', 'hih hih' and so on. The particles are designed to represent as closely as possible the sounds emitted by the participants:

(15) [Goodwin:GR:40]

```
1    J:   So I said look Gurney, yer just a big ass
2         kisser, (0.4) en ⌈yer  getting  yer   wa:y,⌉
3→   B:               ⌊AAHh hah-uh hah-uh huh⌋=
4    J:   =⌈I(h)    ju(h)st⌉ lai⌈d it a:⌉ll on,
5→   B:   ⌊.hhhhhhhhhhh⌋    ⌊hhah⌋
6         (.)
7→   B:   ehh huh uh-huh uh-huh
```

One of the difficulties with transcribing laughter is that participants frequently laugh *together*. This can make for a highly complex transcribing job, especially when the recorded talk involves more than two people. In the following fragment, there are only three participants; but their extended stretch of laughing together leads to a rather daunting-looking section of transcript:

(16) [Goodwin:AD:56:r]

```
 1   B:   he:uh⌈he-uh-ha⌉
 2   C:        ⌊he⌈ha:  :⌉ah ha-ha-ha-ha-ha-ha-a-ha⌉
 3   L:          ⌊ah!ah!⌋ah!ah!ah!ah!ah!ah!ah! ⌋=
 4   C:   =⌈.hhh ⌈he⌉he⌈:h=
 5   L:   ⌊ah!a!⌊a!
 6   B:         ⌊ah hh⌋
 7   C:   =he⌈:h he-ehh-e⌉he-⌈he-⌈.e⌈.hhee⌈hh!⌉
 8   B:      ⌊ Oo:::::ps, ⌋  n⌊he ⌊u ⌊huh ⌋
 9   L:                                 ⌊eh!⌋=
10   C:   =⌈ e::::a::yee: ⌈ee::°
11   L:   ⌊uh!ah!ah!ah!⌋
```

We have used these features of speech production to illustrate some of the reasons why conversation analysts have developed the transcription system currently in use. However, this is not an exhaustive description; other symbols are explained in the glossary of transcription conventions found at the front of the book.

One final thing to mention is that the transcriber may some-times be in doubt as to what actually occurs on the tape. For instance, it may be that a speaker evidently says something, but it may not be clear precisely what it is he or she has said. (One place in which this is likely to occur is during stretches of over-lapping talk.) In such cases, the standard convention is to enclose one's best hearing of what was said in brackets (if no actual words are discernible, the brackets may enclose empty space, signifying at least that *some* sound occurred at that point). On other occasions, the transcriber may want to record some descriptive properties of the speaker's voice, such as that it is 'gravelly', or 'smiley'. This is usually done as an aid to the memory for those occasions when the transcript is being observed without the accompanying tape. Such descriptions are enclosed within double brackets, for instance, ((smiley voice)).

To summarize this section, then, the transcription system used in CA is designed to produce transcripts that are accurate at the relevant levels of detail (levels of turn-taking and actual speech delivery), while avoiding being technically inaccessible to the majority of readers. The purpose of the transcription conventions, however, is not merely to produce accurate representations of talk, but to focus attention on those features of talk-in-interaction that are analytically significant from the standpoint of CA. We have illustrated that point in brief outline in this section. How the transcription system is used to bring out the finer analytic points in a stretch of talk can be illustrated in more detail by means of the following exercise.

A comparative exercise

A good way of showing up the features of talk that are highlighted by a CA transcript is to compare such a transcript with one produced in a different way. On pp. 86–7 we reproduce two transcriptions of the same stretch of talk, in which two middle-aged, middle-class English women are talking on the telephone. Transcript (A) aims to present the words that were spoken, and some non-verbal activities such as laughter, in a standard orthography which makes the text look like a script for a play. Transcript (B) shows how the CA conventions introduced above are used to transcribe the same stretch of talk.

A Comparison between Two Treatments of the Same Conversation

Transcript (A)
[Holt:Xmas 85]

1	L:	Are you not feeling very well?
2	J:	No I'm all right.
3	L:	Yes.
4	J:	Yes I'm all right.
5	L:	Oh. You know I . . . I'm broiling about something.
6		(Laughs)
7	J:	What.
8	L:	Well that sale. At the vicarage.
9	J:	Oh yes.
10	L:	Your friend and mine was there. Mister 'R'.
11	J:	Oh yes.
12	L:	And um, we really didn't have a lot of change that
13		day because we'd been to Bath and we'd been
14		Christmas shopping, but we thought we'd better go
15		along to the sale and do what we could. We hadn't
16		got a lot of ready cash to spend.
17		(Pause)
18	L:	In any case we thought things were very expensive.
19	J:	Oh did you?
20		(Pause)
21	L:	And we were looking round the stalls and poking about,
22		and he came up to me and he said, 'Oh hello Lesley,
23		still trying to buy something for nothing!'
24	Both:	(Sharp intake of breath)
25	J:	Ooo Lesley!
26	L:	Ooo! (Laughs)
27	J:	Isn't he . . .
28	L:	What do you say?
29	J:	Oh isn't he dreadful.
30	L:	Yes.
31	J:	What an awful man.

Transcript (B)
[Holt:Xmas 85]

```
 1   L:   Are you not feeling very ⌜we:ll,
 2   J:                            ⌊°(  ⁻  )°
 3        (.)
 4   J:   No I'm all ri:ght
 5        (.)
 6   L:   Yes.
 7        (0.6)
 8   J:   °Ye:s I'm all right,°
 9   L:   °Oh:.°⁻.hh Yi-m- You know I- I- I'm broiling about
10        something hhhheh⌜heh .hhhh
11   J:                   ⌊Wha::t.
12   L:   Well that sa:le. (0.2) At- at (.) the vicarage.
13        (0.6)
14   J:   Oh ye⌜:s,
15   L:        ⌊.t
16        (0.6)
17   L:   u (.) ihYour friend 'n mi:ne was the:re
18        (0.2)
19   J:   (h⌜h hh)
20   L:    ⌊mMister:, R:,
21   J:   Oh y(h)es, °(hm hm)°
22        (0.4)
23   L:   And em: .p we (.) really didn't have a lot'v cha:nge
24        that (.) day becuz we'd been to Bath 'n we'd been:
25        Christmas shoppin:g, (0.5) but we thought we'd better
26        go along t'th' sale 'n do what we could, (0.2) we
27        hadn't got a lot (.) of s:e- ready cash t'spe:nd.
28        (0.6)
29   L:   In any case we thought th' things were very
30        expensive.
31   J:   Oh did you.
32        (0.9)
33   L:   AND uh we were looking round the sta:lls 'n poking
34        about 'n he came up t' me 'n he said Oh: hhello
35        Lesley, (.) still trying to buy something f'nothing,
36        .tch! .hh⌜hahhhhhhh!
37   J:            ⌊.hhoohhhh!
38        (0.8)
39   J:   Oo⌜::::  ⌜:L e s l e y⌉
40   L:     ⌊OO:!  ⌊ehh heh heh⌋
41        (0.2)
42   J:   I:s⌜n  't⌉  ⌜he
43   L:      ⌊What⌋ do y⌊ou sa:y.
44        (0.3)
45   J:   Oh isn't he drea:dful.
46   L:   °eYe::s.°
47        (0.6)
48   J:   What'n aw::ful ma:::n
```

The first thing that will be noticed about these two renditions is the sheer amount of detail that the CA transcript shows up which is absent from transcript (A). For instance, the CA transcript includes a large number of pauses, overlaps, word stresses and other production features which the first transcript has edited out or 'cleaned up'.

However, we have emphasized that the transcription system is not just aimed at accuracy of detail. Like all transcription systems, it is designed to highlight analytically relevant features of talk-in-interaction. We can illustrate this point by focusing on a particular section of the interchange transcribed in these two extracts. It will be clear that what happens during this interchange is that L tells a story to J about having been insulted by someone referred to as 'Mister R' (this pseudonym is used on the tape itself, not just in transcription) at the local vicarage sale. The story is introduced at the beginning of the extract as something that L is 'broiling about'; just what she is broiling about, it turns out, is Mister R's comment that L, by rummaging about in the stalls at this charity sale, is 'trying to buy something for nothing' (that is, pick up a bargain).

What we are interested in is what happens immediately after L has delivered the punchline of her story: that is, the sequence which begins in line 24 of transcript (A), and line 36 of transcript (B). In each of these transcripts, what happens here is represented radically differently. In Transcript (A), we find the following:

```
22  L:    and he came up to me and he said, 'Oh hello Lesley,
23        still trying to buy something for nothing!'
24  Both: (Sharp intake of breath)
25  J:    Ooo Lesley!
26  L:    Ooo! (Laughs)
27  J:    Isn't he . . .
28  L:    What do you say?
29  J:    Oh isn't he dreadful.
```

While transcript (B) gives us the following:

```
34  L:    about 'n he came up t' me 'n he said Oh: hhello
35        Lesley, (.) still trying to buy something f'nothing,
36        .tch! .hh ⌈hahhhhhhh!
37  J:              ⌊.hhoohhhh!
38        (0.8)
39  J:    Oo⌈: :  ʝ: L e s l e y⌉
40  L:      ⌊OO:!⌊ehh heh heh⌋
```

```
41       (0.2)
42   J:  I:s[n  't]    [he
43   L:     [What] do y[ou sa:y.
44       (0.3)
45   J:  Oh isn't he drea:dful.
```

There are two immediately noticeable differences. The first is that what is discursively represented in transcript (A) (line 24) as: 'Both: (Sharp intake of breath)' is represented typographically in transcript (B):

```
36   L:  .tch! .hh [hahhhhhhh!
37   J:            [.hhoohhhh!
```

The second difference is that transcript (B) shows up how the reactions to the story do not occur simply as a series of utterances following one after another, as suggested by transcript (A). Rather, they occur in three couples, separated by short pauses. Moreover, each of the coupled reactions occurs in *overlap* with its partner.

What is the relevance of this? First of all, we have mentioned that CA transcripts have moved from representing laughter (and other non-lexical phenomena) discursively to developing distinctive typographic representations. What occurs immediately after L's story in this interchange is not laughter but something similarly non-lexical: emphasized, open-mouthed in-breaths which are conventionalized expressions of moral indignation (and so are quite well fitted to the character of the punchline).

However, it is not clear that on reading transcript (B) alone (that is, without the tape) we would be able to interpret these vocalizations in the way they were produced. This appears to be one advantage that transcript (A) has over the CA transcript. In describing what happens as a 'sharp intake of breath', it informs us in a way that transcript (B)'s line of h's does not. But this only serves to emphasize the importance, for CA, of the original data tape, as we stressed earlier on in this chapter. Without the tape it is difficult to 'hear' what is going on at this point in transcript (B). With the tape, however, that problem disappears. So transcript (A) only has an advantage over transcript (B) on the assumption that the analyst does not have access to the tape, which is not the case in CA research.

At the same time, transcript (B) allows us to analyse the

interactional production of this stretch of talk in ways which are not possible with transcript (A). The fact that we can see the set of coupled reactions each being done in overlap brings out the *collaborative* nature of these expressions of indignation. That is, it is not just that both speakers react with sharp intakes of breath, followed by indignant 'Ooo!'s, but they do so almost simultaneously. By this means, the story recipient, J, displays for the storyteller the fact that she understands and empathizes with L's sense of being insulted by Mister R. She does this by vocalizing, on two closely timed occasions, precisely the indignant reaction which L's punchline requires.

The fact that their reactions are not *exactly* simultaneous is itself important in this respect. Looking closer still, we find that on the first occasion, L, as the storyteller, is momentarily the first to embark on a response:

```
36→   L:   .tch! .hh⌈hahhhhhhh!
37     J:         ⌊.hhoohhhh!
```

On the next occasion, however, J takes over the first starter role:

```
38         (0.8)
39→   J:   Oo⌈: : :⌈: L e s l e y⌉
40     L:    ⌊OO:! ⌊ehh h̄eh heh⌋
```

The point is that not only are these reactions closely coordinated; there is even more delicate interactional work going on which is revealed in the timing. Remember that L had set the story up as something she is 'broiling about'. One question that J faces as the story recipient is what form of response would be appropriate to Mister R's comment. This issue is resolved when L herself embarks on a response by manifesting the feeling she had at the time. Having heard the beginning of this sharp intake of breath, J is able to join in (line 37), in a way treating L's response as a 'cue' to show how the story should be treated. After the pause in line 38, J is able to take over the leading response role without waiting for a further cue from the teller. This in turn can then be treated as a cue by L, with which *she* can coordinate a matched response.

By these means the two women display for one another that they are 'with' each other on this tale. But there is evidence to suggest that this does not just happen by accident. They are, it seems, actively coordinating their actions by cueing each other, so that their talk is brought off as closely matched both in timing and in content. This sort of matching is likely to continue only for a short time without becoming a joke (interestingly, notice that L breaks into laughter as early as the second 'round': line 40). Consequently, after the next short pause in line 41, they both go off on separate paths:

```
41        (0.2)
42→  J:   I:s⌈n  't⌉    ⌈he
43→  L:      ⌊What⌋ do y⌊ou sa:y.
44        (0.3)
45   J:   Oh isn't he̲ drea̲:dful.
```

These fine-grained observations about the interactional production of this sequence are only made possible because of the CA transcript's focus on features of detail such as overlap. At the same time, we only notice the overlapping production of the in-breaths following the punchline because the CA transcript favours the typographic representation of sounds over their discursive representation. In short, it is clear that the more complex CA transcript gives us access to the interactional management of talk at a much deeper analytic level than the 'cleaned up' version.

In the way that transcripts are laid out on the page, as well as in the kinds of phenomena that are represented, we find a reflection of CA's distinctive perspective on talk-in-interaction. It has not been our aim in this chapter to discuss the relative merits of the various transcription systems that currently exist, nor to compare their different theoretical underpinnings. But we have emphasized that different research interests will require different selections from the vast range of features of talk-in-interaction that can possibly be transcribed. CA has a specific set of research interests, and the transcription system is extremely well fitted to the associated requirements.

We have also stressed the intrinsic relationship between the processes of transcription and the analysis of data. The development of the transcription conventions themselves testifies to that relationship. The system was not just invented in the abstract, but evolved as analysts sought to understand new features of interactions recorded on tape, leading to the development of new means of transcribing these features.

Overall, this suggests that the CA transcription system is not a finished object, but one that may develop and evolve as new analytic themes themselves emerge. Transcripts, too, develop and evolve. They are not intended as 'objective' representations of social reality, as Graddol, Cheshire and Swann (1994: 181) somewhat critically propose. Transcripts are necessarily impressionistic: they represent the analyst/transcriber's hearing of what is on the tape. And of course, that hearing may alter. Repeated listening to tapes almost always throws up phenomena which were simply missed the first time round. So as a piece of data is subjected to closer and closer analysis, the transcript itself evolves as part of that analytic process. This again illustrates the close connection between data, transcription and analysis.

A final point is that transcripts play a key role in the claim of CA to be a rigorous empirical discipline. An important aspect of this is that analyses produced by one researcher do not amount merely to idiosyncratic and untestable assertions about what is going on in a stretch of talk. Rather, the analysis is projected into a public arena in which it can, if necessary, be challenged and even altered. This is made possible not only by the fact that publications in CA routinely contain examples of data transcripts (as, indeed, we do throughout this book); but also by the fact that conversation analysts' transcripts (and, ideally, the data they are transcriptions of) are made publicly available to anyone who requests them in order to test the accuracy of the analysis, or to reanalyse the data. By this means, transcripts are central to guaranteeing the cumulative and publicly verifiable nature of conversation analytic research.

CHAPTER 4

Analysing Phenomena I
Building a Collection

Having introduced the transcription procedures of conversation analysis, we begin in this chapter to look at some of the basic techniques with which researchers approach the analysis of their data. Conversation analysts place great emphasis on building 'collections' of instances of a particular conversational phenomenon. The aim is to produce analyses of *patterns* in the sequential organization of talk-in-interaction. Analysing patterns in this way enables the analyst to make robust claims about the 'strategic' uses of conversational sequences: the ways in which culturally available resources may be methodically used to accomplish mutually recognizable interactional tasks.

In this chapter we look in detail at the principal analytic techniques which are used in building collections. Using case studies of three pieces of CA research, ranging in time between an early 1968 study and a more recent 1992 paper, we focus on techniques for the identification, description and analysis of singular conversational devices, which can be shown to function in robustly patterned ways within talk-in-interaction. In different ways, these case studies allow us to illustrate the steps by which an analysis of such patterned phenomena can be built up.

However, it is important to emphasize that while this chapter is concerned with analytic procedures and techniques, we do not aim to provide a set of guidelines for doing CA of a 'manual' type. The reason for this is simple. Although as chapter 3 showed, CA has adopted a relatively strict and systematic style of data transcription, the techniques with which researchers approach the actual analysis of data rely as much on what Schenkein (1978) described as the 'conversation analytic mentality' as on any formal rules of research method. Like most forms of qualitative research in the social sciences, CA cannot readily be reduced to a formula which can be applied to data in order to generate appropriate findings. In fact, conversation analysts employ a wide range of essentially interpretive skills in their research. The conversation analytic mentality involves more a cast of mind, or a way of seeing, than a static and prescriptive set of instructions which analysts bring to bear on the data. The best way of describing this and the following chapter, therefore, is as an illustration of the practical application of the conversation analytic mentality.

Collections and patterns

The main research procedure in CA progresses through three stages. The first is to locate a potentially interesting phenomenon in the data. This might be a particular type of turn, for example, one in which the item 'Oh' is used (Heritage 1984b). Or it might be a noticeable kind of sequence, such as opening sequences in telephone conversations (Schegloff 1979b), or sequences in which an invitation is made and responded to (Drew 1984). One thing that it is important to stress here is that the data is not necessarily approached with a particular question in mind. Indeed, conversation analysts try to avoid letting preconceptions about what may be found in some set of transcribed recordings direct their mind when first encountering the data. The preferred policy is one of 'unmotivated' looking. As Sacks once put it:

> When we start out with a piece of data, the question of what we are going to end up with, what kind of findings it will give, should not be a consideration. We sit down with a piece of data, make a bunch of observations, and see where they will go.... I mean not merely that if we pick any data we will find something, but that if we pick any data, without bringing any problems to it, we will find something. And how interesting what we may come up with will be is something we cannot in the first instance say. (Sacks 1984a: 27)

Thus, in each of the cases to be discussed in this chapter, the analysis grew out of the researchers' noticing of a potentially interesting, possibly orderly phenomenon: Schegloff's (1968) study of a particular 'deviant' opening in a large collection of telephone conversations; Drew's (1987) analysis of serious or 'po-faced' reactions to teases; and Hutchby's (1992a) account of a device for accomplishing scepticism in arguments.

First, then, identify a possibly interesting phenomenon. The second step, having collected a number of instances, is to describe one particular occurrence formally, concentrating on its *sequential context*: the types of turn which precede and follow it. If patterns can be located in the sequential contexts in which the potential phenomenon occurs in the data, then there begins to be the basis for a robust description. The third step is to return to the data to see if other instances of the phenomenon can be described in terms of this account. In the process, the description will need to be refined and, gradually, a formal account of a sequential pattern can be developed.

The aim in this type of work is to produce formal descriptions of large collections of data which can account for the whole set of examples which the researcher has collected. But this is not the only analytic technique that is used. As we show in chapter 5, a no less significant aspect of CA is the description and analysis of singular sequences of talk-in-interaction. But particular methodological lessons can be learned by looking at how large collections of data are used in conversation analysis. Consequently we begin by discussing one classic early study using this technique: Schegloff's (1968) analysis of opening sequences in telephone calls.

There is a particular reason why this is a significant case. It illustrates especially clearly CA's insistence on building analytic accounts which are both *particularized* and *generalized*. In other words, conversation analysts aim to be able to describe the specific features of individual cases, and at the same time bring those specifics under the umbrella of a generalized account of some sequential pattern or interactional device.

Schegloff's interest was in how participants coordinate their entry into interaction at the very beginnings of telephone calls. Starting with a collection of 500 examples of telephone openings, he described a pattern which turned out to account for all but one of his cases. But rather than simply accepting that this one was a 'deviant' case which proved the rule, Schegloff wondered whether there might be a better alternative which would account for even the deviant case. In other words, was there a description of the organization of telephone openings which would describe this activity generically, even in cases which seemed out of the ordinary?

Schegloff's initial attempt at describing the management of telephone openings took the form of a rule that 'answerer speaks first' in telephone conversation. He described this as a 'distribution rule', because turns with which telephone calls were opened in his corpus were distributed in a certain way between participants in the respective roles of 'caller' and 'answerer'. This rule accounted for 499 of his cases, in which the first turn of the call was indeed an answerer's 'Hello', or equivalent.

The one case in his collection of 500 which did not fit this pattern was one in which the *caller* spoke first:

(1)   **[From Schegloff, 1968]**
       (Police make the call. Receiver is lifted and there is a one-second pause)
       1 Police: Hello.
       2 Answerer: American Red Cross.
       3 Police: Hello, this is Police Headquarters . . . er,
                      Officer Stratton ((etc.))

Since it is the caller, rather than the answerer, who speaks first in this case, the distribution rule does not apply. Schegloff suggests that there are two analytic strategies for dealing with this. The first is to treat this as a 'deviant case', and develop an analysis focusing on its particular features: describing how it might be that this case came to differ from the rule. This would represent what Schegloff calls an 'ad hoc' attempt to save the distribution rule.

The second alternative is to go back to the corpus as a whole and see if the original analysis can be reformulated in such a way that this case could be accounted for in the same way as all the others. This was the strategy that Schegloff adopted. His solution was to describe the openings of telephone conversations not in terms of the 'answerer speaks first' rule, but as a form of adjacency pair called *summons–answer sequences*. Thus, whereas we might think of the answerer's first 'Hello' as an initial greeting, Schegloff suggests that whatever the answerer says in their first turn is an answer to the summons issued by the telephone's ring. As Schegloff pointed out in a later analysis, it is therefore the *caller's* first turn (that is, the second utterance of the call) that, typically, represents a first greeting (Schegloff 1986). Consider the following typical telephone conversation opening:

(2)   **[HG:1]**
(Hyla and Nancy are teenage friends)
```
1              (Ring)
2    Nancy:  H'llo?
3    Hyla:   Hi:,
4    Nancy:  Hi::.
5    Hyla:   How are yuhh=
6    Nancy:  =Fi:ne how er you,
7    Hyla:   Oka:ry,
8    Nancy:        ⌊Goo:d,
9              (0.4)
10   Hyla:   .mkhhh⌈hh
11   Nancy:        ⌊What's doin',
```

Note that here we have included the telephone ring as part of the transcript. Thus lines 1 and 2 represent the summons–answer sequence, in which Nancy issues an answer to the phone's ring. Only after that, in lines 3 and 4, do the two speakers engage in an exchange of greetings, in which the first greeting comes from Hyla (the caller). Schegloff (1986) shows that this kind of structure is extraordinarily robust in a large collection of telephone conversations involving different participants in different social relationships across varying contexts.

Thus the new summons–answer description enabled Schegloff in his earlier analysis to account for the one case where the answerer did not speak first. This was done by treating the caller's 'Hello' as a *repeat* summons. That is, having made an initial summons via the telephone ring but received no answer, the caller issues another summons (line 1 of extract (1)) which, this time, receives an answer: 'American Red Cross' (the organization that was called). More than that, however, the new version also accounts for all the other cases in the corpus, since in those 499 cases, the initial summons issued by the telephone's ring gets answered in the next move in the sequence, immediately after the answerer picks up the telephone.

Schegloff's analysis of this single 'deviant case' thus resulted in a revision of the analysis and a new, more adequate formal description. By this means he was able to explicate the organizational basis which was common to all the cases in his data. We have used this example to begin with because it is a particularly clear-cut one. Not many studies in the CA literature start off with such a well-defined problem and come to such an elegant answer. And, more importantly, not all patterns or phenomena in talk-in-interaction are so economically describable, as we will show in

the following sections. But the case illustrates three very important principles of the conversation analytic method:

- The insistence on rigorous, formal description;
- The attempt to maximize the generalizability of analytic
  accounts;
- The serious attention given to 'deviant' cases.

With regard to the last point, this study also nicely illustrates a
further important analytic notion in CA. There is another major
importance given to deviant cases, which is connected to what we
introduced in chapter 2 as *conditional relevance*. As we explained
previously, given the initial condition of a first pair part being
uttered, the second part of that pair is then relevant; consequently, the absence of such a second part is a 'noticeable
absence', and the speaker of the first part may search for a reason
for that absence. Adjacency pairs such as question–answer, or
greeting–greeting, display the property of conditional relevance.
The summons–answer sequence also has this property, and Schegloff (1968) lists a number of examples of how speakers may pursue an answer following no response to a summons (for instance,
repeat the summons), and of the kinds of inferences that may be
drawn on in order to account for the absence of an answer (for
instance, the target did not hear/is asleep/is being intentionally
rude).

As we have said, with certain kinds of sequences, conditional
relevance can assist the analyst in defining the sequence as a
robust interactional phenomenon, precisely because of this
accountability feature. If someone displays in their conduct that
they are 'noticing' the absence of a certain type of turn from a co-
participant, then that demonstrates their own orientation to the
relevance of the sequence that the analyst is aiming to describe.
It is important to stress, however, that not all patterned
sequences will exhibit conditional relevance. In other cases, alternative techniques will have to be used in order to produce an
analysis which is generalized and which attends to the participants' orientations to the phenomena being described. In the following sections, we use two further case studies to illustrate in
closer detail the ways in which such rigorous analyses may be
built.

Conversational devices

It is important to stress at this stage that the aim in CA is not simply to build descriptions of patterns in large collections. Underlying the research is a sociological interest in the social and interactional functions of identifiable conversational phenomena. In other words, what interactional work is the phenomenon, or device, being used to do? When we add this to the emphasis introduced in the previous section on how the participants themselves can be said to recognize and use (to *orient to*) the device being described, we have the two core analytic questions in CA:

* What interactional business is being mediated or accomplished through the use of a sequential pattern?
* How do participants demonstrate their active orientation to this business?

We will illustrate the first question through a discussion of Drew's (1987) analysis of 'po-faced' responses to teases.

Drew begins by observing a recurrent phenomenon in his data: people who are the object of a tease will frequently react with a serious, or 'po-faced', response. Why might this be so? First of all, Drew describes the features of the po-faced responses themselves. This shows that it is not the case that people respond seriously because they do not realize they are being teased. Rather, indications that they recognize the humour of the prior turn are visible even as they produce the response. Consider the following example from Drew's paper:

```
(3)   [Goodwin: Family Dinner]
 1    Dot:     Do we have two forks cos we're on television?
 2    Mother:  ⌈No we-
 3    Father:  ⌊Huh hh ⌈huh  hh ⌈h ( )
 4    Angie:         ⌊Yeahah ⌊h hah .hh
 5→   Mother:                ⌊Uh huh ⌈huh huh
 6    Angie:                         ⌊heh heh heh
 7    Father:                        ⌊Right yeh
 8             pro⌈bably the answer right the⌈re
 9    Angie:      ⌊Eh hah hah                 ⌊
10    Mother:                                 ⌊.hhh You have
11             pie you have pie:: tonight.
```

Here Dot's tease in line 1 refers to the fact that this family dinner is being videotaped (hence, 'on television'). Mother starts to respond by saying 'No we-', which appears to be the beginning of a serious account for the presence of two forks. At this point, however, laughter starts among the other participants, and Mother herself joins in (line 5). Yet at the end of the extract, Mother completes the serious response she began earlier: 'You have pie you have pie:: tonight'. Thus, although she has laughed at the joke, her immediate response is a serious or literal one, and that response is completed following the laughter with which she joins in.

The same pattern of a recognition of the joke produced within the immediate environment of a serious response can also be seen in the following extracts.

(4)   **[AL:83 002]**
       (B has just come into the house with A's mother.)
       1 A: Hell⌈o:
       2 B: ⌊He:llo:: how are you:⌈:.
       3 A: ⌊All right thank you?
       4 B: I saw your mum at the bu:s stop so
       5   I ⌈ (give her a li(h)ft-⌉
       6 A: ⌊And you started ya⌋-cking
       7 B: N(hh)o I gave her a lift back

A's tease in line 6, that B 'started yacking' to her mother at the bus stop, is responded to in a 'serious' way with a negation in line 7. Notice, however, that the 'N(hh)o' actually has a small laugh particle embedded within it, thus exhibiting B's recognition of the playful nature of the tease.

In the next extract, Nancy extols the virtues of a man she has met, and responds to Edna's tease which playfully suggests that the man is the type who pays attention to a woman only prior to his sexual conquest of her (line 9) by first laughing (line 11), then producing a serious answer (line 13):

(5)   **[NB:II:4:R:14]**
       1 Nancy: VERY personable VERY SWEET. .hhh VE:RY
       2   CONSIDERATE MY GOD ALL I HAD TO DO WAS LOOK AT
       3   A CIGARETTE AND HE WAS OUT OF THE CHAIR LIGHTING
       4   (h)IT Y(hhh)OU KNO(h)W ⌈.hehh .hh One of those=
       5 Edna: ⌊I: KNO:W IT
       6 Nancy: =kind .hhhh

```
 7 Edna:  ⌈Yes.
 8 Nancy: ⌊A:nd so⌈: but we were
 9 Edna:        ⌊THEY DO THAT BEFORE AND A:FTER THEY
10        DO:n't
11 Nancy: HAH HAH .hhh
12 Edna:  (Or he's-)
13 Nancy: NO:? e-MARTHA HAS known Cli:ff . . .
```

In developing his account of the production of po-faced responses to teases, Drew next describes some features of the sequential environments in which the teases occur. Focusing first on the types of responses found in the data, he notes that not all teases are reacted to seriously. Occasionally a recipient will go along with the tease, as in the next example in which Bill describes symptoms of a current illness.

(6)   [Campbell: 4:5]
```
 1    Bill:    ee I think it was food poisoning (last night)
 2             cos I was ... I'm still gettin:g you know,hh
 3             .hh stomach pains I spewed last ni:ght, . . .
 4             chronic diarrhea as we-e-ell, just before I
 5             went to bed and ... this morning (well) I've had
 6             this bad stomach. So I guess the same thing's
 7             gonna happen tonight ... I've been getting funny
 8             things in front of my eye:s actually. .hh
 9             A bi:t, just slightly, Li:ght flashes.    ((...))
10    Bill:    But uh, (0.3) .tsk (sti:ll.)
11    Arthur:  Well you probably got at least a week.
12             (0.4)
13    Bill:    What of thi:s.
14             (0.3)
15    Arthur:  No a week before you die:,
16             (0.7)
17    Bill:    Ohh yhhe heh heh uh⌈.hhh-hh
18    Arthur:                      ⌊It's a rare disea:se
19             see,
20    Bill:    Yeh yeh yeh.
```

At first Bill does not seem to recognize the tease about having a week left to live (line 13). But once Arthur explains it to him (line 15), he responds by laughing, thereby both recognizing and going along with the tease. Noticeably, unlike the speakers in the previous two extracts, he does not make any attempt to attach a serious response to his laughter.

Drew describes a 'continuum' of responses in which there are four main types: '(i) initial serious response . . . prompted to laugh by others, [but] returning to po-faced rejection; (ii) simultaneously laughing at tease and rejecting its proposal; (iii) laughing acceptance, followed by serious rejection of the proposal in the tease; (iv) going along with the tease' (1987: 225). But he notes that, overwhelmingly, there is some component of po-faced rejection of the tease. In order to address why this might be the case, Drew next looks at the prior turns or actions which have occasioned the tease.

Here we find that a feature common to many (but not all) of the cases is that the tease follows a stretch of talk which is recognizably overdone or exaggerated. For instance, in extract (6) above Bill describes the symptoms of his illness in quite graphic terms. Arthur's tease in line 11 pokes fun at the over-elaborate nature of the description by suggesting that Bill is in fact close to death. Similarly, in the conversation from which extract (5) was taken, Nancy's glowing appreciation of her new male friend has been going on for an extended period of time prior to Edna's tease, and the 'nice guy' virtues of the man have been described in elaborate, if not exaggerated terms. For instance, in prior talk Nancy has referred to him as 'a real, dear, nice guy, just a real nice guy ... real easy going ... he was a captain in the marines ... he's got a real good job ... he's intelligent ... not handsome but he's nice looking ... just a real nice, personable ...' and so on.

In both these cases, the teases produce a non-serious gloss or upshot of the exaggerated talk by the prior speaker. In (5), Edna's tease undermines the elaborate recommendation of Nancy's potential boyfriend by suggesting that these qualities will evaporate once he has succeeded in winning her over. And in (6), Arthur's tease undermines the apparent severity of Bill's illness by sarcastically suggesting that Bill is about to die. Although Bill does not in fact offer a po-faced rejection, this none the less suggests one account for the production of po-faced responses to teases: the respondent is attempting to reassert the seriousness or warrantability of the stretch of talk which the teaser has targeted.

However, not all the cases in Drew's data fall into this pattern. He next looks at other instances which suggest a more general account. This focuses on the way that the design of the tease subtly ascribes a 'deviant identity' to the recipient. For instance, consider the following example of an entirely po-faced response to a tease.

(7) **[Northridge:2:JP/DP:1]**
(A telephone conversation in which Del is the caller.)
1 Del: What are you doing at ho:me.
2   (1.7)
3 Paul: Sitting down watching the tu:ʃbe,
4 Del: ˡkhnhhh:: ih-huh
5   .hhh Wa:tching n-hghn .h you nghn (0.4)
6   watching dayti:me stories uh?
7   (.)
8 Paul: No I was just watching this: uh:m: (0.7) .h
9   .khh you know one of them ga:me shows,

Here, the tease in lines 5–6, 'you ... watching dayti:me stories
uh?' focuses on the fact that Del has called Paul in the daytime
and found him at home 'watching the tu:be', as against, say, being
at work, college, or whatever. So the tease trades on the negative
or 'deviant' identity which can be attributed to Del of being
slobby or lazy. This is found in Del's 'teasing characterization
of infantile, pulp, noninformative, noneducational television,
"dayti:me stories"' (Drew 1987: 234).

We find a similar pattern of the suggestion of negative identities on the part of the tease target in other examples. To return
to extract (3), Dot's tease, 'Do we have two forks cos we're on
television?' implies that Mother is being pretentious by laying
out two forks just because of the presence of the video camera.
In extract (4), 'And you started yacking' proposes the frivolous
or gossipy nature of the encounter at the bus stop (in contrast,
for instance, to 'started talking' which could suggest greater por-
tent in the words or topics involved than 'yacking' could possibly
imply). While in extract (5), Edna's 'THEY DO THAT
BEFORE AND A:FTER THEY DO:n't' implies naivety on
Nancy's part about the wiles of men.

Thus a common pattern has been discovered in this collection
of teases. The pattern is not so much that they follow recognizably exaggerated stretches of talk, but that they implicate negative or 'deviant' identities for their recipients. And although
recipients often exhibit that they can see the joke, the po-faced
response is designed to counter that implication of a negative
identity.

Drew finally draws out some of the sociological implications of
this account. Beginning with the question of why teases may be
responded to in a po-faced manner, the analysis has ended up
suggesting that a recursive pattern in conversational teasing is

that the tease ascribes a mildly deviant identity to its recipient. The implication of scepticism and the suggestion of negative qualities about the teased person serve to act as a subtle form of social control for these minor forms of deviant behaviour. And as Drew points out, like any form of social control, it can be resisted. In these cases, the resistance takes the form of a po-faced response.

Participants' orientations to a conversational device

We mentioned the two core questions with which to approach data: what interactional business is being mediated or accomplished through the use of a sequential pattern or device; and how do participants demonstrate their active orientation to this business? Addressing the first question, we showed how po-faced receipts of teases are a way for teased parties to resist the attribution of tease-implicated deviant identities. We now want to look at a device used in arguments, in order to show more clearly how participants can display their orientations to the interactional work that is being accomplished with a sequence.

Why is this important? So far, we have stressed how analysts bring interpretive resources to bear on data in order to develop a general account of the interactional business being negotiated in collections of data extracts. As in all CA, the essential way in which these accounts are grounded is by looking at how an utterance is responded to in the next turn. But as we suggested with the earlier discussion of conditional relevance, an account of the ways in which a particular conversational device is used to accomplish specific interactional business will be strengthened if we can show that recipients display an orientation to those properties of the device which the analytic account emphasizes. By this means, we can get a deeper sense of the robustness of interactional devices.

We will illustrate this by way of the analysis of a device for exhibiting scepticism which Hutchby (1992a) found to be recurrent in arguments on radio phone-in shows (though the device is one that is generic to argument, rather than being restricted to talk in this particular setting). The device takes the form of a contrast between what the prior speaker has just said ('You say X') and what the current speaker suggests is the case ('What about Y'). By this means, speakers subtly undermine their opponent's claims by using the Y component to suggest that the X claim could not be true – or at least, is at fault – as opposed, say, to actively negating the prior claim.

Following is an example, from Hutchby's paper, of how the device appears in arguments on talk radio.

(8)   **[H:30.11.88:2:1]**
```
 1   Caller:  I think we should (.) er reform the la:w on
 2            Sundays here, (0.3) w- I think people should have
 3            the choice if they want to do shopping on a
 4            Sunday, (0.4) also, that (.) i-if shops want to
 5            open on a Sunday th- th- they should be given the
 6            choice to do so.
 7   Host:    Well as I understand it thee: (.) the la:w a:s
 8            they're discussing it at the moment would allow
 9            shops to open .h for six hou:rs, .hh ⌈ e:r ⌉ on a=
10   Caller:                                      ⌊Yes.⌋
11   Host:    =Sunday,
12   Caller:  That's righ⌈t.
13   Host:               ⌊From:, midda:y.
14   Caller:  Y⌈es,
15   Host:     ⌊They wouldn't be allowed to open befo:re that.
16            .hh Erm and you talk about erm, (.) the rights of
17            people to: make a choice as to whether they
18            shop or not, ⌈o:n ⌉ a Sunday,=what about .hh the=
19   Caller:              ⌊Yes,⌋
20   Host:    =people who may not have a choice a:s to whether
21            they would work on a Sunday.
```

Here, the caller begins by putting forward a position on the issue of whether British laws forbidding general trading on Sundays should be repealed, so that shops could legitimately open for business seven days a week. The host responds to this initially by clarifying a point of detail (lines 7–15). The 'You say X' device appears in lines 16–21, where we find that the host first attributes a position to the caller: 'you talk about ... the rights of people to: make a choice as to whether they shop or not, on a Sunday' (lines 16–18), followed by a challenge in which he seeks to undermine the caller's view: 'what about the people who may not have a choice a:s to whether they would work on a Sunday' (lines 18–21). Thus the host uses a contrast structure which juxtaposes an attributed position ('You say X') with a competing version ('What about Y').

One of the principal ways in which we can ground the claim that 'You say X but what about Y' is an argumentative device for exhibiting scepticism is by showing that recipients actively orient, in the design of their talk, to the two principal properties of the device: first, the fact that it is a contrast, or at least, that it consists of two main parts; and second, the fact that it is used to undermine and exhibit scepticism about the recipient's prior assertions.

First of all, it can be shown that recipients (who are mainly callers, since it is almost always the host who makes use of this device) recognize the 'compound' nature of the device. This means that the device takes more than one turn-construction unit to produce. For instance, in the previous extract, the host's quotation in lines 16–18, 'you talk about ... the rights of people to: make a choice as to whether they shop or not, on a Sunday', *could* constitute a possibly complete turn, since it is a technically complete sentence. However, notice the caller's action just before the completion of this sentence, in line 19:

```
16    Host:     ... you talk about erm, (.) the rights of
17              people to: make a choice as to whether they
18              shop or not, ⌈ o:n ⌉a Sunday,=what about .hh the=
19→   Caller:                ⌊Yes,⌋
20    Host:     =people who may not have a choice a:s to whether
21              they would work on a Sunday.
```

The 'Yes' here may be seen as a *continuer* (Schegloff 1982: 80). Continuers are tokens such as 'mm hm', 'uh huh', 'yes' or 'right', which display a recipient's understanding that a turn-in-progress is not complete, even though a possible transition-relevance place may have been reached. Goodwin (1986) shows that continuers are frequently placed at a particular point in the course of an ongoing turn: namely, at or near the end of one phrase or sentence and extending into the beginning of another. In this way, continuers act to 'bridge' turn-construction units, and show their producers passing on what is a possible opportunity to take the floor. Using this analysis, we can see the continuer in line 19 above as a bridge between the first part of the contrastive device, 'You say X', and its second part, 'What about Y'.

Extract (9) shows up the same features.

(9) **[H:21.11.88:11:3]**
```
1  Host:     You sa:y that you would not force people to do
2            it. You do however accept that there is prejudice
3            against .hh er certain kinds of, homes and
4            er, ⌈ .hh ⌉hospitals in communities ⌈ .hh ⌉so .h=
5  Caller:      ⌊Yeh⌋                           ⌊Yeh⌋
6  Host:     =if: that prejudice exists people aren't going
7            to gi:ve ti:me. Or money for that matter.
```

In this extract, the caller's first continuer (line 5) comes after the host has projected the continuation of the turn with 'and er ...' But the second once more occurs precisely at the bridge between the two types of unit: sentences and contrast parts. Both continuers, like the 'Yes' in the previous extract, signal the caller's acceptance of the host's attributed version of his position. But what they also exhibit is the caller's recognition that, having produced this attribution, the host has not yet completed his turn, and is going on to produce a further component: in other words, the host is doing something more than simply quoting their assertions back at them.

The second type of evidence for callers' orientation to the use of this device is found when callers attempt to *resist* the sceptical potential involved in an attribution. This can operate at very subtle levels of detail in the talk. For instance, in the following extract host and caller are arguing about the problems caused by dogs fouling public walkways:

(10) **[H:2.2.89:12:1–2]**
```
1  Caller:   U:sually when a dog fouls:, .hh e::r it, it
2            lea:ves-=the scent that is left behind even if
3            you, clean up with boiling water an'
4            disinfectant,.hhh is a marker. .h An' when 'e
5            comes on 'is e::r, w:-wa:lk the next da:y, when
6            'e gets to that ma:rk, he does the same thing
7            again.((...))
8  Host:     er you s-seem to be suggesting that they go to
9            the same place every ti:me. Because they've been
10           there before.
11 Caller:   Ooh yes,=quite often ye:s.=
12 Host:     =Yeah but er(h)n(h) then:, .h e:r=
13 Caller:   =An⌈d other dogs will °also°.⌉
14 Host:        ⌊this- this  mea:ns that⌋ they never go in
15           a different pla:ce,=doesn't it.
```

The host attributes to the caller the claim that dogs 'go' to 'the same place every ti:me' (line 8). In the second part of his contrast he casts doubt on this position by pointing out that 'this mea:ns that they never go in a different pla:ce' (lines 14–15). Thus the host uses the 'You say X' device to imply that the caller's claim is erroneous because common sense tells us this could not be so.

Notice, however, that the host is actually *reformulating* the caller's claim. The caller began in a qualified manner by using the word 'usually' (line 1); and his argument remains qualified in the sense that what he is saying amounts to something like 'if the dog passes his own mark on another walk, he'll do the same thing again.' This is somewhat different from the host's version: 'they go to the same place every ti:me.' It thus becomes interesting that the caller, in line 11, not only agrees (apparently) with the host ('Ooh yes') but modifies the attribution by adding 'quite often'. Thus, while appearing to go along with the host, the caller is actually sustaining the more cautious version of his position. Clearly, if the caller's more cautious version were to be allowed to stand as a modification of the host's version, then the host could no longer complete the sceptical contrast he has begun. That is, 'quite often' could not be effectively contrasted by 'never go in a different pla:ce'.

The host deals with this by utterly ignoring the 'quite often' component and treating the prior turn simply as an affirmation. In line 12, the host displays his intention to go on to do the second part of the contrast he has set up. The caller, however, having heard the initial 'Yeah but', interpolates a further modifier: 'and other dogs will also' (line 13). This time, the host simply overrides his opponent, pressing on to complete the second contrast part in overlap with the caller's talk.

Thus there are quite subtle ways in which we can observe callers displaying their orientation to the sceptical uses of the 'You say X' component by attempting to resist the contrastive implications being set up by the host. The following extract is a more straightforward example of this form of resistance.

(11) [G:26.11.88:3:1]
```
     1  Caller:  Uh, what was supposed to happen yesterda:y, it
     2           was an org- it was an o:rganised lobby of
     3           Parliament by: the National Union of Students.
     4  Host:    °M:mm,°
     5  Caller:  And the idea was to make, .hh the public of
     6           England, an' Great Britain, .h awa:re, .h of
     7           thee loans proposals.((...))
     8  Host:    You say it was an organised demonstration by the
```

```
 9              National Union of Students.=⌈do y-
10   Caller:                                ⌊No it was an or- it
11              was an organised lobby, .hh a:nd a ma:rch, which
12              was supposed to go ⌈to (  )
13   Host:                         ⌊Well you- you can organise a
14              lobby or a march it still amounts to a
15              demonstration=d'you think it got out of hand?
```

Again, the host attributes to the caller a reformulated version of what was originally said. In this case, the caller's description 'organised lobby' (line 2) is transformed into the more confrontational 'organised demonstration' (line 8). The caller detects this substitution and seeks to combat it in lines 10–12 by reasserting his own milder version and adding further modulating components: that the lobby was accompanied by 'a march', which was 'supposed' to conduct people to a particular location. In this way, what the host implies was a militant demonstration is reasserted as a legitimate and peaceable protest: the lobby is shown to be the central activity, and it is implied that the march was stopped by outside forces (which the caller later describes as 'a breakaway group') from reaching its destination.

However, the host again displays clearly his intention to go on and complete the contrast in spite of the caller's interjection (lines 13–15). But rather than simply ignoring or overriding the interpolation, he begins by assimilating the caller's more cautious version within his own: 'You can organise a lobby or a march it still amounts to a demonstration'. He then rapidly goes on to produce the second contrast part, 'd'you think it got out of hand?', by which, of course, he seeks to undermine the caller's original claim that the lobby was 'organised'.

There are thus two sorts of evidence of how callers orient to the contrastive and the sceptical nature of the 'You say X' device. First, the use of continuers demonstrates callers' recognition that such units can and indeed should project some further talk from the host. Secondly, callers' occasional attempts to modify hosts' reformulated attributions show that they also recognize the potentially damaging scepticism achieved through this device, and resist by reasserting their own more cautious versions.

Analysing phenomena: further issues

In the foregoing we have illustrated a basic three-stage model for building an analytic account:

- First, identify a potential object of analytic interest – a conversational device or a sequence type.
- Second, produce a formal description of an empirical example, concentrating in particular on the sequential environment, in order to try and define what the device or sequence type is *doing*.
- Third, return to the data collection to refine the description until it becomes a generalized account.

Our discussion has focused on the second two, more analytic stages. Less attention has been given to the question of what 'a phenomenon' is for CA. We will end this chapter by discussing this issue and some other, related questions, including the attitude of conversation analysts towards quantifying phenomena in reporting their findings.

Different types of phenomena

First of all, it may be noted that in our discussion of the studies by Drew (1987) and Hutchby (1992a), the sorts of phenomena that are analysed are different in a variety of ways. For instance, Drew discusses a particular kind of response to a particular kind of action (a po-faced response to a tease). Hutchby, on the other hand, looks at a special kind of turn format which is used to accomplish a certain interactional effect ('You say X' as an indication of the speaker's scepticism).

Similarly, on the one hand, Drew's po-faced responses do not take any generalized form. Rather, each of the examples he discusses is quite particular: there are no defining characteristics of po-faced responses in themselves, but the collection is built up through each response being analysed in terms of what it is a response *to* (that is, a tease). Hutchby's device, on the other hand, takes a much more regular form; indeed, it is the form itself which accomplishes the interactional work. This, of course, is the point of demonstrating that recipients recognize the sceptical work being done even before the 'What about Y' part of the device. However, note that although the device itself is described in a formal way, in each of the cases we have discussed the way that the device appears is different. For instance, Hutchby (1992a) treats both the utterance '*You say* you would not force people ...' and the linguistically quite different, '*You talk about* the rights of people to choose ...' equally as instances of the 'You say X' phenomenon.

A further point that emerges here is that Drew's analysis relies on his (and his readers') ability to recognize commonsensically where a 'tease' occurs in his data, and where a response may seek to treat the tease 'seriously' as opposed to going along with the tease. Hutchby's analysis relies less on this sort of commonsense interpretation, with the collection being built more on the basis of linguistic occurrences of 'You say ...' and its variants in his data. However, there is still, of course, a commonsense element in the identification of when a speaker is being 'sceptical' or a recipient is displaying 'recognition' of possible scepticism.

Do these differences constitute a problem in the CA method? Is it problematic that devices can be identified in quite divergent ways, or that building a collection to identify a phenomenon relies in such a way on the analyst's commonsense understanding? The answer is no, for a number of reasons. First, and most importantly, as we have tried to emphasize, it is not the phenomenon as a linguistic object which is the focus of interest for CA, but the interactional work being accomplished via turns at talk. So whether devices are identified by means of their formal features (an item such as 'Oh' (Heritage 1984b) or a construction such as 'You say X') or purely in terms of their sequential placement in relation to some other turn (such as a reaction to a tease) is irrelevant as long as the analysis focuses on regularities in how the items in a collection achieve their interactional effects.

Second, it is clear that even when the device in question is described in relatively abstract terms, such as the 'You say X' device, no two cases are exactly the same. As we have said, there are great disparities between the ways in which the examples in the study by Hutchby are actually verbalized. However, the analytic account focuses on the regularities and therefore develops a more formal or abstract description of the phenomenon that is of interest.

But it is important to bear in mind that both in Hutchby's paper and in Drew's, as in CA generally, the analysis is actually carried out on a case-by-case basis. Each instance in the data corpus is treated in its own right, attending to its particular as well as its general features. This is because in the real world, in the course of naturally occurring interaction, the cases that were recorded were themselves produced on an individual basis. Participants in talk-in-interaction produce their utterances, and understand those of others, in the here and now. The regularities in talk which we can identify when, as analysts, we locate a phenomenon or device and observe its use in a collection of instances can thus only be described if we build an account that is more general, while continuing to pay close attention to the particularities.

The role of commonsense knowledge

This brings us to the further question of the role of commonsense knowledge in developing analyses. It is inevitable that the analyst's commonsense knowledge will be brought to bear, first of all because as analysts of talk-in-interaction we are, for the most part, members of the same culture as the people we are studying. (There are exceptions to this, which we come to below.) Indeed it is difficult to imagine how it would be possible to do conversation analysis on data involving interactants whose language the analyst did not understand. For instance, of the studies we have mentioned only Schegloff's (1968) analysis of summons–answer sequences in telephone openings conceivably does *not* rely on understanding the actual words that are spoken. Whatever the word people used to answer the phone, that initial sequence would still be crudely analysable in terms of the telephone ring as a 'summons' and the receiver's first turn as an 'answer' (although that interpretation itself would rely on cultural knowledge about what telephones are used for, presumably).

But Schegloff's paper is anomalous in that respect. Both the other studies mentioned above, as well as the vast majority of available CA work, rely fundamentally on the analyst's ability to understand, and to come to some informed interpretation of, what it is that the participants in the data are doing. Of course, as we have emphasized, the aim is actually to come to an understanding of what the participants themselves take it they are doing; but in order to do that, we need to have some access to the interpretive and inferential resources which the participants are relying on. In other words, it is absolutely necessary that conversation analysts are either members of, or have a sound understanding of, the culture from which their data have been drawn.

This is emphasized by Moerman (1972; 1977; 1988), whose research represents the most systematic attempt to apply CA to a culture which is foreign to the researcher, namely, Thai culture. Himself an American, Moerman (1988) remarks that doing research on a culture and language in which the researcher is not native foregrounds the amount that we have to rely on cultural knowledge, for otherwise the practices of interactants may not be understandable at all. But he also points out that when researchers focus on their native language (as conversation analysts mostly do), there is no less a reliance on cultural knowledge – it is simply that such knowledge is more commonsensical and therefore makes things seem more natural than they may be in cultures with which we are less familiar. Moerman in fact argues that conversation analysts should become more overtly aware of the culturally contexted nature of all talk-in-interaction, not just the supposedly 'exotic' or alien.

The relevance of culture

Some work in CA does make explicit reference to cultural specifics. The kinds of points made tend to focus on two issues: the existence of cross-cultural similarities in conversational practices, and the nature of intercultural differences in certain practices. For instance, Moerman (1988) found systematic similarities in techniques for establishing reference to others in Thai and American conversation. In earlier work, Sacks and Schegloff (1979) had found that there are two basic rules for referring to other persons in Anglo-American interaction: first, use as few descriptive terms as possible; and second, seek the recipient's alignment in the description. These rules can be seen to operate in the following extract:

(12)   [Sacks and Schegloff 1979: 19]
```
1   A:   ... Well I was the only one other than the uhm
2        tch Fords? Uh, Mrs Holmes Ford? You know
3        uh ⌈the the cellist?
4   B:      ⌊Oh yes. She's she's the cellist.
5   A:   Yes.
6   B:   Ye⌈s
7   A:      ⌊Well she and her husband were there ...
```

Speaker A makes three attempts to establish reference to a couple named Ford (lines 2–3), each of them focusing on different ways that the recipient might be able to recognize who is being referred to: 'the Fords', 'Mrs Holmes Ford', and 'you know ... the cellist'. The aim is to establish recognition at the first attempt; but having failed with 'the Fords?', the speaker then has to think of other suitable alternatives.

The second rule, that the recipient's affiliation should be sought, is found in the 'try-marking' intonation that the speaker uses: that is, using an upward or questioning intonation to invite B's acknowledgement that the reference form has succeeded (indicated by the question marks in lines 2–3). Moerman (1988) takes this description of an American conversational pattern and applies it to conversations in Lue, a Thai dialect, and interestingly finds that both rules apply in a similar way in his data where not only is the culture quite different, but also the language itself is unrelated to American English. Thus Moerman demonstrates that similar patterns of talk-in-interaction exist in different cultures and distinct languages.

Focusing on differences, Houtkoop-Steenstra (1991) found some basic divergences between the ways that Dutch speakers open telephone conversations and the way Americans typically do. As we noted earlier, Schegloff's work in this area (1968; 1979b; 1986) has identified a robust pattern in American English telephone calls, in which the answerer's first turn takes the form of 'Hello' or some equivalent answer to the summons issued by the telephone ring. The second sequence following the summons–answer sequence is an 'identification/recognition' sequence, which may take the form of the participants exchanging names, or simply greeting each other and relying on voice recognition.

Houtkoop-Steenstra (1991) finds that Dutch speakers tend to answer the phone not with 'Hello' but with a self-identification. For instance:

(13) **[HH:18:245]**
     1→   A: It's Reina de Wind?
     2   B: Hello:, it's Bren.

(14) **[HH:12:98]**
     1→   A: It's Catrien?
     2   (0.7)
     3   B: It's Maarten.

Just as Schegloff (1986) finds that the summons–answer sequence of (ring) + 'Hello?' is typical for American English calls, so Houtkoop-Steenstra finds that the sequence in which the ring is answered by a self-identification is typical for her Dutch data. Thus there is a sense in which the cultural context can be important for identifying and understanding differences, as well as similarities, in the patterns of talk-in-interaction.

Quantification

Mention of these latter studies brings us to our final point: the relevance of quantification in CA. Both these studies of telephone openings base their findings at one level on rudimentary forms of quantification. For instance, Houtkoop-Steenstra states that 'out of 87 cases ... 78 [answerers] ... self-identify in first turn' (1991: 246). And she quantifies her remaining cases in terms of four other categories. Schegloff's (1968) earlier study has its foundation in part in a crude quantification exercise: out of 500 cases, only 499 were covered by the initial hypothesis. Yet for the most part, conversation analysts have a reluctance to treat quantification as the ultimate aim, or even a preliminary stage, of analysis. Indeed, for Houtkoop-Steenstra, her counting of cases is merely a way of strengthening her account of the robustness of her selected phenomenon, rather than an analytic technique in itself.

The reasons for this reluctance are related to the points we have outlined above. Although this chapter has been about the importance of collections in CA, and the ways in which large numbers of instances come to be used in the analysis of a phenomenon or device, we have also stressed the significance of discovering the orderliness of talk from the participants' perspective and the role of commonsense interpretation in generating analyses. Although conversation analysts, like quantitative researchers, engage in developing categories and classifying data extracts in terms of those, both the ways in which those categories are assembled and the role they play in analysis are different from quantitative approaches.

CA employs a methodology in which exemplars are used as the basis on which a generalizable description is built (see Hopper 1989b). This is different from techniques in which a hypothesis is first made and then tested using large collections of data. This is sometimes thought of in terms of the distinction between inductive and deductive research methods. However, the more significant point to stress is that, as we have shown, CA places great emphasis on the close description of empirical examples, and often the analysis of a phenomenon will grow from the careful description of one instance, which then, through the process we have described, becomes a description capable of covering a whole collection of cases.

Conversation analysts use collections in order to reveal systematic patterns in talk-in-interaction across differing contexts and involving varying participants. But that aim is underpinned by a recognition that while there may be regularities across cases, each case is ultimately unique. A related point, which we have mentioned previously and which we come back to in later chapters, is that CA avoids treating the phenomena of talk-in-interaction as statistical variables. Such an approach may seek to show, for instance, that Drew's (1987) po-faced tease receipts are more likely to occur when a participant with a 'serious' personality is involved in the interaction. This could be described as an 'experimental' approach. For CA, such an approach would be to move away from the aim of explicating, on a case-by-case basis, the systematic competencies that participants in naturally occurring talk-in-interaction rely on to understand one another's actions and to generate interactionally appropriate responses.

As an illustration of these distinctions we can consider the quantitative experimental approach as it is adopted in social psychology. In that field, researchers who are interested in interpersonal communication tend to use recorded conversational data (though of conversations recorded in a laboratory setting rather than in naturally occurring interaction) in order to test hypotheses about the nature of speech phenomena (Hopper 1989a). These hypotheses are tested using statistical techniques which involve coding certain speech phenomena into pre-established categories. We can demonstrate the differences between the social psychology (SP) approach and CA by focusing on the issue of speech overlap, and especially 'interruption', since this is an area that has interested both social psychologists and conversation analysts (Drummond 1989).

In SP, interruption tends to be seen as one type of the more general category of overlapping speech. The aim is to distinguish between these different types in order to count the number of interruptions that occur in a given set of data. Underlying this is a theoretical assumption that interruption can be treated as an indicator of interpersonal factors such as dominance, power or control. The technique is to code each of a collection of examples of overlapping speech on the basis of pre-established criteria. These criteria can be very extensive. For instance, in one of the most well-known systems, the 'simultaneous speech coding system' (Roger, Bull and Smith 1988), interruptions are divided into basic 'simple' and 'complex' forms, and then these types are again subdivided into no fewer than seventeen distinct subtypes of interruption.

In another well-known study, Beattie (1983) classifies all 'attempted speaker switches' in his data corpus on the basis of three criteria. First, the *success* of the attempt (whether or not the incoming speaker succeeded in gaining the floor); second, whether or not there is *simultaneous speech*; and third, whether or not the first speaker's utterance is *complete* at the point when speaker change takes place. Thus a category such as 'simple interruption' is defined as a successful speaker switch, in which there is some simultaneous talk, but the first speaker's utterance is not completed.

From a CA perspective, these approaches can lead to the premature categorization of an interactional event as a subtype of interruption, when closer analysis would lead us to see a different kind of orderliness in the example. For instance, while many SP studies of interruption have focused on the occurrence of simultaneous speech as the basis of interruptions, Jefferson shows how large amounts of simultaneous speech which look like interruptions in fact occur in the environment of legitimate transition-relevance places. Thus these may not be appropriately describable as interruptions at all, but rather as attempts to gain the floor which show close attention to the local sequential contexts of

talk-in-interaction. As Jefferson puts it: 'The overlap could ...
be seen as a byproduct of two activities: (1) A recipient reason-
ably, warrantedly treats some current utterance as complete ...
and starts to talk, while (2) the current speaker, perfectly within
his rights, keeps going' (1986: 154).

For instance, in the following extract, a focus purely on the
existence of simultaneous speech would lead a coder to code
Doreen's utterance in line 5 as an interruption. Notice, however,
precisely what is happening in the talk at that point:

```
(15)  [Her:0II:2:7:5]
  1      Doreen:  Yes well pop in on the way back 'n pick it
  2               up
  3      Katie:   °Thhank you ve'y much° eh ha- how are you
  4               all. ⌈Yer a little ti:red⌉ °nah°
  5→     Doreen:      ⌊Oh wir all fi:ne,⌋ Yes I'm jus:
  6               sohrta clearing up
```

Although Doreen's turn overlaps some continuing talk by Katie,
to describe this as an interruption would miss the fact that it
occurs at a legitimate transition-relevance place: namely, after
Katie's inquiry, 'how are you all.' In fact, what happens is that
Katie goes on to provide a candidate response to her own
inquiry, 'Yer a little ti:red'. So that while one speaker starts to
talk at a legitimate place, as opposed to an interruptive one, her
talk ends up looking like an interruption because the first
speaker, equally legitimately, carries on talking.

Other instances which appear more clearly interruptive can
also be described as quite orderly if we focus not on the appearance of the extract but on the local sequential context of the talk:

```
(16)  [UTCL A21:4]
  1      Pam:     O:h that's what I really need is a lid.
  2      Gloria:  For your cake pan?
  3      Pam:     Ye:s.
  4               (.)
  5      Pam:     So that no roaches will stick on
  6               the ⌈on the frosti:ng.⌉
  7→     Gloria:      ⌊O::h-  I  kno:w⌋ what you're talking
  8               about ...
```

Here Pam's utterance begun in line 5 is certainly not complete
when Gloria starts to talk in line 7. So on one level, this could be
classified as an interruption. But in another sense, it is clear that

Gloria's turn is an example of what Jefferson calls 'recognitional onset' of overlapping talk. That is, Gloria has evidently caught the gist of what Pam is saying – that she needs a cake tin lid to keep the roaches off – and starts her talk at that point in order to demonstrate cooperatively her recognition of the point. Rather than being a disruptive interruption, then, this case is more appropriately describable as a display of close cooperation between the two participants.

The point here is that by focusing purely on the coding and counting of instances, the SP approach inevitably counts as 'interruptions' things that may not be that at all. This is not to say that such things as interruptions somehow do not exist (see Hutchby 1992b). But the focus on quantification tends to lead the analyst away from considering, closely and on a case-by-case basis, how the participants themselves are orienting to one another's actions.

In this chapter we have introduced some of the principal conversation analytic techniques used for developing robust accounts of conversational phenomena. The focus has been on how conversational devices and other sorts of phenomena are located in large collections of data. The following chapter comprises the second part of our discussion of techniques for analysing phenomena. There we turn to look at procedures involving a sustained analytic focus on extended sequences of talk, including the widely used technique of single case analysis.

CHAPTER 5

Analysing Phenomena II
Extended Sequences and Single Cases

This chapter focuses on further ways in which the analysis of data can be approached. What we are concerned with here is the analysis of extended sequences of talk and, relatedly, the technique of single case analysis. Thus the focus shifts away from finding recursive features in collections of data, and towards the techniques of seeing significant interactional detail in the ongoing production of singular sequences of talk-in-interaction. In that sense, we now become more centrally involved with exemplifying the 'conversation analytic mentality': the distinctive way of seeing the world of talk-in-interaction that the conversation analyst develops in the course of working through specific pieces of data.

For the most part, the sequences discussed so far have been relatively short, and each turn has been analysed as doing essentially one action. But obviously this is not always the case. Turns at talk are often very long, and accomplish many different actions. At the same time, conversational sequences themselves can be much more extended than the ones discussed in the last chapter. A technique that can be applied in the analysis of extended sequences of talk is 'single case analysis'. In contrast to the analysis of collections, this technique involves tracking in detail the production of some extract of talk, which can be drawn more or less at random from any interactional context, to observe the ways in which particular conversational devices are used in its production. Unlike the building of collections, then, single case analysis is not necessarily aimed at producing new findings (although that can be an outcome), or at generalizability. Rather, it is more like a test-bed for the robustness of findings generated using the more systematic techniques described in chapter 4. As Schegloff puts it, the aim is principally 'to assess the [analytic] capacity of [CA], using its past results' (1987b: 101).

What it will also enable us to do is to illustrate in finer detail how the conversation analytic mentality may fruitfully be applied to any piece of data, wherever it may have been drawn from. This will stand us in good stead when we come in the next part of the book to a discussion of the often subtle and complex inferential work that can be accomplished by single utterances or parts of utterances (chapters 7 and 8). In order to explicate such features, the analyst needs to develop a sensitivity to very close levels of detail in the talk, and analysing single cases is a very good way of accomplishing that. Single case analysis will be the focus of attention in the first half of this chapter.

In the second part of the chapter we turn to a common form of talk-in-interaction which involves not only relatively extended sequential patterns, but also extended single turns at talk: storytelling. Of course, we all recount stories on a routine basis, about what happened to us during the day, or what we saw on the way to and from work or university, or whatever. We might think that these stories are merely ways of relaying information or of entertaining our friends or partners. But viewing stories using the conversation analytic mentality shows that they are in fact highly organized social phenomena, the methodic production of which is finely tuned to display the teller's orientation to the specific details of the current interactional context.

Analysing single episodes

Single case analysis involves looking at a single conversation, or section of one, in order to track in detail the various conversational strategies and devices which inform and drive its production. In his original lectures on conversation, Sacks (1992) used this technique often, stressing that the fundamental aim of CA is to be able to describe, adequately and formally, singular events and event sequences. Analysing singular sequences can be a key starting point in research, and even by beginning with relatively innocuous data, this technique can be used to discover a great deal about how the 'technology of conversation' (Sacks 1984b:

413) operates in particular instances. Furthermore, single case analysis shows how general features and patterns in talk, described using the collection technique, can be seen to inform the turn-by-turn production of talk in singular sequences of events.

In one sense, the kind of research described in chapter 4 itself involves the detailed analysis of single cases. The patterns that we looked at there are not seen just as patterns: they are regularities observable across a range of singular instances. To return to Schegloff's (1968) paper on telephone conversation openings, the reason why that paper is significant is not simply because Schegloff took one deviant case seriously enough to reformulate his analysis so as eventually to describe a pattern which accounted for all 500 cases in his data. Rather, the significance lies in *why* that was done. As Schegloff himself writes:

> Although the 'generalisation' did not apply in [one] case, [the participants] had also achieved, somehow, the outcome in question (getting a telephone conversation underway). How? ... [The second account] was found because one had to respect the fact that the 500th case was also, and equally, orderly for its participants, even though it was anomalous in the aggregate. (Schegloff 1987b: 102)

To illustrate further, Schegloff invites us to consider lectures as interactional occasions:

> Lectures ... have familiar organisational forms and practices which recur with great regularity on the multiple occasions on which they are delivered. But if a lecturer should begin producing bizarre behaviour, it is unlikely that those present would find it sufficient to set this aside as just a statistical anomaly. It would not suffice to consider that all the previously attended lectures followed one or another canonical form; that there was bound to be a case which deviated; and that this was it. Rather, observers find themselves making some sense or other of what is going on, and find some way of conducting themselves that deals with the situation. On reflection, of course, that is what is done on each of the *ordinary* such occasions in which persons participate. They find on each singular occasion whether and when to laugh, when to nod or knit the brow, whether and when to applaud, when and how to leave early if it is a bore ... (Schegloff 1987b: 102–3)

In other words, although conversation analysts are interested in the patterned nature of talk-in-interaction, it is recognized that the locus of order is always the single case. What we want to do in this section is to show how this aspect of the conversation analytic mentality can be brought to bear on one apparently trivial fragment of naturally occurring interaction, with some interesting and sociologically relevant results.

We focus on the following extract from a telephone conversation between two middle-aged, middle-class white American women, 'Nancy' and 'Edna'. We begin at the very start of the telephone call (Edna is caller).

```
(1)   [NB:II:2:1–2]
            (Ring)
  1  N:   Hello:,
  2  E:   .hh H̄I::.
  3       (.)
  4  N:   Oh: hi:::='ow a:re you Edna:,
  5  E:   FI:NE yer LINE'S BEEN BUSY.
  6  N:   Yea:h (.) my u-fuhh! h- .hhhh my fa:ther's wife
  7       ca:lled me,h .hhh So when she ca:lls me::, h I
  8       always talk fer a lo:ng ti:me cuz she c'n afford it
  9       en I ca:n't.hhh⌈hhhh ⌈huh⌉
 10  E:                  ⌊↑OH:⌊: : :⌋: my ⌈go:sh=Ah ↑th⌉ought=
 11  N:                       ((falsetto))  ⌊↑AOO:::::hh!⌋
 12  E:   =my phone wuz outta order:
 13       (0.2)
 14  N:   n⌈:No::?
 15  E:    ⌊I called my sister en I get this busy en then I'd
 16       hang up en I'd lift it up again id be: busy.
 17       (0.9)
 18  E:   .hh How you doin'.
 19  N:   .t hhh Pretty good I gutta rai:se.h .hh⌈hh
 20  E:                                         ⌊Goo:u⌈d.
 21  N:                                               ⌊Yeh
 22       two dollars a week.h
 23       (.)
 24  E:   Oh ⌈wo:w.
 25  N:   ‾ ⌊↑Īh:::huh hu⌈:h huh,
 26  E:                 ⌊Wud̄ee gun: do with it a:ll.
 27  N:   Gol' I rilly I jis' don't know how Ah'm gunnuh
 28       spend all that money.
 29       (0.2)
 30  E:   Y'oughta go sho:pping,
 31  N:   .hhhh Well I should but (.) yihknow et eight
 32       dollars a mo:⌈n:t̄h:,   anything   I'd⌉ buy'd, be using=
 33  E:              ⌊hm hmm hm-mm-hm.⌋
 34  N:   =up my raise fer ‾alf ⌈a YEA:R:⌉ ((smiley voice))
 35  E:                        ⌊Ye:a:h.⌋
 36  E:   .hhhhh Bud j's lef' t' play go:lf he's gotta go tuh
 37       Riverside . . .
```

What happens here is on one level entirely trivial. Edna calls her friend Nancy and indicates that she has had some trouble getting through. Nancy then complains about a paltry pay rise she just received; then as the extract ends Edna announces that her husband Bud has gone to play golf. What could be more commonplace? However, using the conversation analytic mentality we can come to see how the activities which make up this fragment are delicately accomplished through the use of interactional techniques which both transcend this particular conversation, yet at the same time are specifically designed for use within it.

So how do we go about using the findings of conversation analytic studies in order to explicate the underlying interactional organization of this fragment? One technique is simply to focus on some point in the talk and attempt to explicate the interactional work that is being done and the conversational resources being used in that work. We will focus first of all on Edna's utterance 'FI:NE yer LINE'S BEEN BUSY' (line 5). Later, we will look at the second half of the extract, following Nancy's utterance 'Pretty good I gutta rai:se' (line 19). One reason why we focus on these two turns is that both are done in response to an entirely conventional 'How are you?' inquiry (Nancy's ''ow a:re you Edna:' in line 4, and Edna's 'How you doin'' in line 18), yet both take very different forms. A second reason is that each of the utterances constitutes a form of *complaint*: yet these complaints are accomplished in different ways, which in turn have specific consequences for the talk which immediately follows. A number of CA studies can be brought to bear in helping us to understand how those utterances are designed to achieve the interactional effects that they do.

Let us note to start off with, then, that the fragment begins with a version of the standard telephone conversation opening described by Schegloff (1968; 1986): a summons-answer sequence of (ring) + 'Hello:', followed by an exchange of greetings, 'HI::' + 'Oh: hi:::'. This in turn is followed by the initiation of a how-are-you sequence: 'Oh: hi:::='ow a:re you Edna:' + 'FI:NE . . .'

To get a sense of how routine this form of opening is, note the almost identical structure of the opening we discussed briefly in the previous chapter:

(2)   [HG:1]
                   (Ring)
       1 Nancy: H'llo?

```
2  Hyla:    Hi:,
3  Nancy:   Hi::.
4  Hyla:    How are yuhh=
5  Nancy:   =Fi:ne how er you,
6  Hyla:    Oka:y,
```

This opening exemplifies what Schegloff (1986) has identified as the four 'core sequences' that are characteristic of telephone conversation openings in Western (and some non-Western) cultures:

- The *summons/answer sequence* (lines 0–1) This consists of the telephone ring (the summons) and the answerer's first 'Hello'.
- The *identification/recognition sequence* (lines 2–3) This is accomplished in extract (2) as the caller recognizes the called party's 'Hello', and uses a vocal signature to identify herself and invite reciprocal recognition.
- The *greetings sequence* (lines 2–3) In extract (2), this is accomplished simultaneously with identification/recognition; but in other calls, the participants may need to identify each other before engaging in greetings.
- The *initial inquiries sequence* (lines 4–6) Following greetings, participants regularly engage in an exchange of 'How are you's. These may lead straight into a first topic: for instance, if a response to a 'How are you' inquiry is either very negative ('Terrible') or overly positive ('Fantastic!'), the inquirer may ask 'Why?' Alternatively, as in extract (2), the responses can be neutral ('Fine' or 'Okay') and then a first topic needs either to be introduced or solicited.

In his large-scale study, Schegloff found this core set of sequences to be present in various forms and permutations throughout his data collection.

Like the two speakers in example (2), Nancy and Edna are friends who call each other up on a regular basis. Thus, in both examples, the caller (Edna in (1), Hyla in (2)) takes it that there is no need to identify themselves; rather, they assume that the answerer (a different 'Nancy' in each case) can recognize them by means of the sound of their voice alone. Consequently, the greetings exchange is minimal and the speakers rapidly move into the ensuing how-are-you exchange.

Here, however, the two calls start to differ. A major difference is that the how-are-you exchange in extract (2) is completed in what is the standard way for such an exchange (that is, two adjacency pairs, adjacent to each other: 'How are you'/Response + 'How are you'/Response), whereas in extract (1) that little sequence of two adjacency pairs is disrupted after the first response. Edna, instead of returning the how-are-you inquiry after her response, 'FI:NE', produces a comment about the fact that she has apparently been struggling to get through: 'FI:NE yer LINE'S BEEN BUSY'.

What interactional work is this utterance doing? Clearly, one way of viewing this statement is as a form of mild complaint. Edna is complaining, in an indirect way, about the fact that she has been unable to get through; in fact, she later implies, the situation had been so bad that she 'thought [her] phone wuz outta order:' (lines 10–12). Yet why does she produce this 'complaint' in the way she does: by stating a fact – the line's been busy – rather than objecting more overtly? We can account for this using a study by Pomerantz (1980) of the interactional strategy of 'fishing'.

Pomerantz notes that while speakers may request information in a straightforward way – for instance, by saying, 'Are you coming to the party tonight?' – another routine way in which requests for information are made is indirectly. One technique is to provide a factual report on the relevant events seen from the speaker's point of view, in order to 'invite' the recipient to provide the sought-after information by telling their side of events. So, with the party example, you might say, 'I hear Jeff's having a party tonight' as a way of *fishing* for information about whether your co-interactant has been invited. Pomerantz refers to these fishing statements as 'my side' tellings.

In telephone conversation, a common form of 'my side' telling is one which reports on the answerer's failure to answer their phone, as a way of fishing for information about where the answerer was, or who she was talking to. Clearly, this sort of information is open to being treated by its holder as entirely private; that is, it could be said that it is none of the caller's business why the phone was not answered. Therefore there are good reasons why such information should be sought indirectly. As Pomerantz shows, by producing a 'my side' telling, a speaker implies that they are intrigued to know more, but does not put the recipient in the position of having either to answer or find a reason for not answering, as would be the case with an explicit request.

In this sense, as Pomerantz says, 'the design of the "my side" telling poses this problem for the recipient: to determine what the co-interactant is suggesting or meaning in and through describing "my side"' (1980: 194). A significant feature of 'my side' tellings is thus that they provide an environment in which the next-turn proof procedure becomes especially relevant. In the turn following a 'my side' telling, the recipient displays her understanding of what the prior speaker was intending.

To return to our example, then, Edna's utterance 'yer LINE'S BEEN BUSY' is a clear example of a 'my side' telling: it reports the state of events from Edna's point of view as a person trying to make a telephone call. But if she is intending this as a form of mild complaint about the length of time she has been trying to get through, there are good reasons to use such a fishing device to do so, since there may be much more negative interactional implications associated with a more direct formulation.

But what exactly leads us to characterize this utterance as a complaint? As Pomerantz points out, discussing the same exchange, there is nothing in the formulation of Edna's utterance itself which necessarily makes it into a complaint: 'Certainly one possibility is that it is "merely" [Edna's] sharing of her experience of trying to get through to [Nancy]. Such a telling may also be done as an elicitor of information, for example, Were you talking on the phone and with whom.' However, she notes something quite specific about the way Edna's utterance is formulated:

> Those possibilities do not exhaust what can be heard as possibly 'behind' the telling. This telling, which formulates the 'my side' report as a product of the speaker's *repeated* attempts to get through (note the tense of the description), is hearable as a comment on the *length of time* the line was busy . . . (Pomerantz 1980: 195; second emphasis added)

It is this aspect which Nancy orients to as important in the construction of her response. We see this in the way that she reacts in the next turn by providing an *account* for the length of time the line has been busy: 'my fa:ther's wife ca:lled [and] when she ca:lls me::, I always talk fer a lo:ng ti:me cuz she c'n afford it en I ca:n't'.

Thus, by focusing in detail on this utterance, on the sequential environment in which it is produced, and the sequential implications which operate in the next turn, we begin to see two things. First, the way in which the speaker in this singular instance utilizes a general conversational resource in order to engage in a specific, locally situated activity; and secondly, the way in which conversation analytic studies of such general resources can be brought to bear in explicating the interactional organization of singular sequences. We can pursue these themes further by looking at a second instance of a 'complaint' in this extract, this time accomplished using quite different resources.

The talk occasioned by Edna's complaint goes on for a few more turns. It peters out when, after further talk by Edna about the number of calls she's been trying to make, there is no response from Nancy: merely a 0.9-second silence (line 17). This silence is broken by Edna returning eventually to the business of the how-are-you exchange (which, somewhat like an adjacency pair into which an insertion sequence has been slotted, has thus retained its conditional relevance): 'How you doin'' (line 18).

In line 19, Nancy's response to Edna's inquiry begins: 'Pretty good'. This, it turns out, is a significantly different kind of response to 'How are you?' than Edna's earlier 'FI:NE'. Indeed, the way Nancy responds to Edna's 'How you doin'' can be seen to be consequential for the particular kind of activity that follows: complaining about her raise. We can expand on this using another analysis of a general conversational resource.

As part of a major analysis of talk about troubles, Jefferson (1980) focused on responses to how-are-you inquiries, and began from Sacks's (1975) remarks that 'Fine' represents the conventional response to 'How are you'; it is a 'no-problem' response. 'Pretty good', on the other hand, represents what Jefferson describes as a 'downgraded conventional response'. Although it appears very similar to 'Fine', one kind of work which 'Pretty good' does that 'Fine' does not is to suggest or foreshadow bad news. Basically, Jefferson (1980) shows that if a speaker has some bad news to report or some trouble to tell, they will tend to use 'Pretty good' in this sequential environment in order to set up a trajectory in which the trouble might be elaborated on. By contrast, use of 'Fine' in this position, although it may be followed by news of some sort, is specifically *not* followed by bad news.

Adumbrating bad news, then, is a potential property of a 'Pretty good' response to 'How are you'. It is only potential, because bad news may or may not follow. The claim is not that 'Pretty good' is always followed by bad news, only that that is one of its routine uses. More than that, even when there is bad news, it may not be told straight away. For instance, Jefferson discusses cases where the troubles talk adumbrated by a 'Pretty good' response at the beginning of a conversation does not emerge until some minutes into that conversation. This potentiality makes it a perfect kind of resource for Nancy to engage in complaining about her raise ironically. Its ambivalence also makes it a good place for us to trace analytically the sequential trajectory of how it is understood.

The first mention of the raise immediately follows the 'Pretty good' response; it takes the form of a straightforward, unelaborated announcement: 'I gutta rai:se'. At this stage, then, the news that is being offered is, it appears, good news. And Edna indeed understands that to be the case, as exhibited in her response in line 20: 'Goo:ud'. It is only in the next two turns (lines 21–4) that the sense of Nancy's news being in fact not so good emerges. But notice that there is nothing in Nancy's next turn itself – 'Yeh two dollars a week' – which overtly suggests that Edna may need to revise her initial understanding of the news. She does not say, for instance, 'It's not that good – it's only two dollars a week'. Rather, her turn begins with 'Yeh', and then goes on to name the amount. In other words, the turn *implicitly* does the work of making the news ironic: it is left up to Edna to recognize the significance of 'two dollars a week' and so to detect the irony in Nancy's talk.

Now we come to the crux of the issue. Edna's reinterpretation of the announcement appears in the next turn, in line 24. Here, in the same way that her initial reaction was fitted to the form of the announcement as good news, this second reaction, a downward-intoned 'Oh wo:w.', equally is fitted to the new, revised status of the news. The fact that the turn begins with 'Oh' is significant in itself. As another collection-based analysis has shown, the discourse marker 'Oh' routinely performs the interactional work of displaying that 'its producer has undergone some kind of change in his or her locally current state of knowledge, information, orientation or awareness' (Heritage 1984b: 299). Edna's use of the item therefore connects with the way she is exhibiting a new understanding of her co-participant's talk. More importantly, the particular kind of new understanding being exhibited is marked in how the 'wo:w.' is said. The downward intonation (shown by the period) marks the negative status that the raise deserves, just as an upward and animated inflection ('Oh wow!') would mark the news in a positive way (see Local 1996).

Following that, and Nancy's burst of laughter in line 25, there is a sequence in which both speakers now adopt a heavily ironic mode of talking. Edna sustains the joke about the paltriness of the raise by asking, 'Wudee gun: do with it a:ll' (line 26) and by suggesting that Nancy 'oughta go sho:pping' (line 30). Nancy's responses are similarly ironic: for instance, 'Gol- I rilly I jis don't know how Ah'm gunnuh spend all that money' (lines 27–8).

These two complaint sequences repay close analysis partly because they are very well bounded. The first begins with a response to a how-are-you inquiry, and ends with the eventual production of a return how-are-you. The second sequence begins with a response to that inquiry, and ends when Edna explicitly changes the subject to mention that Bud (her husband) has just left to play golf (line 36). As we have shown, there are many features of this extract which illustrate the ways in which attending to the turn-by-turn organization of singular instances can lead to revealing insights into the orderliness of interaction. By focusing on the sequential management of complaints in these instances, we have illustrated two central themes in CA. First, that there is a close relationship between particular social actions and the sequential resources by which they are accomplished. Secondly, we have seen how the pervasive orderliness of interaction can be detected in singular sequences, simply by describing, in detail, the turn-by-turn unfolding of talk.

Another aspect of talk-in-interaction which repays detailed single case analysis is the activity of storytelling. In the following section, we introduce some of the key findings which conversation analysts have made about the interactional organization of storytelling, by means of an analysis of a single case of a story told in a telephone conversation.

Storytelling sequences

Stories involve extended, multi-unit turns at talk. One of the issues that arises when we begin to think about stories told in conversation is how we can subject such extended turns to analysis using the fundamentally sequential perspective of CA. This raises both empirical and methodological questions. We address some of the methodological questions in chapter 7, when we discuss the ways in which a CA perspective can be applied to extended, monologic utterances such as those where speakers recount stories about personal experiences in response to interview questions. However, most CA work on stories has focused on a second issue: the fact that stories are not produced in a vacuum, but their telling is always situated within interactional and sequential contexts. Given the overarching concern of CA with the sequential organization of talk, the analysis of stories merges into the analysis of story*telling*, which in turn becomes a focus on the production of storytelling sequences.

The linguists Labov and Waletsky (1966) were among the first to show systematically that stories told in conversation could be subjected to formal analysis. Their approach primarily involved soliciting stories from subjects by means of an interviewer asking them informally to recall any 'life-threatening experiences' they may have had. By looking at the overall structure of these stories as recounted in such a 'semi-natural' situation, Labov and Waletsky were able to show that unscripted stories have formal structures which can be analysed in a way similar to classical linguistic analyses of written stories such as fairy tales.

However, Labov and Waletsky's study took a fundamentally linguistic approach: they were interested in 'recurrent patterns characteristic of narrative from the clause level to the complete simple narrative' (1966: 12). Consequently, they focused on the story as a unit viewed, for the most part, in isolation from the surrounding sequential context in which it was produced. But from a CA perspective, one of their most interesting observations, which they mention only in passing, is that the production of a story in fact always occurs in some specific interactional context.

At around the same time as this study was produced, Sacks was developing an alternative analysis of the ways stories in conversation can be built, which focused on the question of interactional contexts. Sacks's concerns centred around two issues. First, how do stories get to be told in the first place? That is, how do speakers who want to tell a story go about starting to tell it? Given that most stories told in conversation are not produced in response to such a question as 'Have you ever been in a life-threatening situation?', how do putative storytellers establish an audience for their telling? The second issue, correspondingly, is: how do story recipients *respond* to the storytelling? This includes the kinds of actions produced by recipients during the storytelling itself; as well as the question of how the end of a storytelling is established. Both these processes turn out to involve highly systematic conversational phenomena.

We can illustrate these phenomena, again, by means of a single case analysis of a story told in the course of a telephone conversation. The following extract is one on which we have previously commented, in chapter 3. There, however, we focused on it principally in terms of how it is transcribed, whereas here we are concerned with how the storytelling is put together in sequential terms. Prior to the beginning of the extract, Lesley has been trying to persuade Joyce to accompany her to a meeting, which Joyce has declined but in a vague way, without providing any reason. It seems that this declination would be an appropriate point at which to conclude the call. Lesley, however, carries on the conversation in the following way.

(3) [Holt: Xmas 85:4:2–4]

1 L: Are you not feeling very [we:ll,
2 J: [°( )°
3 (.)
4 J: No I'm all ri:ght
5 (.)
6 L: Yes.
7 (0.6)
8 J: °Ye:s I'm all right,°
9 L: °Oh:.° .hh Yi-m- You know I- I- I'm broiling about
10 something hhhheh[heh .hhhh
11 J: [Wha::t.
12 L: Well that sa:le. (0.2) At- at (.) the vicarage.
13 (0.6)
14 J: Oh ye[:s,
15 L: [.t
16 (0.6)
17 L: u (.) ihYour friend 'n mi:ne was the:re
18 (0.2)

```
19   J:    (h⌈h hh)
20   L:     ⌊mMister::, R:,
21   J:    Oh y(h)es, °(hm̄ hm)°
22         (0.4)
23   L:    And em: .p we (.) really didn't have a lot'v cha:nge
24         that (.) day b̄ecuz w̄e'd been to Bath 'n we'd b̄een:
25         Christmas shoppin:g, (0.5) but we thought we'd̄ better
26         go ālong t'th' sale 'n do what we coūld, (0.2) we
27         hadn't got a lot (.) of s:e- ready cash t'spe:nd.
28         (0.6)
29   L:    In any case we thought th' things were v̲ery
30         expen̲sive.
31   J:    Oh dīd you.
32         (0.9)
33   L:    AND uh we were looking round the sta:lls 'n p̲oking
34         about 'n he came up t' me 'n he said Oh: hhello
35         Lesley, (.) still trying to buy something f'noth̲ing,
36         .tch! .hh ⌈hahhhhhhh!
37   J:            ⌊.hhoohhhh!
38         (0.8)
39   J:    Oo⌈::: ⌈: L e s l e y⌉
40   L:     ⌊OO:!⌊ehh h̄eh heh⌋
41         (0.2)
42   J:    I:s⌈n 't⌉  ⌈he
43   L:      ⌊What⌋ do y⌊ou sa:y.
44         (0.3)
45   J:    Oh isn't he drea:dful.
46   L:    °eYe::s.°
47         (0.6)
48   J:    What'n aw::ful ma:⌈:::n
49   L:                     ⌊eh heh heh heh
50   J:    Oh:: honestly I cannot stand the m̄an it's j̲ust
51         (no⌈: )
52   L:       ⌊I thought well I'm gon' tell Joyce that, ehh heh
```

The story here consists of Lesley's recounting of the social insult or 'squelch' inflicted on her by 'Mister R' (in his implication that she is using a charity sale to hunt for bargains) and the circumstances surrounding that. One way of seeing this is as an extended turn which runs from line 12, when she introduces the context for the story ('that sa:le ... at the vicarage'), to line 35, when she recounts the squelch ('still trying to buy something f'nothing'). However, it is not simply a single turn of extended length: as we can see, at various points her recipient, Joyce, produces utterances which 'break up' the story turn (lines 14, 21 and 31). We return to this point shortly. First, we need to address the question: how does this story come to be told? In other words, how is the story *occasioned* in the sequential unfolding of the talk?

Story prefaces

In a series of lectures on storytelling in conversation, Sacks (1992, vol. 2: 222–68) began with a basic observation: 'Stories routinely take more than one turn to tell' (p. 222). By this, he meant to draw attention to the fact that in order to tell a story, the prospective teller has to engage in work to align their co-interactant as a story *recipient*. There are various reasons for this. One is that stories are designed in numerous ways 'for' their particular recipients, and the telling provides opportunities for recipients to react to, display understanding of, or otherwise become involved in the telling. We discuss some of these features as they can be found in our focus extract later.

More importantly, the telling of a story involves the teller in keeping possession of the conversational floor for longer than the basic rules of turn-taking ordinarily allow. That is, the story-telling turn consists of more than one turn-constructional unit, and there has to be some way of indicating to the recipient that such an extended turn is underway, in order for them to refrain from taking the floor themselves at what might otherwise be a legitimate transition-relevance place. The most routine way of accomplishing this is to produce a *story preface*. This is a turn in which a speaker, often indirectly, proposes to tell a story. Following the preface, the recipient can then respond by indicating whether they wish to hear the story; and finally, the story can be told with the recipient appropriately aligned. The canonical format for story prefaces is thus a three-part structure:

> *Teller*:   Story preface
> *Recipient*: Request to hear story
> *Teller*:   Story

For example:

(4) **[Trio:2:1:1]**
(A calls B, who is an employee at 'Bullocks' department store)
1→   A: Well I thought I'd jus' re- better report
2   to you what's happened at Bullocks today
3→   B: What in the world's happened?
4   A: Did you have the day off?
5   (.)
6   B: Yah?
7→   A: Well I:- (.) got outta my car at fi:ve thirty ...
           ((Story continues))

By indicating that she'd 'better report what's happened', A proposes to tell a story. In line 3, B appropriately aligns herself as a story recipient by inviting A to go on and tell 'what in the world's happened', which A then proceeds to do.

Sacks makes a number of observations on this sequence in terms of how it sets up the story to follow and aligns the recipient in the appropriate way (1992, vol. 2: 157–87). For instance, 'I thought I'd jus' re- better report to you what's happened at Bullocks' displays that speaker A is designing this telling specifically 'for' her recipient. Given that Bullocks is B's place of work, but not A's, then her reporting of something that happened there on what she believes to be B's day off (note the way she checks this in line 4) is a way of doing the activity of 'showing that I had my mind on you' (p. 174). This is a common feature of recipient design in conversational storytelling. We find another, more explicit example of it towards the end of extract (3), our focus extract:

```
48    J:   What'n aw::ful ma:ɹ::n
49    L:                        ᶫeh heh heh heh
50    J:   Oh:: honestly I cannot stand the man it's just
51         (noɹ: )
52→   L:        ᶫI thought well I'm gon' tell Joyce that, ehh heh
```

Having told her story, and gone with her recipient through an extended response sequence, Lesley makes an announcement which claims that, even at the time the events were happening, she was thinking of Joyce as a suitable and in fact necessary recipient of this story.

Returning to extract (4), there are further features of interest in the way the story preface is designed. Note that the speaker actually executes a self-repair in the course of this preface; she begins to say 'I thought I'd jus' re[port] ...', but then changes that to a formulation which brings to the forefront the urgency and importance of the story: 'I thought I'd ... *better* report to you what's happened'. This way of putting it also implicates the recipient as someone who actually has some stake in this story: she is not just any recipient, but one to whom the events had 'better' be reported. When speaker B produces the second part of the story prefacing sequence (request to hear the story), she too orients to the seemingly momentous nature of this story, thereby situating herself as a suitably awed recipient. She does this by saying, not simply, 'What happened?', but 'What in the world's happened?', thereby focusing on the extraordinariness of these (so far undisclosed) events. (In fact it turns out that A had seen a policeman wielding a 'great big long gun' outside the store where B works, but could not discover why he was there. Subsequently the two participants engage in a series of phone calls involving a third person who also works at the store but did not, like B, have the day off, in an attempt to discover what was happening.)

Aligning recipients, then, is one of the key functions of story prefaces. But it is not the only significant function. They can also be involved in another key aspect of conversational storytelling: indicating to the recipient what *kind* of story this will be. This is important because one of the interactional tasks of a story recipient is to respond to the story in appropriate ways once it is over. Thus the recipient needs to have some idea of what it will take in order for the story to be complete: in other words, an idea of the likely payoff or punchline for this particular story. This element of story prefaces is illustrated well in the preface which occurs in our focus extract:

```
 9→   L:   ... You know I- I- I'm broiling about
10         something hhhhehₜheh .hħhh
11→   J:                    ⌊Wha::t.
12→   L:   Well that sa:le. (0.2) At̄- at (.) the vicarage ...
```

What is noticeable here is that the preface, in lines 9–10, gives a very clear indication not only of the kind of story this is, but also, crucially, of how Joyce, as recipient, might monitor for a suitable conclusion to the story. We can notice in particular the use of the word 'broiling' in 'I'm broiling about something'. Why might Lesley select this word to describe her state of mind? The *Shorter Oxford English Dictionary* defines 'broil' as 'to be in a confused state, a turmoil'; it can also mean 'to subject to high heat', as in cooking. However, given the story Lesley goes on to tell, neither of these usages would seem to be particularly appropriate. Rather, it is possible that she coins the word as an ad hoc combination of 'brewing' and 'boiling'. As Goffman (1981, ch. 5) has suggested, making a slight twist on Freud's ideas about slips of the tongue, mispronunciations or 'wrong' uses of words can frequently be closely tied to questions of interactional design. It may be that Lesley's use of the word 'broiling' is interactionally sensitive in that it neatly conveys a sense of her being about to boil over with anger, and at the same time brewing up a desire to tell this story to Joyce.

More than that, 'I'm broiling about something' indicates to the recipient how she might monitor for an appropriate conclusion to the story. In a word, it poses a question for the recipient: 'What kinds of things might the teller legitimately be broiling about?' The kinds of things to which 'broiling', in the sense we have suggested, is a relevant reaction include having been insulted, embarrassed, made to feel foolish, belittled and so on; in other words, just the kind of social 'squelch' which Lesley's story reports Mr R inflicting on her.

Another point is that the very way in which the story is responded to on its completion links back very neatly to the way it was introduced in the preface. That is, the sharp intakes of breath and exaggerated, indignant Oooh's have an almost ono-matopoeic connection to the states of 'brewing' and 'boiling'. They are sounds which are reminiscent of steam and of sudden, heated expulsions. In this way, the coordinated verbalized reac-tions of Lesley and Joyce can be seen as concomitant with the *physical* reaction ('broiling') which Lesley has described herself as undergoing as a result of the story's events.

Clearly, these last few points are speculative: there is little sys-tematic evidence in the transcript itself which would support such an interpretation of Lesley's use of 'broiling'. However, our remarks here relate to an issue with which Sacks was concerned in his lectures on conversation: what he referred to as the 'poet-ics' of everyday talk (1992, vol. 2: 291–331). Often, in looking repeatedly at a particular segment of talk, Sacks noted that the analyst can begin to find certain poetic resonances and relation-ships between the words used. He speculated that there may be a principle of 'locally historical searches' that speakers use in com-ing up with their words. They may somehow rely on echoes of words produced moments earlier to cue other words or phrases. In the lectures given during the second half of his career, Sacks discussed a number of intriguing cases to support this notion.

This way of proceeding may seem to go against the rigorous reliance on the next-turn proof procedure which we have stressed in previous chapters. However, what it in fact does is to illustrate a significant benefit of single case analysis: that it provides the analyst with an entirely open opportunity to develop and explore analytic themes and ideas. As Sacks put it: 'When we start out

with a piece of data, the question of what we are going to end up
with, what kind of findings it will give, should not be a considera-
tion. We sit down with a piece of data, make a bunch of observations, and see where they will go' (1984a: 27). One implication of
this is that we should not initially feel constrained in the observations we make by what common sense might suggest is possible
or not. In the very first of his lectures, Sacks was at pains to point
this out to his students:

> When people start to analyse social phenomena ... then, if you
> have to make an elaborate analysis of it – that is to say, show that
> they did something as involved as some of the things I have pro-
> posed – then you figure that they couldn't have thought that fast. I
> want to suggest that you have to forget that completely. Don't
> worry about how fast they're thinking. First of all, don't worry
> about whether they're 'thinking'. Just try to come to terms with
> how it is that the thing comes off. Because you'll find that they can
> do these things. ... So just let the materials fall as they may. Look
> to see how it is that persons go about producing what they pro-
> duce. (1992, vol. 1: 11)

Recipient's actions during the storytelling

We noted earlier that the story turn itself is not a single unbro-
ken utterance, but one which is punctuated by turns from Joyce,
the recipient. However, these turns cannot be seen as utterances
which 'break up' the story turn, to use our earlier words. They
are sequentially organized features of the storytelling itself.
Obviously, the 'Wha::t' in line 11 functions as the second part of
the story preface sequence. Let us now turn to Joyce's next two
utterances: 'Oh ye:s' in line 14, and the similar 'Oh y(h)es' in line
21.

Like the 'Wha::t', but in a different manner, these two turns
are invited or solicited by Lesley. Recall in the last chapter that
we briefly discussed some generalized, cross-cultural procedures
by which speakers seek to establish mutual recognition of the
identity of someone or something they are referring to. This
comes under the heading of *recipient design* (Sacks and Schegloff
1979): the way in which all turns at talk are in some way designed
to be understood in terms of what the speaker knows or assumes
about the existing mutual knowledge between him or her and the

recipient. In chapter 4 we observed that in the following extract, speaker A makes three attempts to establish mutual reference to a couple named Ford (lines 2–3), each of them focusing on different ways that the recipient might be able to recognize who is being referred to:

(5) **[Sacks and Schegloff 1979: 19]**
```
1  A:  ... Well I was the only one other than the uhm
2         tch Fords? Uh, Mrs Holmes Ford? You know
3         uh ⌈the the cellist?
4  B:        ⌊Oh yes. She's she's the cellist.
5  A:  Yes.
6  B:  Ye⌈s
7  A:     ⌊Well she and her husband were there ...
```

Having failed to establish mutual reference with the general term 'the Fords?' (line 2), the speaker then proceeds to more specific labels: 'Mrs Holmes Ford' – which again does not immediately work – and finally 'the cellist'. Note that it is this third reference which appears to be most closely designed in terms of the two participants' mutual knowledge: when B finally recognizes who is being referred to, she herself affirms that recognition (line 4) by repeating the categorization: 'she's the cellist.'

There are close similarities here with our focus extract (3):

```
12→  L:  Well that sa:le. (0.2) At- at (.) the vicarage.
13        (0.6)
14  J:  Oh ye:s,
```

And a moment later:

```
17→  L:  u (.) ihYour friend 'n mi:ne was the:re
18        (0.2)
19  J:  (h⌈h hh)
20→  L:    ⌊mMister::, R:,
21  J:  Oh y(h)es, °(hm hm)°
```

On both these occasions Lesley makes successive attempts to get Joyce to recognize (1) the context of the story, and (2) its key protagonist. It is notable that both her first attempts are very vague: 'that sa:le' (line 12) and 'Your friend 'n mi:ne' (line 17); also, that both these attempts fail. The first, 'that sa:le', could potentially refer to any sale in any place, although clearly Lesley believes that Joyce is capable of pinpointing the precise sale in question, perhaps because of its recency, the fact that it had been discussed in a previous conversation (this is the first mention of it in this particular call), or some other aspect that gives it salience. Equally, Lesley's first mention of the key protagonist in the story (line 17) is extremely vague: 'Your friend 'n mi:ne'. While this is a conventionally ironic way of referring to someone who is not a friend at all, it leaves the recipient a lot of work to do in order to establish which person exactly is being mentioned.

One other thing to notice about Lesley's turn, 'Your friend 'n mi:ne was the:re', is its slight upward intonation (indicated by the underlined colon in 'the:re'). Sacks and Schegloff (1979) observed that one way of attempting to achieve the most economical form of reference is for speakers to use upward intonation, which they called 'try-marking' (since it is a way of marking a try at establishing mutual reference). Speaker A in extract (5) uses try-marking three times (indicated in the transcript by question marks), and a similar phenomenon is found in our focus extract.

A further thing to observe is that in our focus extract (3) a pause follows this try-marked reference (line 18). This appears to be a place in which Lesley is monitoring for a response from Joyce indicating that she has 'got' the reference. In the absence of any such indication, Lesley then produces her next attempt, which is also try-marked: 'Mister::, R:,' (line 20): note again the underlined colon. At this point, Joyce recognizes the referent (line 21), and the story subsequently proceeds.

Thus, in this case, 'interjections' into the storytelling turn can be seen to result from interactionally organized forms of invitation by means of which Lesley, rather than merely recounting the incident, is actively seeking to *involve* Joyce in the telling. Furthermore, this segment illustrates the carefully designed ways in which storytellers may display that they are designing their telling for this *particular* recipient (see Goodwin 1984). Notice, for instance, the way that both of Lesley's attempts to establish reference are designed to point up the common knowledge of the interactants. In the first case this is done by the use of pronouns: '*that* sale ... at *the* vicarage'. Implicit here is the claim not only that Joyce knows about the sale, but also that she knows about the vicarage in question.

In the second case, Lesley twice uses euphemisms rather than a name; furthermore, each of those figurative references in turn foregrounds common knowledge: 'Your friend and mine', and the familiarism, 'Mister R'. A final point on this is that Joyce not only recognizes the person being referred to as 'Mister R', but appears to do the correct *kind* of recognition for what turns out to be the point of this story. That is, by appending a slight laugh to her affirmation: 'Oh y(h)es, °(hm hm)°', Joyce exhibits that she sees Mister R in the appropriate way; that is, as someone who may be expected to have done something amusing, embarrassing or possibly insulting.

Conversation analysts, then, consider stories not just as single turn narratives, but as multiple unit turns which occur in concrete sequential contexts. One thing that is clear about storytelling sequences is that they can be relatively extended, as compared, say, to the classical adjacency pair structure. But as we have seen through this discussion of a single storytelling sequence, it is possible also to show that other structures – for instance, story preface sequences or recognitional sequences – are used in specific ways in putting together a storytelling sequence. In other words, one of the main objectives of a CA approach to storytelling as a conversational phenomenon is to analyse how the various structural patterns in talk can be deployed as the 'building blocks' for other, more extended sequences.

This takes us back to an idea mentioned briefly towards the end of chapter 1: that the resources of talk-in-interaction are both context-sensitive and context-free. What we have done in this and the preceding chapter is to demonstrate how that feature of conversational resources can be seen empirically, and how it informs the analytic procedures of CA. In chapter 4 we focused on the building of collections of similar extracts which are organized using certain techniques to demonstrate the existence of patterns in interaction. This procedure relies on the idea that different conversationalists, at different times and in different situations, have available essentially similar resources for accomplishing their actions. These resources (such as the po-faced receipt of a tease, for instance), while they are not tied to the specific occasion of their use, are none the less utilized in a way which attends to the unique features of that local occasion. In this sense, talk-in-interaction can be described as an abstract, structural phenomenon, without going against the idea that participants are knowledgeable agents who are not somehow 'caused' to act by that structure but actively use it to accomplish particular communicative actions.

In a similar way, the present chapter has demonstrated how abstract structural resources such as the story preface sequence, or sequences for inviting recipient's reactions or establishing mutual reference to a third party, are used in locally situated ways to accomplish activities such as telling a story. We also demonstrated how conversation analytic studies of structural patterns themselves can be fruitfully deployed in making sense of how participants are managing interaction in single cases or extended sequences.

In conclusion, it is important to say that while these chapters have aimed to introduce some of the key 'how to' techniques in CA, it has not been our aim to provide an exhaustive account of all the possible research practices employed by conversation analysts. This is because, for one thing, there are simply too many minor variations to make such an exercise worthwhile; also, specific techniques which work well for one researcher will not necessarily work in the same way for another. Therefore, what we have done is introduce the *basic* means of beginning on a piece of CA research. For the beginning researcher, thinking in terms of systematic, formal similarities between data extracts which appear to be involved in certain classes of social action is perhaps the most useful starting point. But as we have shown in this chapter, a great deal can also be learned simply by sitting down with a transcript, and the associated tape, and trying to describe what is going on in that talk. However trivial it may appear, the lesson is that this talk is an orderly, methodic accomplishment. Approaching data in terms of 'What are the participants doing here?', 'How are they accomplishing that?' and 'How do they display the orderliness of the talk for each other?' is at the root of the conversation analytic mentality, and will virtually always yield results.

In the following chapters, we turn away from issues specifically to do with the process of analysis and towards the question of how a conversation analytic approach can be applied to some of the broader questions of social life. We begin in chapter 6 with an account of how CA approaches the nature of institutionalized and workplace interaction.

PART III

Applications

CHAPTER 6

Talk in Institutional Settings

What does conversation analysis have to say about interaction in the larger-scale, institutional contexts of social life? CA's hallmark seems to be the analysis of small sequences of talk often recorded in the most mundane settings of everyday life. But can this perspective be applied to studies of talk in institutional settings such as courtrooms, classrooms, the media, medical consultations, psychiatric interviews and other forms of lay–professional interaction? In recent years a great deal of research has been carried out on such settings. Our aim in this chapter is to introduce the central issues involved in this work, in which the approach of CA is applied to relatively specialized sets of data.

There are a number of reasons why it is important to study interaction in institutional settings. First of all, in modern society a vast amount of people's time is spent in broadly institutional or organizational contexts such as workplaces, educational establishments and service settings like shops, banks and doctors' consulting rooms. In all these routine social spaces, talk is a central activity. We also listen to an enormous amount of talk that has been produced within the institutional and organizational context of television and radio studios. Studying such settings therefore tells us more about the key role of talk in the production of social life.

However, CA's contribution goes further than simply describing the talk that people produce in such settings. In line with its general approach, where participants in conversation are seen as actively accomplishing the orderly nature of conversation itself, CA argues that institutional talk is centrally and actively involved in the accomplishment of the 'institutional' nature of institutions themselves. We have seen how participants can be observed to display an orientation to the rules of turn-taking for conversation, thereby constituting the very activity of 'having a conversation', as opposed to, say, 'doing an interrogation'. By focusing on the relatively specialized ways in which turn-taking and turn design are accomplished in institutional settings, conversation analysts show how participants similarly constitute 'non-conversational' interactions by the same process of displaying an orientation to the relevance of specific types of activity.

We therefore begin this chapter by looking at how CA approaches the issue of participants' orientations to institutional contexts. In later sections, we move on to address a series of related questions such as the different forms of interaction in institutional settings that can be discovered. Lastly, we outline a conversation analytic perspective on the nature of asymmetry and power in institutional interaction.

Orienting to context: the comparative approach

As we have seen, a central feature of CA is a focus on the turn-by-turn unfolding of talk-in-interaction. This approach is linked to the view that participants themselves use that sequential development as an interpretive resource in order to make sense of one another's actions. In analysing talk-in-interaction, then, CA places great emphasis on the immediate sequential context in which a turn is produced.

But there is a broader sense of 'context' which can be invoked. Talk does not occur in a vacuum. It is always, somehow, situated. These situational contexts range from chance meetings in the street, through conversations with friends and family members, to larger-scale organizational settings such as workplaces, schools and various kinds of service institutions, including even more specialized settings such as doctors' consulting rooms, courts of law, or TV and radio studios. The question is, what can CA's essentially local idea of context tell us about these wider social contexts?

To answer this question we need to understand what characterizes institutional interaction itself. As Goffman (1961) once pointed out, institutions are things that social scientists spend a great deal of time trying to describe and explain, but which they have not found a very apt way of classifying. CA has found one way round this problem. As far as CA is concerned, what characterizes interaction as institutional is to do not with theories of social structure, as in most sociology, but with the special character of speech exchange systems that participants can be found to orient to.

This idea has its roots in the seminal paper on turn-taking by Sacks, Schegloff and Jefferson (1974). In that paper, the authors proposed that different forms of talk could be viewed as a continuum ranging from the relatively unconstrained turn-taking of mundane conversation, through various levels of formality, to ceremonial occasions in which not only who speaks and in what sequential order, but also what they will say, are pre-arranged (for instance, in wedding ceremonies). By selectively reducing or otherwise transforming the full scope of conversational practices, concentrating on some and withholding others, participants can be seen to display an orientation to particular institutional contexts.

This involves moving beyond a commonplace conception of context, in which the contexts of interaction are thought of as 'containers' which people enter into and which, at the same time, exert causal influences on the behaviour of participants within them. This is an assumption which underlies a good deal of work in sociology and sociolinguistics (Coulter 1982; Schegloff 1991). However, it raises the problem of the 'cultural dope' (Garfinkel 1967). Basically, the 'container' view of context fails to pay sufficient attention to the active knowledge that participants have of the production of their behaviour. Rather than seeing contexts as abstract social forces which impose themselves on participants, conversation analysts argue that we need to begin from the other direction and see participants as knowledgeable social agents who actively display for one another (and hence also for observers and analysts) their orientation to the relevance of contexts.

This is not to deny that the wider social contexts of interaction may have an overarching relevance for the participants. Intuitively, we know that a lively sense of context routinely informs our actions in the various social scenes of everyday life. For instance, if we were to call a radio phone-in programme, it is unlikely that in the midst of that activity we would suddenly be under the impression that we were calling a friend about a dinner invitation. In general, it seems, we 'know what we are doing', and are aware of the social settings for our actions.

But for conversation analysis, this intuitive view is inadequate. By relying on the private realm of individual awareness, it fails to account for the essentially *public* means by which participants display for one another their orientation to context and their understanding of each other's actions. As in mundane conversation, CA looks for a proof procedure which will show how participants make available for each other (and hence for the analyst too) the relevance of an institutional setting. That proof procedure is found in the observable details of talk-in-interaction.

CA has developed a distinctive means of locating participants' displayed orientations to institutional contexts. This is done by adopting a broadly comparative perspective in which the turn-taking system for mundane conversation is treated as a benchmark against which other forms of talk-in-interaction can be distinguished. By 'mundane' conversation, of course, we refer to a technical category which is defined by a turn-taking system in which the order, size and type of turns are free to vary. By contrast, other, more institutional forms of talk-in-interaction involve either the reduction or the systematic specialization of the range of practices available in mundane conversation.

The significance of this approach is that it succeeds in revealing what is distinctive about interaction in different types of environment. This is the most basic way in which CA aims to locate participants' active orientations to institutional contexts. Using this method, two basic types of institutions have been defined. They are described as *formal* types and *non-formal* types (Heritage and Greatbatch 1991). The formal types of institutional setting are represented by courts of law (Atkinson and Drew 1979), many kinds of interview, particularly the broadcast news interview (Clayman 1988; Heritage 1985; Heritage and Greatbatch 1991) but also job interviews (Button 1992), by some more 'traditional' or teacher-led styles of classroom teaching (McHoul 1978), and most sorts of ceremonial occasion. Non-formal types include more loosely structured, but still task-oriented, lay/professional encounters such as GPs' consultations (Frankel 1990), counselling sessions (Perakyla 1996), various other kinds of social work encounters (Heritage and Sefi 1992), business meetings (Boden 1994), service encounters in places such as shops (Lamoreux 1988–9), radio phone-in conversations

(Hutchby 1996a) and so on. We can look at each of these basic types in more detail.

Formal institutions and question–answer sequences

The distinctiveness of formal types of institutional settings is based on the close relationship between the participants' social roles and the forms of talk in which they engage. As Heritage and Greatbatch put it: 'The institutional character of the interaction is embodied first and foremost in its *form* – most notably in turn-taking systems which depart substantially from the way in which turn-taking is managed in conversation' (1991: 95). Studies of settings such as courtrooms and broadcast news interviews have focused on the ways in which participants orient to a strict turn-taking format. Atkinson and Drew (1979) coined the notion of 'turn-type pre-allocation' to characterize the organization of interaction in these settings. Turn-type pre-allocation means that participants, on entering the setting, are normatively constrained in the types of turns they may take according to their particular institutional roles. Typically, the format involves chains of question–answer sequences, in which the institutional figure asks the questions and the witness, pupil or interviewee is expected to provide the answers. This format is pre-established, and normative rules operate which mean that participants can be constrained to stay within the boundaries of the question–answer framework.

This, of course, is very different from turn-taking in mundane conversation, where roles are not restricted to those of questioner and answerer, and where the type and order of turns in a given interaction may vary freely. But the question–answer pre-allocation format is only a minimal characterization of the speech exchange system for courtroom interaction. As Atkinson and Drew (1979) point out, any of a range of actions may be done in a given turn, provided that they are done in the *form* of a question or answer. For instance, consider extract (1), which is taken from the transcript of a rape trial.

(1)   [Levinson 1992: 83]
    1   A: You have had sexual intercourse on a previous
    2   occasion, haven't you.

```
 3  B:  Yes.
 4  A:  On many previous occasions?
 5  B:  Not many.
 6  A:  Several?
 7  B:  Yes.
 8  A:  With several men?
 9  B:  No.
10  A:  Just one?
11  B:  Two.
12  A:  Two. And you are seventeen and a half?
13  B:  Yes.
```

Here, A and B are respectively the defence attorney and the alleged rape victim. As we see, they restrict themselves to producing questions and answers, and by this restriction of turn-taking behaviour, we gain a powerful sense of context simply through the details of their talk.

However, when we look more closely at the questions asked by speaker A, we find that they are of a peculiar type. Searle (1969) introduced a distinction between two types of question: 'real' questions which are designed to inform the questioner about something which he or she does not know, and 'exam' questions which are designed to test the answerer's knowledge about something which the questioner already knows. The questions in extract (1) seem to represent neither of these types. First of all, they are not designed to inform the questioner. When asking about B's sexual experience, or about her age, A clearly knows the answers already. Neither, though, are the questions designed to test B's own knowledge. Rather, they are designed to get B to *admit* to something: namely, to having had sexual intercourse with 'several men' at the age of seventeen and a half.

By these means, the questions are designed to construct, piece by piece, a certain social image of B: as a woman with 'loose morals'. Levinson (1992) observes that it is not any one question in particular which accomplishes this, but rather the juxtaposition between the questions as a series (especially in the last case, in line 12) and their answers. In other words the *style* of questioning is itself a significant part of the participants' displayed orientation to the context of a courtroom.

Of course, in making these observations, we are relying on our commonsense knowledge about what a 'trial' consists of. In particular, we are using commonsense knowledge about how defence attorneys might go about cross-examining witnesses. For instance, in a rape trial, the defence may want to build up a picture of the alleged victim's 'loose morals' in order to suggest complicity on her part. On this basis, we are able to recognize A's questioning strategies in extract (1) as those of a cross-examining defence attorney.

But does this reduce our analysis to the level of 'mere' common sense? The answer is no, because for CA, what is of interest are the ways participants manage their interaction. This means that we aim to describe what it is that participants display to one another as relevant to their interaction, on a turn-by-turn basis. Inevitably, some of the features we rely on to anchor our descriptions will seem intuitive. This is because they are the very same resources as those used by the participants in the occasion. In fact, if we did not begin from the standpoint of these resources, we would face the problem of explaining why our analyst's notion of the relevant contextual features differed from the relevancies that were observably oriented to by the participants themselves. The point is that, as in mundane conversation, the details of turn-taking reveal the procedures by which participants in institutional interaction display for one another their mutual understandings and their corresponding sense of context.

Going further than this, orientation to pre-allocated turn-taking systems such as the question–answer format can have important implications for the specifically 'institutional' character of actions in formal settings. We can focus on one of the most significant of these: the fact that in settings such as courtrooms and broadcast news interviews, powerful constraints operate to restrict the distribution of rights to express a personal opinion on the matter being discussed. In both settings, questioners are required to avoid stating their opinions overtly. Rather, their task is to elicit the stance, opinion or account of the one being questioned, but to do so at least technically without bias or prejudice. This is because both courtroom and broadcast news talk are intended to be heard principally by an audience: the jury in a trial court, and the public in broadcast news. For different reasons, the audience in each case is supposed to draw inferences and make judgements about the one being questioned without undue influence from the questioner. As well as constraints on the form of questioners' turns, then, there are restrictions on their content, in that a questioning turn should not be hearable as putting forward a personal opinion.

·

However, questioners clearly have ways of undermining this constraint. We have already observed how the questioner's strategies in extract (1) serve to construct a negative social image of the witness, and hence are implicitly critical in their assessment of her behaviour. In broadcast news, interviewers can similarly produce talk that is critical and challenging towards interviewees by adopting various kinds of strategies. For instance, they can embed critical or evaluative statements within questions; or they may cite the 'facts' so as to emphasize their contrastive relationship with an interviewee's statement; alternatively, they may attribute opposing points of view to others and then offer them for comment (Pomerantz 1988–9). These strategies enable interviewers to take up critical stances on their own behalf; yet through being framed within a question, allow them formally to adhere to the journalist's norm of neutrality (Clayman 1988; 1992).

Another strategy involves selectively 'formulating' the gist or upshot of the interviewee's remarks, usually in pursuit of some controversial or newsworthy aspect. Heritage describes the practice of formulating as: 'Summarising, glossing, or developing the gist of an informant's earlier statements. Although it is relatively rare in conversation, it is common in institutionalised, audience-directed interaction [where it] is most commonly undertaken by questioners' (1985: 100). Formulations can be used both in a relatively benign, summarizing role, and also as moves in which the interviewer seeks somehow to evaluate the interviewee's remarks. Extract (2), taken from Heritage's paper, provides an illustration of the latter type of use:

```
(2)    [TVN: Tea]
1      C:   What in fact happened was that in the course of last
2           year, .hh the price went up really very sharply, .hhh
3           and uh the blenders did take advantage of this: uh
4           to obviously to raise their prices to retailers. (0.7)
5           .hhh They haven't been so quick in reducing their
6           prices when the world market prices come down. (0.3)
7           .hh And so this means that price in the sh- the
8           prices in the shops have stayed up .hh really rather
9           higher than we'd like to see them.
10          (0.7)
11→    Int:  So you- you're really accusing them of profiteering.
12     C:   .hhh No they're in business to make money that's
13          perfectly sensible.=We're also saying that uh: .hh
14          it's not a trade which is competitive as we would
```

```
15          like it.=There're four (0.2) blenders which have
16          together eighty five percent of the market .hhh
17          and uh we're not saying that they (.) move in
18          concert or anything like that but we'd like the
19          trade to be a bit more competitive.=
20→   Int:  =But you're giving them: a heavy instruction (.) as
21          it were to (.) to reduce their prices.
22    C:    .hh What we're saying is we think that prices
23          could come down without the blenders losing their
24          profit margins
```

The interviewee here is the chairman of the Price Commission (C), who is being interviewed about the commission's report on tea prices. Looking at the two interviewer turns (lines 11 and 20), what we find is a dispute over what C is 'actually saying'. In line 11, the interviewer formulates the long turn in lines 1–9 as 'accusing (the blenders) of profiteering'. Formulations tend to be followed by responses in which a recipient either agrees or disagrees with the version being put forward. In this case, C disagrees with the 'profiteering' formulation and moves on to address another issue, lack of competitiveness. In line 20, the interviewer formulates these remarks, again using much stronger terms than C; and once again, C rejects the formulation.

The point is summarized by Heritage:

> The interviewer's two formulations ... restate the interviewee's position by making overt reference to what might be treated as implicated or presupposed by that position.... Further, in this case and many others like it, the interviewee is invited to agree to a characterisation of his position that overtly portrays him as critical of, or in conflict with, some third party. (1985: 110)

Formalized speech exchange systems can also impact on the management of overt disputes, as detailed in Garcia's (1991) analysis of mediation hearings in a small claims court, and in Greatbatch's (1992) study of the panel set-up in some broadcast news programmes, where a number of participants with varying stances on an issue act jointly as interviewees with the interviewer as chair.

In both these environments, disagreement is an intrinsic feature of the encounter. In Garcia's data, the official task of the mediator is to hear and arbitrate between two sides in an ongoing dispute which arose in circumstances external to the hearing, and which is now being put forward for an independent judgement. In a similar sense, Greatbatch notes that in panel interviews, interviewees are selected precisely on the basis of their differing standpoints on issues. Panel formats thus 'allow interviewers to facilitate combative interaction through the airing of disagreements between the interviewees themselves' (Greatbatch 1992: 272).

However, the specialized distribution of speaker roles and rights in both settings leads to the disputes taking distinctive forms. In both settings, an institutional agent (the arbitrator in Garcia's data, the interviewer in Greatbatch's) is accorded a central mediating role, with two main consequences. First, the institutional agent is allotted the task of eliciting, through questions, the position or version of events supported by each antagonist. Consequently, oppositional turns are generally not adjacently positioned, since each side's opportunity to put forward its case needs to follow an intervening question from the mediator.

Therefore, opposing sides in the dispute tend not to address their disagreements directly to each other, but instead to direct their talk at the mediator as a third party. Garcia (1991) points out that in mediation hearings, this feature takes the form of a sanctionable norm. Disputants who shift into direct person-to-person opposition will be required by the arbitrator to redirect their utterances to him or her, and return to referring to co-disputants in the third person. In the case of panel interviews the convention is less stringently observed. Interviewers may allow interviewees to argue with each other directly for short periods of time. But as Greatbatch (1992) shows, there are various ways in which the interviewer retains overall control of the course of the dispute, and at any point he or she may re-establish the mediated format.

These studies illustrate clearly how formal institutional interaction involves 'specific and significant narrowings and respecifications of the range of options that are operative in conversational interaction' (Heritage 1989: 34). The specialized turn-taking systems found in formal types of institutional setting show us how participants orient to the relevance of an institutional context. But formalized speech exchange systems also have an impact on the ways in which social activities such as disputing or generating controversy are accomplished in these settings.

Non-formal institutions: tasks, identities and turn design

We have spent some time discussing settings in which interaction is characterized by a strict question–answer turn-taking format. However, such settings are comparatively rare. More common are institutional settings where the interaction is less formally structured. Talk that has been studied in locations such as doctors' surgeries, social service settings and other workplace environments (see, for example, the papers in Drew and Heritage 1992a) appears much more 'conversational' than courtroom or interview talk. Certainly, if we aggregate the number of questions asked by professionals and by clients in such settings, we find that professionals ask by far the most, and often clients ask virtually no questions (Frankel 1990; ten Have 1991). But unlike in formal settings, there is no norm that says one person 'must' ask the questions and the other must answer. Therefore, participants' orientations to context, as a result of which these patterns of asymmetry emerge, must be located in other aspects of talk.

How can we approach this task? One way is to look at how the same interactional task can be accomplished in systematically different ways in different settings. We can illustrate this by means of some data used in an analysis of interaction in one non-formal institutional setting: telephone calls to a radio phone-in broadcast (Hutchby 1996a). Comparing the opening sequences of these calls with opening sequences in everyday telephone calls, we find further evidence of how orientations to context can be displayed in the details of talk.

In general, telephone openings are a useful thing to study, for the following reason. Since participants do not have visual access to one another, in order to be sure with whom they are interacting they need to engage in purely verbal forms of identification and recognition (Schegloff 1979b). Thus the way speakers design their first utterances will begin to reveal how they categorize themselves in relation to the other. This categorization issue is a key one in conversation analysis, because categories of personal identity and of reference to others are necessarily selective. There are innumerable ways in which we could legitimately describe ourselves and our relationship to someone else with whom we might be interacting. For instance, on the telephone, someone may present themselves as a 'friend' (calling another friend), a 'colleague' (calling a workmate), an 'inquirer' (calling a service agency), a 'family member' (calling another family member) and so on. Similarly, those who pick up the phone in any of these scenarios will aim to present themselves in the appropriate way, possibly using aspects of the caller's talk as a cue to what their own identity is for the purpose of the present conversation. Thus, by examining the design of the talk we can locate the *relevant* identities to which speakers are orienting at that moment (Schegloff 1991).

Looking at extract (3), it is clear that the two participants in this telephone conversation rapidly establish their identities as 'friends':

```
(3)   [HG:1]
      1         (ring)
      2    N:   H'llo?
      3    H:   Hi:,‾
      4    N:   HI:‾:.
      5    H:   How are yuhh=
      6    N:   =Fi:ne‾ how er you,
      7    H:   Oka:⌐y,
      8    N:        ⌐Goo:d,
      9         (0.4)
     10    H:   .mkhhh⌐hh
     11    N:             ⌐What's doin',
```

One thing to notice here is that the two speakers establish one another's identity, and start chatting about 'What's doin',' (line 11) without exchanging names at all. Hyla (the caller) recognizes Nancy's voice as Nancy answers the phone in line 2. Hyla's first utterance, 'Hi:,' in line 3, exhibits that recognition; and at the same time, invites Nancy to recognize the caller's voice (note that she does not self-identify by saying, 'Hi, it's Hyla'). After Nancy's enthusiastic return greeting (line 4), they move into a 'How are you' exchange without needing to check their mutual recognition in any way. Following that, Nancy invites Hyla to introduce a first topic by saying 'What's doin'' (Button and Casey 1984).

This opening sequence can be described in terms of the four 'core sequences' that Schegloff (1986) found to be characteristic of mundane telephone call openings (recall that we discussed Schegloff's work on telephone openings in chapter 5). This set of sequences enables callers and answerers economically to establish their relevant speaker identities, and to negotiate the initial topic that the call will be about.

Turning to an institutional setting, the talk radio show, we find a strong contrast in the form of opening sequences. Rather than passing through a set of four relatively standard sequences, calls on talk radio are opened by means of a single, standard two-turn sequence, which is exemplified by extract (4):

(4)   **[H:21.11.88:6:1]** (H = Host, C = Caller)
   1   H: Kath calling from Clapham now. Good morning.
   2   C: Good morning Brian. Erm:, I:: I also agree that
   3   thee .hh telethons a:re a form of psychological
   4   blackmail now. .hhh Because the majority of
   5   people I think do know ... ((continues))

Here, identification and recognition, greetings, and topic initiation are accomplished in rapid succession in two turns occupying lines 1 and 2. In line 1, the host announces the caller, and then provides a first greeting which invites her into the speaker role for the next turn. In line 2, after returning the greeting, the caller moves without ado into introducing her 'reason for the call'. Typically for this setting, that reason consists of her expressing an opinion on some issue: 'I also agree that thee .hh telethons a:re a form of psychological blackmail'.

Clearly, the kinds of tasks and issues around identification and first topic that are involved in calls on talk radio are different from those arising in mundane conversational calls. In everyday telephone calls, prior to the talk getting started, it is not unequivocally clear for either participant who will be talking at the other end. Nor is it clear, at least for the answerer, that there will be any specific reason for the call. It is for these reasons that the core sequences are used locally to negotiate mutual identification and the introduction of a first topic.

On talk radio, by contrast, caller and host are, for all practical purposes, pre-identified before talk even begins. This is because callers, who of course have called the host specifically, typically first encounter a switchboard operative who takes details of their name, and passes these on to the host, who in turn first encounters each caller as an item on a list of callers waiting to get on the air. Once that has happened, the expectation of the host is that the caller has called in with something specific to say, and so it is not strictly necessary for the initial topic to be solicited.

The basic difference, then, is that in mundane telephone talk, participants need to select from among an array of possible relevant identities and a range of possible things that the call may be about. The structure of the opening in extract (3) allows those tasks to be done. In the institutional setting of the talk radio show, the opening is designed in such a way that the participants can align themselves in terms of given institutional speaker identities ('host' and 'caller'), and move rapidly into the specific topical agenda of the call.

If we look more closely at the construction of the opening turns, however, we find more detailed evidence of the participants' orientations to the specialized features of their interaction. Here are some further examples:

(5) **[H:23.1.89:2:1]**
```
1  H:  Bob is calling from Ilford. Good morning.
2  C:  .hh Good morning Brian. (0.4) .hh What I'm phoning
3      up is about the cricket ...
```

(6) **[H:30.11.88:10:1]**
```
1  H:  Mill Hill:: i:s where Belinda calls from. Good
2      morning.
3  C:  Good morning Brian. .hh Erm, re the Sunday
4      o:pening I'm just phoning from the point of
5      vie:w, .hh as a:n assistant ...
```

(7) **[H:21.11.88:11:1]**
```
1  H:  On to Philip in Camden Town. Good morning.
2  C:  Yeh guh morning Brian. Erm (.) Really what I
3      wanted to say was that I'm fascinated by watching
4      these telethons by the anuh- amount'v
5      contradictions that're thrown up by them ...
```

(8) **[H:2.2.89:12:1]**
```
1  H:  Michael from Uxbridge now. Good morning.
2  C:  .h Er, g'morning Brian. .hh Emm:, I have some
3      advi:ce that might be, a little bit more practical,
4      to people ...
```

In these opening sequences, the design of each turn exhibits clearly the speaker's orientation to the specialized nature of the interaction. For instance, the host's first turns already have an institutional quality to them in that they are constructed as *announcements*. In most types of telephone call, the answerer's first turn is an answer to the summons represented by the telephone's ring. We thus find typical responses such as a simple 'Hello?' (see extract (3)); or, more commonly in some Scandinavian countries (Houtkoop-Steenstra 1991; Lindstrom 1994), self-identifications in which the answerer recites their name. In institutional settings, once again answerers self-identify, but this time usually in organizational terms: for instance, 'Police Department', 'Sociology', or 'Simpson's car hire, how can I help?' In the talk radio data, the host begins by identifying not himself but the *caller*: for instance, 'Kath calling from Clapham'.

This apparently has not always been the case. In examining recordings of an American talk radio show broadcast in 1968, Hutchby (1996a) found that the host answers the telephone using the more conventional organizational self-identification format (line 2):

(9)   **[BCII: Red]**
1   H: Thirteen minutes before ten o'clock here o:n
2→   W.N̄.B.C., ((click)) Good evenin:g, W.N.B.C:,
3   (0.3)
4   C: A:h. (0.2) Is that Brad Crandall?=
5   H: =Yes sir good evening.

Possibly, callers in this early form of talk radio got straight through to the host, without first encountering a switchboard and being put on hold or on call back, as tends to happen now. None the less, this example serves to point up the way in which the host's first turn in extracts (4) to (8), in which the caller's name and geographical location is announced, displays that it is designed principally for reception by the overhearing audience. By constructing this turn as an announcement, the host exhibits an orientation to the broadcast nature of the conversation.

Callers' turns too are designed to fit the institutional properties of the talk radio show. In each case, callers introduce topics on which they propose to offer opinions: 'What I'm phoning up is about the cricket'; 're the Sunday o:pening'; or 'Really what I wanted to say was that I'm fascinated by watching these telethons'. But there is a sense in which those topics get introduced not just as topics but as *issues*. One way this is done is by referring to them using the definite article: 'the cricket', 'the Sunday o:pening' and so on. Using this form of reference, callers can provide their topics with a sense of being generally recognizable. As Clark and Haviland (1977) observed, to refer to a topic with the definite article is to invoke some degree of shared knowledge between speaker and recipient(s). This way of introducing topics constructs them as given themes in the public domain. In this sense, callers specifically introduce topics which are the 'right' kind of thing to be discussing in the public sphere of a talk radio show.

This point is illustrated further by the fact that callers do not phone in about personal or private problems and complaints; not, at least, unless these can be explicitly related to an identifiable public concern. For instance, in the following extract the caller begins by stating that 'We've got a real problem he:re', but that problem is immediately linked to the public issue of 'dogs fouling our footways'.

(10) **[H:2.2.89:4:1]**
```
 1   H:   And good morning to Ma:ndy from Ruislip. Good
 2        morni ng.
 3   C:          ͟Good mor:ning Brian. .hhh We've got a real
 4        problem he:re with dogs fouling our footway,
```

In various ways, then, the design of turns and sequences allows us to locate the participants' orientations to context in non-formal institutional settings such as talk radio, where the type and order of turns are not pre-allocated. Our remarks here fit with research in a wide variety of these settings, where, as Drew and Heritage report:

> Systematic aspects of the organization of sequences (and of turn design within sequences) having to do with such matters as the opening and closing of encounters, and with the ways in which information is requested, delivered, and received ... emerge as facets of the ways in which the 'institutionality' of such encounters is managed. (1992b: 28)

Aspects of asymmetry in institutional interaction

A central theme in a great deal of research is that institutional interaction is systematically asymmetrical, in contrast to what is seen as the ideally equal nature of mundane conversation. Of course, participation in conversation is not necessarily equal at all. For instance, a speaker who asks another's advice on some matter, or one who intends to recount a story about an event they witnessed, automatically places himself or herself in a position of asymmetry in relation to the recipient. Asking for advice situates the recipient in a position of 'holder of knowledge' about, say, a course of action. Similarly, the aim to recount a story assumes that the recipient is not already aware of the events. This, of course, is part of the function of story prefaces as discussed in the previous chapter.

However, in institutional discourse, as Drew and Heritage point out, there does often seem to be a 'direct relationship between status and role, on the one hand, and discursive rights and obligations, on the other' (1992b: 49). For instance, analysts of doctor–patient interaction have observed that doctors typically ask far more questions than their patients, and those questions tend to be much more topic-directing than the few that patients do ask (Maynard 1991; ten Have 1991).

But the conversation analytic perspective seeks to go much deeper than making assertions about relationships between status and relative discursive rights. Beginning from the basic level of the organization of turn-taking in medical consultations, conversation analysts have shown how patients are often complicit in maintaining a situation in which the doctor is able not only to determine the topics that will be talked about, but also to define the upshots and outcomes of those discussions. For instance, Frankel (1984; 1990) observes that while there is no institutionalized constraint against patients asking questions and initiating new topics, overwhelmingly these two activities are undertaken by doctors and not by patients. His analysis reveals that this asymmetry emerges from two tacitly negotiated features of the talk. First, doctors tend to ask certain kinds of questions, usually information-seeking questions which require strictly factual responses. By this means, they routinely open up restricted options for patients to participate in the encounter. Patients are situated as the providers of information about their current physical state; and not, say, as individuals who can contextualize their state of physical health within a broader narrative of life events (Mishler 1984). Yet at the same time, patients themselves orient to and reproduce this asymmetry in participation options when they seek to offer additional information to the doctor. Frankel shows that this new information is offered almost exclusively in turns which are responses to doctors' questions. By this means, patients 'ensure that the new information, if it is going to be dealt with, will be handled via a physician-initiated obligation package, i.e., question–answer sequence' (Frankel 1984: 164).

In a similar vein, Heath (1992) shows how asymmetries are oriented to by patients during the consultation, as patients systematically withhold responses to doctors' announcements of a diagnosis. Given that the diagnosis represents a piece of 'expert' knowledge which the doctor passes on to the patient, then by withholding responses other than acknowledgement tokens such as 'yeh' or 'um', patients display their orientation to the expert status of the doctor. Heath shows that this withholding is even done when the patient has an opportunity to respond through the doctor leaving a gap following the announcement of diagnosis, as in the following extract:

(11) **[Heath 1992: 242]**
            (Physical examination)
    1 Dr: Yeah.
    2   (0.3)
    3 Dr: That's shingles.
    4   (1.2)
    5 Dr: That's what it is:
    6   (0.6)
    7 Pt: Shingles.
    8 Dr: Yes.

The doctor provides the diagnosis in line 3, then pauses for over a second (line 4); then reiterates that the diagnosis has been made (line 5). After a further pause, the patient responds simply by repeating the diagnosis (line 7), at which point the doctor reconfirms it. Thus the diagnosis is produced over a series of turns alternating with pauses, in which there is no response from the patient other than a single-word repetition of the doctor's conclusion.

As Heath notes, the only times when patients do respond more fulsomely occur either when the doctor mitigates or expresses doubt about the diagnosis, or when the patient appears to have an opinion about what may be wrong and this turns out to be incongruent with the diagnosis. In the first kind of case, typically, patients respond with turns in which they stress their own lack of knowledge and often present their own or others' guesses about the problem, as in the next extract:

(12) **[Heath 1992: 248]**
```
1  Dr:  Well there's a marked er:: (.) conjunctivitis
2       on both si:des there mister Banks, erm:
3  Pt:  °er
4       (0.2)
5  Dr:  .thhhhh What set it off I wouldn't know:
6  Pt:  I wouldn't either I thought it was hay: fever or
7       somit like this:
```

The patient responds to the initial diagnosis with a very brief acknowledgement (line 3). Subsequently, the doctor remarks that he 'wouldn't know' what caused the condition (line 5). After this, the patient responds by, first, announcing his own lack of knowledge, then secondly, mentioning his guess that it was hay fever.

In the second kind of case, patients respond to the incongruence between their own thoughts and the doctor's opinion by using newsmarks such as 'Is it?' or 'Oh really?', which then lead to the doctor reconfirming the diagnosis. The following extract is an illustration:

(13) **[Heath 1992: 250]**
```
1  Dr:  It's not a vein: (.) it's a muscle in spa:s⌈m.
2  Pt:                                             ⌊Is it?
3  Dr:  Yeah.
4  Pt:  Oh.
5  Dr:  And I think what's causing it to be in spasm . . .
```

Here, the patient has previously suggested (in data not shown) that the problem is related to 'a vein'. In line 1 of the extract, the doctor contrasts his diagnosis with the patient's suggestion, asserting that 'it's a muscle in spa:sm'. This is responded to with a newsmark (Jefferson 1981), 'Is it?' (line 2); and the subsequent reconfirmation (line 3) receives the change-of-state token (Heritage 1984b) 'Oh' (line 4).

In these ways, patients preserve, in the design of their turns at talk, the fundamentally asymmetrical nature of the medical consultation. As Heath writes:

> By withholding response, patients not only provide the doctor with the opportunity of developing the consultation as they so wish, but preserve the objective, scientific, and professional status of the diagnosis or medical assessment; the silence or acknowledgement operating retroactively to underscore the significance of the practitioner's 'opinion' of the condition. . . . Even in cases

where the doctor displays uncertainty in diagnosis, and thereby encourages discussion of the medical assessment of the condition, it may be observed how the patient's contribution preserves the contrasting status of the two versions of the illness and in particular embodies the subjective and lay standpoint of their own opinion. (1992: 262)

Asymmetry and power

Many of the asymmetries in institutional discourse can be thought of in terms of the 'power' of institutional agents to establish the participation opportunities of laypersons, and to define the upshots and outcomes of their encounters. It may be claimed that due to the practices outlined above, for instance, doctors exert power over patients by controlling what will count as an acceptable diagnosis (as in 'it's not a vein, it's a muscle in spa:sm'), while patients systematically defer to that institutionalized power.

However, we have to be careful about how we relate asymmetries in institutional discourse to power and authority. For instance, policies of simply counting the number of questions, or coding the types of questions asked, can run the risk of not being sensitive enough to the more basic sense of context stressed by CA: the local sequential context of talk in which utterances are produced. Schegloff (1991) has argued that analysts need to take care to understand the basic conversational functions of utterance types before drawing conclusions about relations of authority and power in institutional talk.

We can illustrate this point by drawing from Schegloff's (1980) discussion of the following extract, which is taken from a doctor–patient consultation. Notice in particular the patient's utterance in line 5:

(14) [Frankel 4–80: LOG 10750]
```
    1     Dr:  Very good. (0.4) Very good=lemme see your ankle.
    2          (2.2)
    3     Dr:  pt. .hhh VERY GOOD.
    4          (1.1)
    5→    Pt:  I wanna ask you som'n.
    6     Dr:  What's that.
    7          (0.6)
    8     Pt:  pt. .hh (0.5) I have- (0.6) this second toe (.)
```

9		that was broken. (0.4) But I went to the pediatrist
10		(.) because I couldn' find a doctor on th' weekend.
11		(0.4) An' he said it wasn' broken.=It was.
12		So it wasn' (.) taken care of properly. .hh 'n when
13		I'm on my feet, I get a sensation in it.
14		I mean is anything (th't) can be do:ne?
15	Dr:	How long ago d'ju break it.
16	Pt:	Mmh two years.
17	Dr:	Yih c'd put a metatarsal pad underneath it . . .

In this extract, the patient's utterance in line 5, 'I wanna ask you som'n', might be seen as a 'request for permission' to speak in the asymmetrical doctor–patient context. In this kind of setting, as we have said, the questioning initiative usually lies with the doctor (Frankel 1990). Therefore, this could be taken as an example of the patient deferring to the institutional authority of the doctor.

Yet this would represent only a superficial analysis; one which *assumed* that patients defer to the authority of doctors. As Schegloff (1980) shows, the utterance at line 5 is in fact of a quite common type in ordinary conversation, where it functions as a particular kind of item: a 'preliminary to preliminaries'. Basically, utterances such as 'I want to ask you something' or 'Can I ask you a question' indicate that whatever it is the speaker wants to ask, it requires some preliminary background detailing before the question can be answered. Schegloff supports this analysis by observing that, generally, what a speaker does immediately after saying 'Can I ask you something' is *not* to ask a question. The question itself comes after some preliminaries: this is what Schegloff means by the phrase 'preliminary to preliminaries'.

This analysis can be applied to extract (14). The actual question the patient wants to ask comes at line 14: 'I mean is anything th't can be do:ne?' The question follows the preliminary detailing, in lines 8–13, in which the patient relates a background story about what happened to his toe. Thus what might seem at first glance to be an orientation to having to ask permission to put a question to the doctor turns out on closer inspection to be an orientation to a common conversational practice whereby a question can be projected following some background details. In other words, it is not enough simply to codify individual utterances on the basis of an assumption about the power relationships in doctor–patient discourse. We need to remain sensitive to the local interactional relevancies that the participants are demonstrably oriented to.

However, this does not mean that CA can say nothing systematic about how asymmetries can be related to power in institutional discourse. Indeed, by focusing on the local management of talk, CA can provide compelling accounts of how power is produced through talk-in-interaction, rather than being predetermined by theoretical features of the context.

One kind of example can be found in some of Drew's work on courtroom interrogation. Drew has observed how the pre-allocated question–answer format of courtroom interaction gives attorneys a certain discursive power which is not available to witnesses, namely, the 'power of summary'. As a questioner, the attorney 'has "first rights" to pull together evidence and "draw conclusions"' (1992: 507); in other words, to define the meaning, the terms and the upshots of a particular set of answers. This is something the witness cannot do:

> The witness is left in the position of addressing and trying to deal with the attorney's selection of which items to pull together: she has no control over the connections which are made between pieces of information or testimony, nor over the inferences which may be drawn from such juxtapositioning – although she may attempt [in her answers] to rebut those inferences (Drew 1992: 507).

This is a kind of power that is available to anyone, in whatever context, who asks a series of questions of a co-participant. The added significance in the courtroom, of course, is that the witness is systematically disabled from asking any questions of her own, or of taking issue with the attorney's final summary.

We will conclude this chapter by looking at a more specific attempt to ground an account of power in a conversation analytic framework. Earlier we discussed aspects of the work carried out by one of us on talk radio (Hutchby 1992a; 1992b; 1996a; 1996b). Recall that we described how, at the outset of calls, callers in this data orient to their role as introducers of topics for discussion. Moreover, we suggested that they introduce topics in such a way that they are treated as 'issues' on which they offer opinions. However, this basic structural feature of talk radio calls, apart from being one way in which callers display an orientation to interaction in an institutional setting, is also closely linked to differences in *power* between hosts and callers.

The principal activity in these interactions is that of argument. Callers offer opinions on issues, and hosts then debate those opinions, frequently taking up opposing stances in the process. As Sacks observed (1992, vol. 2: 348–53), arguing about opinions is a basically asymmetrical activity, in whatever context it occurs. There are significant differences between, on the one hand, setting out an opinion, and on the other, taking issue with that opinion. Sacks described these actions respectively as 'going first' and 'going second' in an argument. Sacks proposed that those who go first are in a weaker position than those who get to go second, since the latter can argue with the former's position simply by taking it apart. Going first means having to set your opinion on the line, whereas going second means being able to argue merely by challenging your opponent to expand on, or account for, his or her claims. Thus, while first position arguers are required to build a *defence* for their stance, those in second position do not need to do so, and indeed are able to choose if and when they will set out their own argument, as opposed to simply attacking the other's.

Sacks observes that in conversation, speakers can often be seen to try and maneouvre their interlocutors into first position, and one of the features of arguments in ordinary conversation is that there may be struggles over who sets their opinion on the line first and who gets to go second. But as Hutchby (1996b) shows, on talk radio this asymmetry is 'built into' the overall structure of calls. Callers are expected, and may be constrained, to go first with their line, while the host systematically gets to go second, and thus to contest the caller's line by picking at its weaknesses. The fact that hosts systematically have the first opportunity for opposition within calls thus opens to them a collection of argumentative resources which are not available in the same way to callers. These resources are 'powerful', in the sense that they enable the host to constrain callers to do a particular kind of activity – that is, produce 'defensive' talk.

One set of such resources is a class of utterances, including 'So?' and 'What's that got to do with it?' which challenge a claim on the grounds of its validity or relevance to the matter in question. We can describe these as powerful resources, since one feature of them is that they need not make clear precisely on what terms the claim is being challenged. They may function purely as second position moves, by which the first speaker is required to expand on or account for the challenged claim.

In the following extract the caller is complaining about the number of mailed requests for charitable donations she receives. Notice that in line 7 the host responds simply by saying 'So?'

(15)   [H:21.11.88:6:1]
```
     1   Caller:   I: have got three appeals letters here this
     2             week.(0.4) All a:skin' for donations. (0.2) .hh
     3             Two: from tho:se that I: always contribute to
     4             anywa:y,
     5   Host:     Yes?
     6   Caller:   .hh But I expect to get a lot mo:re.
     7   Host:     So?
     8   Caller:   .h Now the point is there is a limi⌈t to (      )
     9   Host:                                        ⌊What's that
    10             got to do- what's that got to do with telethons
    11             though.
    12   Caller:   hh Because telethons . . .((Continues))
```

As an argumentative move, this 'So?' achieves two things. First, it challenges the validity or relevance of the caller's complaint within the terms of her own agenda, which in this case is that charities represent a form of 'psychological blackmail'. Second, because it stands alone as a complete turn, 'So?' requires the caller to take the floor again and account for the relevance of her remark.

Another second position resource available to the host enables him to try and establish control over the agenda by selectively formulating the gist or upshot of the caller's remarks (recall our discussion of formulations in news interviews above). In extract (16), we see a particular kind of strategic direction of talk that is related to the argumentative uses of formulations in a setting such as talk radio. The host here uses two closely linked proposals of upshot to contentiously reconstruct the position being advanced by the caller. The caller has criticized the 'contradictions' of televised charity events known as telethons, claiming that their rhetoric of concern in fact promotes a passive altruism which exacerbates the 'separateness' between donors and recipients. He goes on:

(16)   H:21.11.88:11:3
```
     1   Caller:   . . . but e:r, I- I think we should be working at
     2             breaking down that separateness I ⌈think ⌉these
     3   Host:                                       ⌊Ho:w?⌋
     4             (.)
     5   Caller:   these telethons actually increase it.
```

```
 6  Host:    Well, what you're saying is that charity does.
 7  Caller:  .h Charity do::es, yer::s  I  mean-
 8  Host:                         Okay we- so you're (.) so
 9           you're going back to that original argument we
10           shouldn't have charity.
11  Caller:  Well, no I um: I wouldn't go that fa:r, what I
12           would like to see is-
13  Host:                        Well how far are you going then.
14  Caller:  Well I: would- What I would like to see is . . .
```

In line 6, the host proposes that the caller's argument in fact embraces charities in general and not just telethons as one sort of charitable endeavour. This is similar to the inferentially elaborative formulations that Heritage (1985) discusses. Although the caller has not made any such generalization himself in his prior talk, he assents to this in the next turn (line 7).

However, it turns out that the caller, by agreeing, provides the host with a resource for actually *re*formulating the agenda in play here. By using a second formulation to describe the upshot of the caller's position, the host proposes that the caller is going back to an argument which a previous caller had made, namely that 'we shouldn't have charity' (lines 8–10).

The caller rejects this further formulation (line 11). But the point is that by relying on his 'second position' ability to formulate the gist or upshot of the caller's remarks, the host can actually attempt to change the agenda in the caller's remarks. Having changed it, he would then be in a position to challenge – and constrain the caller to defend – this new agenda.

Thus we see a similarity here with Drew's (1992) remarks on attorneys' power of summary, quoted above. Only here, rather than emerging out of a pre-allocated question–answer turn-taking format, the discursive power of the host emerges in an environment where turn-taking is much more 'conversational' (see Hutchby 1996a: 20–40). What seems to be the case on talk radio is that a form of power emerges in the talk as a result of the way calls are structured overall. In particular, the fact that callers must begin by taking up a position means that argumentative resources are distributed asymmetrically between host and callers. The host is able to build opposition using basic second position resources. The characteristic feature of these resources is that they require callers to defend or account for their claims, while enabling hosts to argue without constructing a defence for an alternative view. At the same time, as long as the host refrains from setting out his own position, such second position resources are not available to the caller.

Underlying this discussion is a particular conception of power: as the structurally provided ability to constrain the actions of others. Power is a contested term in contemporary social theory, and we recognize that our discussion of power as a phenomenon in institutional talk-in-interaction does not take on board the whole range of conceptual problems outlined by others (see Lukes 1986). The reason we have discussed the issue in the context of this chapter is because conversation analysts have traditionally been wary of making such claims as that CA represents a means for analysing power. There are good reasons for this: as we outlined above, there is a danger that in being too quick to rely on concepts like power we may lose sight of the more basic question of the structural organization of talk-in-interaction.

That being said, it is clear that a high proportion of CA studies of asymmetry in institutional interaction, although they do not put it in these terms, can be described as showing how the oriented-to structural patterns in talk – such as question–answer sequences or first and second positions in argument – furnish participants with differential resources. And one upshot of these resources is that one participant is often in a more powerful position discursively to constrain the actions of his or her co-participant.

It is important to stress two points about this discussion. First, this approach does not lead us back to the container view in which pre-existing hierarchical features of the context exert causal forces over the available actions of participants. We have emphasized that CA reveals the orientations of participants themselves to the specialized features of institutional interaction. In line with this view, the features of power that we have discussed are rooted in *oriented-to* patterns of action. Hence, the participants could conceivably make things different; although obviously departures from the normative conventions, though possible, would be treated by other participants as accountable and open to challenge.

The second point is that we are not seeking to treat power as a monolithic, one-way process. In line with the views of Foucault (1977), the exercise of powerful discursive resources can always be resisted by a recipient. In the two studies we have mentioned, strategies of resistance play a key part. Drew (1992) discusses how witnesses utilize the many resources that are available for evading or challenging the strategic implications to be detected in attorneys' questioning. In Hutchby (1996b), it is shown how callers may resist the second position challenges of hosts in numerous ways; and indeed, how callers may take the opportunity to move into second position themselves if hosts elect to move away from the challenging mode and express an opinion on their own part.

In this chapter we have begun to introduce some of the applications of a conversation analytic approach. By moving outside the domain of mundane conversation to look at more specialized forms of talk, the researchers discussed here have made significant inroads into an understanding of how institutional contexts function which goes beyond conventional sociological and sociolinguistic notions of context as a container for action. By focusing on the distinctive nature of the speech exchange systems which are oriented to by participants in such settings, and on other aspects of the design of talk, CA demonstrates that institutional contexts are the ongoing accomplishment of the participants in their interactional conduct, rather than external constraints which cause certain forms of conduct to occur.

CHAPTER 7

Conversation Analysis and Interview Data

The interview is one of the most widely used research instruments in the social sciences. Consequently, much of our knowledge about the social world is derived from information generated during interviews. However, research interviews are themselves periods of social interaction between two parties. It has long been recognized that if we are to rely on the interview as a research tool it is necessary to know how the relationship between the interviewer and interviewee influences the nature of the information subsequently gathered. However, even if it were possible to take account of all interpersonal influences on the outcome of an interview, there would still be features of the organization of the talk between interviewer and interviewee which needed to be addressed: the way turns are exchanged, the methods by which misunderstandings and other troubles are repaired, or the effect of letting misunderstandings go unrepaired, and so on. These interactional contingencies impinge on the organization of the interview, and therefore they might also influence the nature of the information subsequently collected. Consequently, however careful we might be to ensure that *interpersonal* factors do not 'contaminate' a research interview, information obtained from interviews can never be gathered in an *interactional* vacuum, and it is for this reason that it may be not only fruitful but necessary to examine the verbal organization of interviews.

In this chapter we will concentrate only on those types of interviews involving verbal exchanges between two people in face-to-face interaction. Therefore, we will not be discussing the relevance of CA for the study of group interviews, or interviews conducted over the telephone (for examples of the latter, see

Houtkoop-Steenstra 1995; Maynard, Schaeffer and Cradock 1995).

We will focus on three types of interviews. First, we will look at standardized or structured interviews, in which the interviewer simply administers a questionnaire or survey to the respondent. This is the most formal kind of interview setting: the interviewer follows the survey or questionnaire much like a script. To ensure consistency across interviews, the interviewer does not ask questions which are not written in the survey, nor is there an opportunity to develop lines of inquiry raised by the interviewee's responses. We will then examine semi-structured interviews. Here the researcher will ask a set number of questions in the same way, and will deal with specific topics in the same order; however he or she does not follow a strict survey or questionnaire, and is therefore at liberty to explore issues generated in the course of the interview. Finally, we will look at focused or unstructured interviews. This is the most loosely organized type of interview. The interviewer comes to the interview with a set of issues to be discussed and can raise them in any order; furthermore, it is not necessary to ensure that questions are worded consistently across interviews. In addition, the interviewees have some control over the range of topics discussed, as they may raise issues not introduced by the interviewer; they will also be encouraged to talk at length, perhaps illustrating an experience or an opinion with a series of anecdotes. Consequently the interviewee may provide long stretches of relatively uninterrupted talk.

In the following discussion we will try to show the broad kinds of empirical contributions conversation analysis can make to the analysis of interview interaction. However, we will also discuss some important methodological issues that follow from the attempt to examine interview data from a conversation analytic perspective.

The structured interview

In a structured interview the interviewer administers a survey to a respondent, and then codes the answers into a number of pre-set categories. The numbers entered into each category then provide the social scientist with the basis for statistical analysis. Because it is necessary to have standardized data for statistical analysis, it is imperative that the interviewer should ask the respondents the same questions in the same way in the same order every time. Consequently, for many social scientists, this interview format is regarded as an essentially neutral instrument for data collection.

However, Suchman and Jordan (1990) argue that the process of administering such a survey is itself to be seen as an interactional event. The interviewer and respondent will be co-present, and the interviewer will elicit the required information by asking the respondent questions written down on the survey or questionnaire. Consequently the structured interview actually relies on very basic features of conversational interaction: turn-taking, question–answer sequences and so on. But Suchman and Jordan argue that because it is necessary to produce standardized answers, the participants in the structured interview also have to suppress some essential characteristics of mundane conversational interaction. So, although the interviewer may appear to be engaging in everyday interaction, the nature of their task is such that they also have to violate certain conversational procedures. Suchman and Jordan show that this has some very important consequences for the nature of the information actually being recorded. We will illustrate their argument by discussing some features of ordinary conversational interaction which are constrained in structured interviews. This discussion will be based on Suchman and Jordan's analysis of recordings of three interviews using the General Social Survey and two interviews using the National Health Survey.

In conversation we design our utterances for their recipient(s). However, in a structured interview, the interviewer must pose the same question in the same way to different respondents: consequently the person (or group) who produces the survey has to ensure that each question must be designed to accommodate everyone who may have to answer it, and it must address a wide range of possible circumstances. The upshot is that questions can become awkward and clumsy. For example:

(1)   **[Suchman and Jordan 1990: 233]**
I.   During those two weeks, did anyone in the family receive health care at home or go to a doctor's office, clinic, hospital or some other place. Include care from a nurse or anyone working with or for a medical doctor. Do not count times while an overnight patient in hospital.
R: (pause) No::

Because questions have to be exhaustive they may contain many clauses, and it is not unusual for a respondent to answer a question after an initial clause. But because of the requirement to ask questions the same way on each occasion the interviewer has to continue with the rest of the question, even after the respondent has answered it.

(2)   [Suchman and Jordan 1990: 234]

I: Was the total combined family income during the past twelve months, that is yours, your wife's Judith's and Jerry's more or less than twenty thousand dollars.

R: More

I: Include money from jobs, social security, retirement income, unemployment payments, public assistance and so forth. Also include income from interest dividends, net income from business or rent, and any other income received.

R: More. it was more income.

In everyday interaction, speakers may monitor and attend to the immediately prior sequence of utterances, or information revealed in earlier stages of the conversation. Subsequent contributions to a conversation can be designed to take account of these prior interactional events, or previously disclosed information. However, the professional interviewer has to take no notice of this local context. They are not allowed to incorporate inferences available from prior turns into the design of subsequent questions. Suchman and Jordan cite an instance in which an interviewer is asking a respondent about health problems. Having established that the respondent has a form of skin complaint brought on by playing the violin, the interviewer asks 'When did you last see or talk to a doctor or assistant about the dermatitis under the neck?' (Suchman and Jordan 1990: 233). The respondent answers that she did not see a doctor in relation to this problem. Some turns later, however, the following sequence happens:

I: Were you ever hospitalized::for
R: ⌊No

In ordinary conversation, a participant would have been able to infer that if a co-participant had not even seen a doctor because of a skin problem, then it was highly unlikely that it was a serious enough condition to warrant institutional care, and a question about hospitalization would not have been asked.

These features of structured interviews may become very irritating to the respondent, leading to a strong desire to finish the interview as soon as possible – an attitude that is hardly going to maximize the effectiveness of the interview as an information-gathering instrument. However, there are more pressing dangers from the suppression of mundane conversational procedures. For example, not only are the questions structured prior to the interview, but so are the kinds of answers that the respondents can give. That is, interviewers are not free to take account of how the respondents may wish to answer the question because responses have to be recorded in terms of the categories or coding schemes built into the survey being administered.

For example, the following segment comes from part of an interview in which the respondent is being asked to assess the appropriateness of the amount of money being spent on problems in big cities.

(3)　**[Suchman and Jordan 1990: 234–5]**
　　I:　. . . solving the problem of big cities
　　R:　hm:: ((long pause)) Some questions seem to be ((little laugh))
　　　　hard to answer because it's not a matter of how much money, it's-
　　I:　Alright, you can just say whether you think it's too much, too
　　　　little or about the right amount, or if you feel you don't know you
　　　　can:: say that of course.
　　R:　Ah from the various talk shows and programs on TV and in the
　　　　newspapers, ah it could be viewed that they're spending maybe
　　　　the right amount of money. but it isn't so much the money that
　　　　they're spending it's the other things that-
　　I:　Well do you think we're spending too much too little, or about
　　　　the right amount.
　　R:　Ahm, I'll answer I don't know on that one.

In this case the respondent tries to formulate an answer to the question which is premised on the idea that the allocation of financial resources is not the major issue. However, because the interviewer needs to have an answer which fits the categories available, she constrains the respondent's actions so that the respondent eventually produces a 'don't know' answer, whereas it is clear from the preceding talk that she does indeed have an opinion on the topic. In this case, then, the respondent's actual opinion, which she tried to volunteer, was lost.

Often respondents will provide a narrative or anecdote as a way of illustrating an answer. But because of the requirement to furnish standardized answers, the interviewer must take no notice of these stories. It is possible, however, that these stories may actually contradict the answer which has been given. The following extract comes from an interview with a doctor.

(4)   **[Suchman and Jordan 1990: 236]**
     I: When you think about other doctors in general, how would you
             compare yourself to them. Are you very similar or different?
     R: I think I'm pretty similar to most doctors. Except that a lot of
             doctors try to stay right in the mainstream of medicine. They
             don't like to be out, away from the drug-oriented type of medical
             treatment. In other words, you have a problem. you have drug for
             it. and that'll take care of it. Or surgery or something. Cut it off.
             and you'll be fine ((laughs)) And most doctors have that attitude.
             Then there's a small group that believe in the reason that you
             have doctors in the first place. And that is that we're more
             holistic. So we can use a more natural approach. The hippocratic
             approach. So I think I'm more like that group

Here the interviewer is faced with two contradictory answers, and she has a problem. If she accepts the first answer, she will be attributing to the respondent an opinion with which he clearly disagrees. If she takes account of his subsequent explanation, and pursues a response in the light of that, then she may end up with an uncodifiable answer (both 'yes' and 'no'); furthermore, she will be transgressing the norm that the interviewer should actively take no notice of 'irrelevant' parts of the respondent's utterances.

Suchman and Jordan consider the implications of these and many other characteristics of interaction in structured interviews. They conclude by suggesting a variety of ways in which the writers of survey questionnaires, and the interviewers who administer them, might benefit from recognizing that 'the survey interview is fundamentally an interactional event' (1990: 240).

Suchman and Jordan's paper is important for the following reasons. First, drawing on CA studies of ordinary talk, they begin to provide a formal analytic description of the ways in which interaction in structured interviews departs from procedures in everyday conversational exchanges. Second, and more important, they point to some of the implications of these departures. They show that in an attempt to ensure that the interview is a neutral and objective instrument, there are requirements that the interview proceeds in a certain way. However, these requirements lead the interviewer into trying to conduct an exchange that has the superficial appearance of a conversational encounter without many central characteristics of talk in everyday settings, for example being able to design utterances for their recipients, clarifying misunderstandings, allowing inferences available from prior utterances to shape subsequent turns, and so on.

Analysts have begun to show how the imposition of these verbal parameters can lead to the respondents' annoyance and disinclination to cooperate fully with the interview (Maynard, Schaeffer and Cradock 1995). But a more serious consequence of these requirements is that the nature of the talk may impinge significantly on the information recorded. That is, Suchman and Jordan show that it is not the case that verbal exchanges in a structured interview are simply a means of eliciting information; rather, these restricted forms of conversational interaction can have an impact on the decision as to what information the respondent is actually offering by way of an answer. In short, the information collected in structured interviews may not be disentangled from the organization of the talk through which the interview was conducted.

Semi-structured interviews

In the previous section we observed how an analysis informed by findings from conversation analysis could reveal how the absence of everyday interactional procedures may lead to significant problems in structured interviews. In this section, we will begin by describing how discursive practices which are common to everyday talk can be deployed in the context of a semi-structured interview. As we stated in the introduction to this chapter, in a semi-structured interview, the interviewer is not reading questions from a written list. Consequently the 'same' questions may be worded differently on each occasion.

We will consider some data from Widdicombe and Wooffitt's (1995) study of semi-structured interviews provided by members of youth subcultures, such as punks, skinheads, rockers and gothics. They used a conversation analytic approach to investigate the first exchanges in their interviews. Before we examine their analysis, however, it is necessary to discuss the background to their study.

Initially the interviews were not collected as data for a conversation analytic study of interaction between interviewer and respondents. The interviews were conducted as part of Widdicombe's doctoral research to test a theory known as social identity theory, which tried to explain the processes of group membership and identification. She wanted to find out if this theory could be used to reveal why young people joined youth subcultures. To test the theory, it was necessary to devise an interview schedule which encouraged the respondents to declare their subcultural affiliation right at the start or early on in the interview. Interviews were conducted 'in the field' at rock concerts, on the streets of London – any venue or place where members of subcultures were known to gather.

Widdicombe and Wooffitt argue that there were good grounds to assume that the respondents would realize that the reason they were approached for an interview was their visibility as members of a specific subculture. In short, they looked the part. Consequently, respondents could infer that the interviewer was inviting them to speak as 'punks' or 'goths' rather than, say, as 'women', 'students', 'people out shopping' or whatever other kind of categorization could logically apply.

The opening question was designed to elicit a subcultural self-categorization. And in some cases the respondents immediately did affirm the relevance of that kind of social identity: they said, 'I'm a punk' (or whatever) in their first utterance in the interview. However, in many cases, the respondents' first turn in the interview was in fact a question. For example:

(5)   [1R:M:T5SB(RRF)]
```
             ((Tape starts))
     1  I:   how would you descri:be (.) yourself
     2       and your appearance and so on
     3       (.)
     4  R:   describe my appearance,
     5  I:   yeah
     6       (1)
     7  R:   su- su- slightly longer than average hair
             ((goes on to describe appearance))
```

(6)   [1P:F:T7SA(KR)]
```
             ((Tape starts))
     1  I:   RIght how would you describe your sty:le,
     2       (0.6)
     3  R:   how would I describe ⌈the style
     4  I:                        ⌊yeah
```

```
5       (0.4)
6  R:   well (0.4) it's:: (.) different it's
7       usually dirty and
        ((continues))
```

In these cases, the respondents' first turns have the character of 'questions-seeking-clarification/confirmation'. This was a recurrent phenomenon in the data. Instead of trying to explain these responses in terms of social identity theory, Widdicombe and Wooffitt wondered if there might be an interactional basis for the respondents' production of these kinds of utterances.

Instead of producing the conversational action that was sought – a self-identification in terms of a subcultural category – the respondent has produced a request for clarification. This is an entirely different kind of action, one which has significant implications for the trajectory of the interaction. To illustrate, let us reconsider extract (5). By producing a request for clarification the respondent has also initiated an insertion sequence. An insertion sequence is simply a spate of interaction which is nested in or embedded in an overarching sequential framework.

```
        ((Tape starts))
1  I:   how would you descri:be (.) yourself        Q1
2       and your appearance and so on
3       (.)
4  R:   describe my appearance,                      Ins Q2
5  I:   yeah                                          Ins A2
6       (1)
7  R:   su- su- slightly longer than average hair    A1
        ((goes on to describe appearance))
```

Significant implications follow from the production of this insertion sequence: through this simple action the respondent is able to re-characterize the business of that part of the interview. So that, instead of being question–answer sequences in which the respondent formulates a description of his subcultural identity, the subsequent utterances now focus on other, perhaps more superficial features: descriptions of his hair, clothes and so on.

There is another interesting feature of the respondent's first turn: it borrows some words from the interviewer's prior turn, but deletes other words. So we find that the component 'describe yourself' has not been recycled as 'describe myself' but 'describe my appearance'. In this sense, the respondent's turn in line 4 formulates a *version* of the interviewer's prior utterance. And that version is crucial because it is designed to make available certain inferences about the social identity of the speaker. That is, he does not address the prior question as a member of a sub-cultural category; instead, his first contribution to the interview is designed to display that he is addressing the question as any normal person would. By producing a turn in which he does not address those parts of the prior turn which make relevant, and invite him to confirm, a particular kind of categorical self-ascription, he makes available the inference that that kind of identity is not relevant to him. He produces a request for clarification, of a kind which would be produced by any normal, unexceptional person who could not infer what it was about them in particular that had motivated the interviewer to approach them and ask a question concerning style, appearance and so on. In this sense, this first turn is designed not to invoke the speaker's identity as a member of some subculture, but instead to warrant his identity as an ordinary person. He is in the business of, as Sacks (1984b) put it, doing 'being ordinary'.

As we said earlier, the use of insertion sequences after the interviewer's first question is not an unusual phenomenon. But why do respondents do this?

Widdicombe and Wooffitt argue that this is a strategy to resist a way of being seen. Doing 'being ordinary', or at least portraying themselves through their actions as not belonging to a specific category or group, is a method by which respondents can counter what must be a routine feature of their everyday lives: that by virtue of an inspection of their dress and appearance, other people assume that it is possible to see what kind of person they are. Regardless of whether such an inference is true or not, another's assumptions about a person's categorical affiliations – one's social identity – mean that whatever is known about that category can be invoked as being relevant to that person, whether as a set of resources for interpreting and accounting for past or present conduct, or as a set of knowledge to inform predictions about likely future behaviour. There is a sense in which this is a form of social control: by virtue of a category membership (either attributed by others or offered by the individual), a person's own behaviour can be glossed, interpreted and characterized in terms of what is known and expected about that category (Sacks 1979).

It is therefore always potentially the case that the sense or purpose of a person's actions, beliefs, opinions and so on may be understood by virtue of what is known commonly about the category to which the individual can be seen to be affiliated. It is this ever-present potential state of affairs which the respondents' first utterances may be designed to resist. By portraying themselves as 'not seeing the category relevance of the interviewer's first turn', the respondents are rejecting the validity of (what they can infer to be) the basis on which they were selected for interview; they are resisting the categorical affiliation which the interviewer's first turn tacitly asks them to confirm. So providing this kind of clarification-seeking question is a method of resistance executed in the design of utterances on a turn-by-turn basis.

There is another point. The production of an insertion sequence allows the respondents to display one instance of their ordinariness: but this action is not produced randomly in the account, but in their first turns in the exchange. So that when the interviewer subsequently asks explicitly if they belong to a specific category, their acceptance of that label merely constitutes one further dimension of their identity. So instead of being a criterial identity – a central component of their social selves – the subcultural identity is produced as merely one of (at least) two relevant identities. Through their talk, then, the respondents display that they do not, in the first instance, see themselves as being punks, or gothics, while not definitely denying the potential relevance of a subcultural identity. This is a useful resource, for it is possible that in some contexts the respondents would affirm their categorical identity as members of a specific subculture: in some of the interviews, the respondents did indeed go on to accept the category term offered by the interviewer, having earlier provided the kind of resistance that we have discussed. Indeed, there is a sense in which an outright denial of a subcultural affiliation could warrant assertions of deliberate mischief, disingenuousness or simple perversity. After all, the kinds of dress and appearance of the respondents invite a certain kind of categorical ascription. The respondents' talk thus displays their sensitivity to the delicate issue of undermining the criterial relevance of their subcultural identity, while at the same time minimizing the likelihood that a simple denial of the relevance of their subcultural affiliation could warrant unfavourable conclusions about themselves and their behaviour.

There is one more interactional benefit to be gained from initiating insertion sequences in this way. There are other ways of resisting category ascription: for example, the respondents can simply question the legitimacy of the interviewer's first question. In the following extract, the first respondent formulates her negative attitude to the prior question, and thereby resists providing any kind of self-identification.

(7) [3:NSG:F:T3SA (FP)]
```
            ((Tape starts: respondents talking to each other
            for approximately 12 seconds))
   1   I:   can you tell me something about your style and the way
   2        you look,
   3        (0.7)
   4   I:   how would you descri:be yourselves
   5        (0.7)
   6   R1:  °huhh°
   7        (.7)
   8   R1:  I dunno >I hate those sorts of questions uhm
   9   R2:            ,                         ⌊yeah horrible
  10        isn't it
```

The first respondent's utterance, 'I hate those sorts of questions', constitutes a complaint about having to provide a characterization of herself. Her reluctance to answer the question has therefore become an explicit feature of the exchange. Although an overt complaint about the interviewer's question does not necessarily index an imminent breakdown of the interview, it certainly constitutes a 'trouble' in the exchange. This is a marked departure from routine conversation in which participants generally rely on various interactional practices to minimize the likelihood of explicit conflict or disagreement. Explicit rejections of questions, then, can jeopardize the smooth flow of the interview, and can undermine the relationship between interviewer and interviewee.

The production of an insertion sequence which seeks clarification, however, does not question the propriety or salience of the prior turn. Yet it does permit the speaker to establish a spate of talk in which the likelihood that they will be expected to produce a subcultural self-identification is minimized. In this sense, producing an 'ordinary person's' kind of response via an insertion sequence is a delicate strategy: it allows the respondents to avoid giving a subcultural identification in such a way that their resistance does not become an explicit focus of the exchange.

Before concluding this section it is worth making a few broader methodological remarks, as they illustrate the power of a conversation analytic approach to semi-structured interview data.

It is important to remember that the interviews with members of youth subcultures had not been collected as part of a conversation analytic project. Instead, they were initially conducted as part of a social psychological project to assess the utility of a theory of group membership. However, in keeping with empirical traditions in cognitive psychology it was originally assumed that the raw data themselves would not be able to tell us anything significant about the processes of group affiliation. Instead, the data had to be transformed: first they were sieved through a coding scheme which transformed them into numerical information. These numbers were then subjected to high-powered statistical tests, the results of which were then interpreted in terms of social identity theory. Only after this series of methodological transformations were the data considered to be suitable to allow the investigator to make inferences about the dimensions of, and processes underlying, group membership and self-categorization.

A conversation analytic examination of the 'raw data', however, indicated that these issues were not of interest simply to academics, but were real concerns for the respondents themselves in the course of the interviews. Furthermore, these issues were not relevant in some removed or secondhand sense, in that they had to be recovered from the interview data via a complex series of methodological transformations: they had a very live and immediate relevance to the respondents in the unfolding exchanges with the interviewer. Analysis revealed that the interviewees' tacit reasoning about their self-categorization and group membership were embodied in the design of their contributions to the interview.

The application of a conversation analytic approach, then, not only illuminated features of the social organization of the interview as a form of talk-in-interaction, but also revealed some aspects of the interactional management of category ascription, resistance and affiliation. On the basis of this, Widdicombe and Wooffitt were able to make some critical points regarding the assumptions underlying social identity theory and the purchase it affords on understanding processes of group affiliation and self-categorization. This is evidence, then, that at least in some cases it is possible for a CA approach to make a contribution to the substantive concerns of a study for which a set of semi-structured interviews had originally been collected.

The unfocused or unstructured interview

Data produced from this kind of interview present a particular set of methodological problems and possibilities. Due to the informal character of the interview, it is common to find that interviewees engage in long uninterrupted stretches of talk. These may consist of anecdotes, explanations, stories and so on. During these accounts the interviewer may be entirely silent, or may contribute no more than an occasional 'mm hm' or 'yeah'. These interviews, then, can generate data which are not so much interactional as monologic, and it is this feature of unstructured interview data which raises some special methodological questions.

Consider, for example, some differences between monologic data and conversational interaction. In the latter, the analyst is easily able to identify the turn as the unit of analysis: he or she can begin to describe how turns are built to display their connection to prior turns, and how they may constrain the kind of next turn which a next speaker may produce. But it is not so simple to isolate a unit of analysis in lengthy one-speaker turns. Does the analyst look for some organizational features which seem to cohere over single uninterrupted turns? Or should the interviewer's utterances, however minimal, be taken as marking the boundary of an analytic unit?

This issue has important implications. The object of conversation analysis is to identify and describe the ways in which participants collaboratively produce recognizable action sequences which exhibit orderly structural and normative properties. Those sequences emerge from the production of alternative turns by two (or more) participants in a conversation. It is for that reason that the turn is the basic analytic unit in conversation analysis. But how can the analyst attempt to identify the sequential properties of monologic, single-speaker utterances when there is no established analytic unit through the examination of which sequential properties can be seen to emerge? Lengthy accounts produced by an interviewee, with little or no contribution from an interviewer, certainly seem more like textual materials than ordinary conversation. And even if it is possible to identify properties of the organization of lengthy accounts, to what degree can we claim that these have any interactional orientation in the absence of any other participants' contributions? How can we compensate for the absence of the 'proof procedure' afforded by turn-by-turn displays of participants' own interpretations? What alternative resources are available to the analyst?

By way of answering these questions we will look at some of the resources used by one of the authors in a study of people's accounts of their encounters with a range of paranormal or supernatural phenomena (Wooffitt 1992). This will allow us to illustrate the kinds of insights generated when we employ a conversation analytic mentality in the study of lengthy, one-speaker accounts produced in informal interview settings.

In chapter 4 we described the preliminary stages in CA. First, find some feature of the data which seems to have some interesting interactional features: for example, a particular sequence of turns. Second, try to describe the organization of this sequence more formally, focusing on its underlying organization. Then, with these initial observations in mind, return to the original data corpus to find any other sequences which appear to have similar properties, thereby building a collection of possible or candidate cases of a specific conversational phenomenon. This procedure can also be applied to the study of interview accounts.

In the following extract the speaker is about to describe his first awareness of the onset of an encounter with a poltergeist in his home. This episode happened while he was walking towards the kitchen.

(8)   [ND:22:159]
```
1   S:   anyway I got to the kitchen door
2        an as ah .hh
3        I had the teapot in my hand like this
4        and I walked through the kitchen door
5        (0.5) .hhh
6        as I was going through the doorway
7        (0.7)
8        I was just (.) jammed against
9        the doorpost (.) like this
10       with the teapot sti(h)ll stu(h)ck
11       out in front of me
```

In this part of the account the speaker is describing his recollection of what he was doing just before the onset of that particular encounter with the poltergeist. This is a crucial part of the narrative, in that it is the first mention of the ostensible 'topic' of the account: the experience, or the particular phenomenon he encountered. How does the speaker actually produce this 'first mention'?

A preliminary observation is that he seems to be using a two-part format, or device. In the first part of this format he describes what he was doing just prior to the onset of the experience (line 6) and in the second part he reports his first actual awareness of the phenomenon: being pushed by an invisible entity (line 8).

Having identified this sequence as potentially interesting, a next analytic step is to produce a more formal description of its properties. We can identify this two-part format as 'I was just doing X ... when Y': the X component is used to describe the speaker's activities at that time just before the experience, and the Y component contains the speaker's first awareness of the phenomenon. So the speaker claims that 'as I was going through the doorway' ('I was just doing X ...') he was 'just (.) jammed against the doorpost' ('... when Y').

Note that the characterization 'I was just doing X ... when Y' does not rely on the specific details of what the speaker actually said. We do this for the following reason. Remember that a preliminary stage in analysis is to build a collection of instances of a pattern. However, it is very unlikely that our data will actually yield other instances which are identical to the first case we have identified. That is, it would be very unusual if all the people interviewed had a paranormal experience as they were walking towards their kitchens. Similarly, as we noted earlier, not every interview in the data corpus concerned poltergeist incidents. Therefore, we need a general, more formal characterization of the properties of the pattern. We can then return to our larger data corpus to see if other sequences seem to fit this overarching pattern.

And indeed, the 'X then Y' format does seem to re-appear when speakers get to that part of their account in which they report their first awareness of a paranormal force or parapsychological happening. Here are two such examples. In extract (9) the interviewee is reporting a vision of her dead husband during his funeral service; and in extract (10) the interviewee describes one of a series of apparitions which appeared in her home.

(9)   [EL:4:29]
```
1  S:   an' I went in there (.) er:m
2       w- with my mother in law and uhm: (0.4)
3       friends that were with me
4       (1.3)
5       .hhh
6       (.)
7       and I was just looking at the coffin            X
8       and there was David standing there (0.3)        Y
9       he was in Blues
```

(10)   [REW 52]
```
1   S:   so I I think I remember I 'ad a dish
2        in hand I was out in the kitchen
3        it was different like (.) y' know (.)
4        to this sort've flat (0.5)
5        an' it ws' like a (.) big entrance hall (0.7)
6        with one (.) door (0.5) and then it came
7        straight the way through
8        there was a door there and a
9        door there (0.5) a door there
10       an (0.5) it was a kitchen
11       (1)
12       and I was right by this unit part
13       (1.5)
14       an'
15       (.)
16       I were lookin' out that way                    X
17       an' it seemed to be like a figure              Y
18       (.)
19       coming through the ↑hall (0.7)
20       all I could see was the ah (a-)
21       the top part
```

In the data we have so far examined, there does appear to be a consistent pattern emerging.

Remember that in ordinary conversation, an analytic claim about an utterance can be supported by reference to the ways in which co-participants themselves responded to it. But in the kinds of interview data we are considering here, we do not have the advantage of such an 'inbuilt' proof procedure. What other resources can we use to strengthen our claim to have discovered a robust device which exhibits regular organizational features?

One strategy is to examine the data corpus to see if there are occasions when interviewees seem to replace one description of part of their experience with another, slightly amended version of ostensibly the same thing. Such cases of self-repair will provide an insight as to the 'design features' of the device.

Instances of self-monitoring also occur in ordinary conversational interaction. (The data corpus from which the following extract was taken was collected in the United States in the early 1960s. Consequently some of the terms and categories may seem somewhat dated.)

(11) [From Sacks 1992, vol. 1: 44]
  1 A: Corliss, the g-this chick I'm hanging around with now
  2   she's real nice she's got a real good personality,
  3   she's not – y'know she's just a real cute kid.
  4 B: mm hm

Notice that at the start the speaker says 'Corliss, the g-this chick I'm hanging around with'. Although we can't be sure, it would seem reasonable to assume that the abandoned word beginning with 'g' was 'girl'. So, the speaker begins to say 'Corliss this *girl* I'm hanging around with', stops himself right at the start of the word 'girl' and produces instead the word 'chick'. There are, then, (at least) two alternative ways of referring to that person, 'girl' and 'chick'. Why would he start with one form of reference and then reject it in favour of another? We can make some speculative remarks based on the alternative but non-equivalent inferences made available by the categories girl and chick. 'Girl' is a largely neutral form of address: it may be taken to indicate gender and an approximate age, but it doesn't reveal much more about the person so described. At that time, however, 'chick' performed a very different kind of work: it is a primarily male description which points to sexual attractiveness, as well as invoking a sense of being 'cool' or 'hip'. So by referring to his girlfriend as a 'chick' rather than a 'girl', the speaker is able to establish that she has the kind of personal and perhaps physical characteristics which would be highly valued among his peers at that time. (And this in turn suggests something positive about himself: that he's the kind of 'cool', 'hip' person a 'chick' would go out with.)

Interviewees will also produce such small self-repairs and amendments to their descriptions or accounts. These kinds of discursive actions can furnish us with the basis for analytic claims about the kinds of interactional or inferential concerns relevant to the speakers' ongoing production of their talk. Let us illustrate this by examining some data relevant to the 'X then Y' pattern. In the cases we have seen so far, interviewees have used the past progressive tense to describe their activities just before the experience occurred, for example, 'was going' and 'was looking', rather than 'went' and 'looked'. Here are some more examples.

(12) **[EM B 88]**
6	an' I was standing right there	X
7	on the platform (0.7) waiting	
8	for this damned train to come (.)	
9	all of a sudden	Y

(13) **[EM A 300]**
1	one night however a friend was with me (.)	
2	and we're just sitting watching the telly	X
3	(0.3)	
4	and she was also very psychic	
5	a:nd urm	
6	(1.3)	
7	its (.) th-the s:ound started	Y
8	the litt(le)m musical (s) tu-	
9	s::ound started again	

(14) **[YB 3:13]**
6	I was sitting in bed one night (.)	X
7	getting ready to go to sleep	
	((goes on to describe precognitive experience))	Y

(15) **[DM 7]**
19	I were just thinkin'	X
20	(0.3) er:m	
21	and then suddenly I was aware of	Y

There are cases, however, in which speakers produce a candidate X component using the simple past tense, but then immediately produce another version using past progressive tense before moving on to produce the Y component. Two examples follow, the first of which comes from extract (8).

(16) **[ND:22:159]**
1	I had the teapot in my hand like this	
2	and I walked through the kitchen door	X_1
3	(0.5)	
4	.hhh as I was going through the doorway	X_2
5	(0.7)	
6	I was just (.) jammed	Y
7	against the doorpost	

(17) **[EM A 10:86]**

1	but my experience was	
2	I got to a certain point in	X_1
3	the (0.3) circle s:circle and the chant	
4	we kept going round slowly	X_2
5	in a circle without stopping	
6	.hh all of a sudden	Y
	((goes on to describe experience))	

In both extracts the speakers provide two consecutive utterances which address ostensibly the same issue: their activity at the time; and in both instances the information in the first version is repackaged in the second. The reformulated versions, however, employ past progressive tenses, whereas the first versions are constructed through simple past tenses. In the way that the speakers amend their first version of their activities just before the experience, they display their tacit knowledge about socially patterned conventions which underpin the production of these particular episodes of extraordinary experiences: that is, they are orienting to the 'design features' of the 'X then Y' device.

Further important features of the X component in the device enable us to examine how it can be used to address interactional or inferential tasks. We can describe these 'I was just doing X' components as *state formulations*. That is, they describe, usually in the past progressive tense, a particular state of activity or state of mind that the speaker was engaged in immediately prior to the onset of the paranormal experience. When we look closely at the design features of these state formulations, we find that they are built to accomplish specific kinds of inferential tasks.

A common characteristic of state formulations is that they seem to report very mundane or ordinary activities. Consider some state formulations we have seen so far:

'.hhh as I was going through the doorway'
'I were lookin' out that way'
'and we're just sitting watching the telly'

All these are very routine activities. However, it is not necessarily the case that the speakers are reporting these events in this way simply because that's what was happening at the time. These formulations have been designed to have this mundane character. We can find evidence for this when we look at those cases in which the state formulation is used to provide a summary of the speaker's own prior talk. Consider the following extract.

(18)　[DM 7]
```
 1   S:   un' I was thinkin' about religion
 2        un' eh (0.5) I was thinkin' well (0.4)
 3        (           ) on the lines of it (0.3)
 4        I(t)- i- it must be very easy
 5        to be Saint Paul because yuh get yer
 6        blindin' light on the road to Damascus
 7        sort u(v) thing un' eh .hh (0.6)
 8        you've no problems (so you) you:: know
 9        as far as you're concerned
10        you measure all things
11        according to that experience
12        the experience was exterior
13        to yourself an' so therefore
14        (1.3)
15        you viewed it (0.7) as a star:t
16        (0.5)
17        (>yu know<) >yeah<
18        I were just thinkin'                              X
19        (0.3) er:m
20        and then suddenly I was aware of                  Y
21        (0.7)
22        almost (.) the sensation was
23        almost as if a veil was lifted
```

The speaker is describing what he was doing just before the onset of a mystical or revelatory experience. In the first part of the extract he provides a lengthy account of the kind of thoughts which were occupying him at the time, and these concerned his reflections on personal faith which results from a direct personal encounter with a mystical presence. These could hardly be called everyday reflections. However, when he comes to that part of the account in which he makes his first reference to the actual phenomenon he is reporting, he builds a very mundane state formulation 'I were just thinkin'' (line 18).

The speaker in the next extract seems to follow similar design features in the construction of the 'I was just doing X' component.

(19)　[EL 5:39]
```
          (The speaker here is describing how she had her husband's
          funeral service video recorded for relatives who were unable to
          attend the ceremony.)
 1   S:   I also wanted it video'd for
```

```
2        my children: who were
3        (1.7)
4        two and four at the time
5        and they didn't come to the funeral
6        (2.4)
7        so perhaps a wee:k later
8        (1.3)
9        >must've bin about< a week afterwards
10       .h I:: (0.5) put the recording on
11       and was: (0.5) watching it
12       I was obviously extremely upset
13       (0.8)
14       and I was sat on a chair                        X
15       (.)
16       uhn:d
17       (0.5)
18       when I looked down David was (.)                Y
19       kneeling at the side of me
```

In this case the speaker is describing how she was watching a video recording of her husband's funeral service – clearly a traumatic and emotional experience. However, when she comes to produce the first reference to the apparition of her husband, her state formulation is the prosaic 'I was sat on a chair' (line 14). Indeed, given these extremely traumatic circumstances, this state formulation seems to be conspicuously routine.

In both these cases the speakers are using their state formulations to provide one of two kinds of summary of their prior talk. 'I were just thinkin'' is a *gist* of 'thinking about personal faith which is verified by direct contact with a deity', and 'I was sat on a chair' is an *upshot* of watching a recording of the service. In both these cases, then, the speakers gloss over or discard those features of their prior talk which are non-ordinary, emotive or traumatic. This deletion of specific features of their prior talk suggests they are actively constructing their state formulations. Given that we seem to have identified this design feature of X components, we can ask: what kind of work is being done when state formulations are built in this way?

One consequence of reporting anomalous events is that there is always the possibility that a sceptical recipient may try to reconstruct the reported experience so as to recast it as an ordinary event which may, for example, have been misidentified. (This is a strategy often employed by sceptics when they appear in television documentaries about the paranormal.)

In extracts (18) and (19) the speakers reveal a lot of information about themselves. For example, in (18) the speaker is describing in positive terms the kind of phenomenon he subsequently claims to have encountered. Consequently it would be easy to suggest that his experience was a form of wish fulfilment and not a truly extraordinary mystical or revelatory experience. In extract (19) the speaker's perception of her husband's apparition can be 'explained' by reference to the trauma of reliving his funeral service as she watched a video recording made at the time. It is precisely this kind of information which could be used to build a sceptical or non-paranormal explanation for the events being reported.

We can argue, then, that the production of distinctly mundane state formulations does important inferential work: such routine formulations ensure that the immediate sequential context for the first reference to the phenomenon is not the kind of information which could support a sceptical reappraisal of the claimed experience.

Admittedly, this is a speculative account: there is no proof procedure through which we can provide a firmer warrant for these claims. However, we can look to see how other structural properties of the 'X then Y' device are used: are similar inferential tasks being addressed in different ways?

In many cases, speakers insert information between the two components of the device. Inspection of these inserted materials reveals that they work to undermine various kinds of sceptical responses. For example, one type of insertion deals with the possible retort that when the speaker encountered a phenomenon, they were not in the best position to observe it accurately. In the following extract the speakers are describing one in a series of poltergeist experiences which were centred in the attic in their house. The insertion reveals that the speakers were directly underneath the source of the disturbance they are reporting.

(20) **[ND 7:49]**
```
     1   S1:   and then the disturbances started
     2          (2.4)
     3          the first thing we
     4          (1.3)
     5          really noticed was: (0.5)
     6          one night
     7          (1.3)
     8          in (0.7)
```

```
 9          I would think September
10   S2:    yeah September ⌈seventy six=
11   S1:               ⌊September
12   S2:    =it would be
13   S2:    yeah that's right
14          (1.5)
15          we were laid (0.7) in the front bedroom      X
16          which was below the front attics            Ins
17          (1.5)
18          and we heard a noise (0.5)                   Y
19          like someone throwing gravel across
20          a piece of (.) hollow hardboard
```

Similar work is done by the insertion in the following case.

(21) [HS 17]
```
 1   S:    ah came home from work at lunchtime
 2         (1)
 3         an' I walked into the sitting room door
 4         (.)
 5         in through the sitting room door             X
 6         (1.5)
 7         an::
 8         right in front of me (.)                    Ins
 9         was a sort of alcove (.)
10         and a chimney breast (.)
11         like this (0.7) ((pointing to wall))
12         and a photograph of our wedding              Y
13         (1)
14         came off the top shelf (0.2)
15         floated down to the ground
16         hh completely came apart
17         But didn't break
```

Finally, consider the following case. This comes from a corpus of naturally occurring telephone conversations recorded in England in the late 1980s. The participants, L and T, are chatting about friends, relatives and so on. Immediately prior to this extract, L has asked about T's 'haunting', a reference to unusual happenings in a house belonging to one of T's friends. T replies that nothing untoward has occurred recently, but then goes on to say:

(22) [Holt:J86:1:2:4]
```
     T:   It's quite funny actually cuz there's someb'dy up
          the road I wz talking to an' uh (0.2) sh'reckoned
          tha(.)t uh: he he bought th'house b't'er bought it
          off his sister.
          (0.5)
```

```
T:   A⌈n' iz sister wz: uh gettin' ready one night t'go out.        X
L:    ⌊Yes.
T:   She hadn't been °drhhinking° .hhh                              Ins
     an' the hairspray apparently lifted itself up 'n went         Y
     t'the other side a' the dressing table.
```

This is a very neat conversational instance of an insertion between the two components of the device which is starkly designed to minimize the possibility of a specific kind of sceptical response to the story. This example is important because it provides clear evidence that the X then Y phenomenon, and at least one way it can be used, is not an artefact of the interview situation.

The structural features of the X then Y device seem to furnish a range of resources, some of which we have examined. Analysis of the design of state formulations, and examination of insertions between the X and Y components, indicates that speakers are using the device to defuse potential sceptical claims about the veracity of the account or the reliability of the speaker. In short, the device is used for inferential work which is sensitive precisely to the possibility that the account might receive an unsympathetic or sceptical hearing.

It is important to keep in mind that the recipient of the story – the interviewer – does not need to be sceptical for the speakers to build their accounts to warrant the claimed paranormality of the event. Regardless of the avowed or assumed beliefs of the interviewer, a speaker's utterances may be designed to address a wider, culturally based scepticism. To a degree, Sacks made a similar argument when discussing the ways in which we may invoke or resist membership of certain kinds of categories, even when we have no reason to care about the opinions of the people we're talking to. Observing that people will lie to market researchers about the amount of time they spend watching television, Sacks says 'It's interesting in that they're controlling an impression of themselves for somebody who couldn't matter less' (1992, vol. 1: 580).

There is a related point. Wooffitt (1992) discusses data taken from an interview with a professional medium, whose everyday work consists of talking to the dead on behalf of the living. At many points during the interview the speaker emphasizes that for her, supernatural experiences are commonplace. An ethnographic or traditional sociological analysis of her account might reflect, and indeed endorse, her claim that she treats supernatural phenomena as ordinary events. However, analysis of a segment of her account revealed that she displayed a tacit sensitivity to the inauspiciousness of reporting paranormal experiences, and the cultural conventions which are associated with paranormal experiences – conventions which she rejects as having no relevance to her. There was, then, a discrepancy between what she explicitly *said* is normal to her, and the kinds of concerns which actually *informed* the way in which she built her account of a specific experience. An analysis of interview data informed by conversation analysis is able to trace the influence of a speaker's orientation to these kinds of cultural expectations and norms, important concerns which may be overlooked in more traditional uses of interview data in sociological research.

Reported speech

So far we have illustrated a CA approach to interview data by examining how speakers produce the first reference to paranormal phenomena they claim to have experienced. This crucial part of the account was accomplished through the use of a small, two-part device. Further investigation of this device revealed that it could be used to address a range of subtle inferential tasks. However, the same analytic approach can be applied to patterns which seem to cohere over larger sections of accounts produced in unstructured interviews. We can illustrate this by looking to see how speakers can use reported dialogue between themselves and other people in their accounts.

One interesting pattern in the use of reported dialogue is illustrated in the following extract. This comes from the conclusion of an account of a series of mysterious noises which had been disturbing the speaker in her home. Until this point in the account the speaker had not explicitly claimed that she knew that the noises were caused by a spirit. In this excerpt, however, she goes on to provide information which clearly substantiates the paranormality of the experiences. The speaker is describing events which happened shortly after the manifestation of the noise.

(23)   **[EM A 307]**
(To mark out the segments of reported dialogue we are using 'speech marks' common to fictional writing.)

```
 1   S:    so: about two or three days later (0.3) ahr (.)
 2         I went to: a seance
 3         (1.3)
 4         the medium came to me ↑almost immediately
 5         and >she sed< '↑oh: (.) by the way'
 6         (0.2)
 7         she >didn't know me< she jus:t (.) came
 8         straight to me however 'nd she said ehm (.)
 9         'you know that ehm musical (.) sound you've been
10         hearing in your ↑living room'
11         'n I dy(eu) h huhh hah
12         I just said 'ye:ah hh'
13         .hhh and she said ehm
14         (0.7)
15         'that was Da:ve (.) a ma:n (.) who passed
16         over quite a lo:ng time ago'
```

Of interest here are the following three sections: the medium's
initial utterance and the remarks leading up to it (lines 4 to 10);
the speaker's subsequent turn (lines 11 to 12); and the medium's
final utterance (lines 15 to 16).

The medium's initial utterance 'you know that ehm musical (.)
sound you've been hearing in your ↑living room' itself constitutes
a mystery: how did the medium know that the speaker has been
hearing strange noises? After all, the speaker interrupts her
report of the medium's talk to make it plain that they did not
know each other. Furthermore, why did the medium approach
the speaker with such urgency, especially as they were not
acquainted? The medium's actual utterance substantiates the
mystery surrounding her reported decision to approach the
speaker. The reference to the phenomenon which the speaker
had been experiencing has an unequivocal character which itself
borders on the extraordinary: she seems to know *exactly* what has
been going on. So, for example, the medium is depicted as referring directly to the phenomenon: she is not portrayed as if she
were unsure whether the speaker had had any encounters with
strange noises. The upshot of this utterance is that the medium is
seen to be intimately familiar with the specific details of the
speaker's experience. So the way that this sequence has been
constructed provides the grounds for the inference that the
medium's remarks are a revelation to the speaker. Despite not
knowing her, she has approached the speaker directly and displayed her detailed knowledge about her experiences.

The speaker's subsequent turn is: 'n I dy(eu) h huhh hah I just said 'ye:ah hh'. In this she reports her rather surprised reactions to the medium's remarks. This also establishes that the medium was correct in her remarks about the strange noise the speaker has been hearing. The speaker begins to say "n I' but then interrupts herself and laughs briefly. This laugh is designed to be heard as a feature of the telling of the account, rather than as an indication of a humorous event at the time of the exchange being reported. Consequently, the speaker's brief burst of laughter is a way of displaying her surprise at the accuracy of the information she received. In this, the speaker is also showing that she behaves as any normal person might: she has claimed that she has received dramatic news, and by reporting her surprise, she shows that she responded as anyone might in that position.

The speaker's response does not explicitly confirm the accuracy of the other voice's utterance; instead, her 'ye:ah' (line 12) acknowledges that she is aware of the events to which the medium has referred, while at the same time returning the floor to the other voice. This provides the warrant for the speaker to report the medium's subsequent turn.

The medium's final turn is: 'that was Da:ve (.) a ma:n (.) who passed over quite a lo:ng time ago'. In this section the speaker uses the reported speech to confirm that the cause of the experience was a spirit agency. An advantage of using another person's voice to do this is that the speaker does not explicitly have to provide the information which underlines the claim that the events she experienced were something genuinely mysterious. Furthermore, the speaker is describing how such important and extraordinary information was revealed to her by *someone else*: she depicts herself merely as a passive recipient of incredible news. By displaying an innocent and passive recipiency towards news which confirms the paranormal character of her own experiences, the speaker is able to portray herself as behaving normally when confronted with an extraordinary situation.

In this short extract, then, the speaker's account exhibits a clear three-part pattern. In the first part, someone else's voice is invoked to reveal information which is a *revelation* to the speaker at that time. The second part reveals the speaker's *response* to this news. The final part of the sequence finds the speaker portrayed as a recipient of further information which provides the *resolution* or denouement of the mystery established by the first part.

Again, inspection of other data reveals that this pattern is not unique to this extract.

(24) [ND 31:216]

(The speakers are reporting a discussion with someone who shared their house at the time of their experiences of poltergeist phenomena, which started in September of the previous year.)

1	S1:	when we left the house we (re) talking to	
2		the lad who lived on the ground floor	
3		(0.6)	
4		and he also had bought a house and he was gonna	
5		leave wasn't he	
6		(0.2)	
7	S2:	°yeah°	
8	S1:	and he said	
9		(1.2)	
10		'somehow the atmosphere in	**Revelation**
11		this house has changed'	
12		'uo:h really Gavin' ah said	**Response**
13		'w͞hen would you reckon ↑that happened'	
14		(0.4)	
15		'oh about September' 'e said	**Resolution**

(25) [EL 9:75]

(Shortly after the death of her husband, the speaker, accompanied by a neighbour, attended her children's school Christmas play.)

1	S:	when I came out and I was driving	
2		my neighbour home she said to me	
3		'I hope you won't be upset	**Revelation**
4		(0.5)	
5		but I think David was there'	
6		and I said	
7		'what made you (0.3) think that	**Response**
8		he was there'	
9		(0.7)	
10		and she said 'because I felt him	**Resolution**
11		on my shoulder'	

When we were describing the three-part pattern in extract (23) we noted some of the inferential benefits to be gained from the use of reported dialogue. The third part of the device seems particularly suited to allow speakers to address scepticism regarding paranormal experiences and the people who have them. The speaker uses that third part to introduce information which is significant to the account in that it confirms the paranormal status of the experience. However, this itself is a sensitive issue: for example, had the speaker not legitimized the introduction of this information through the first two parts of the sequence it may have appeared that this was a clumsy and conspicuous effort to confirm the strangeness of her experience. What appears to be happening, then, is that the speaker has designed this sequence of reported dialogue to allow her to incorporate information which is of crucial significance to the denouement of the account.

In this chapter we have considered three kinds of interview data. To some degree, the kind of findings which can be generated from the application of a conversation analytic approach to these kinds of data depends on the organization of the interview itself. For example, in the structured interview, conversation analysis can tell us about some of the important consequences when everyday conversational conventions have to be abandoned because of the need to administer all questions in the same order and with the same wording. Data from unstructured interviews, however, lend themselves to analysis of the broader organizational devices and patterns through which people structure lengthy, monologic accounts. But there are some methodological features which underpin the application of conversation analysis to all three kinds of interview data.

First, there is an emphasis on the identification and description of recurrent patterns in the data; the focus may be on the organization of exchanges between interviewer and respondent, or on the descriptive devices which inform longer sections in a single speaker's turns.

Second, it is important to explicate the participants' orientation to the normative properties of the sequential unfolding of the exchange; or, in the case of unstructured interview data, the normative properties of larger patterns.

Finally, we have tried to show that, in all the interview data, it is not the case that respondents are simply imparting information to a passive recipient. Whatever the ostensible topic, context or purpose of the interview, the interviewer and respondent are engaged in social action. The participants' utterances, and the accounts generated in unstructured interviews, are the site for a variety of interactional or inferential work. And, as we saw when we discussed Widdicombe and Wooffitt's analysis of interviews with members of youth subcultures, that inferential work may reflect, and provide an alternative focus on, the kinds of issues or topics which in the first instance motivated the use of the interview as a data collection tool.

CHAPTER 8

Analysing Versions of Reality
The Organization of 'Factual' Accounts

Initially, we might think that factual language is rather dull: what analytic benefit is to be gained from examining utterances which simply represent a fact about the world? However, there are a number of issues concerning factual language which merit attention. For example, just because something may be true does not in itself provide an account for reporting it. The utterance 'ice melts in water' is a factual statement yet we do not go around repeating it. Therefore, there is an issue of 'why this now?': why is it that at a particular point in a conversation we produce utterances which report factual statements, and in others we do not?

One feature of facts, or any other state of affairs in the world, is that they do not constrain the ways we may describe them or refer to them. When we describe or refer to an object or state of affairs, there is a (potentially inexhaustible) range of words and combinations of words which may legitimately be used. Even when we are describing something routine or mundane, we can produce an endless list of legitimate or 'logically' correct statements.

Schegloff provides a nice example of this in a paper in which he examines the ways in which people produce descriptions of the location of objects and people. He writes:

> Were I now to formulate where my notes are, it would be correct to say that they are: right in front of me, next to the telephone, on the desk, in my office, in Room 213, in Lewisohn Hall, on campus, at school, at Columbia, in Morningside Heights, on the Upper West Side, in Manhattan, in New York, in the Northeast, on the Eastern Seaboard, in the United States, etc. (1972: 81)

As Schegloff goes on to say, each of these descriptions is correct in so far as it does refer to where his notes were at the time of writing. In this sense, the statement 'At the time of writing Schegloff's notes were in New York' and 'At the time of writing Schegloff's notes were next to the telephone' are both factual statements.

The implication is that even when speakers are describing the most routine and commonplace events or states of affairs they have a wide range of alternative words and combinations of words from which to choose. This means that on each occasion when speakers produce a factual report they have selected which referential item or descriptive utterance they wish to use. If any factual reference or statement involves a process of selection, we can ask: what are the tacit reasoning procedures which led to this specific formulation of a fact at this point in the interaction? This is an issue we shall discuss in the first part of the chapter.

There is another issue which can be explored using conversation analysis. Our everyday lives are often disputatious: in everyday conversation we regularly engage in activities such as 'disagreeing', 'arguing', 'contesting', 'accusing', 'defending', 'criticizing' and so on. In short, it is a perfectly normal feature of everyday life that we enter disputes with other people about something that happened, or didn't happen when it should, or the implications and consequences of events. On these occasions people will be using language to warrant their perspective, position or point of view.

A related point is that there are times when we are talking to someone who may simply be sceptical of the claims we are making. Imagine someone with liberal views talking to someone with strong right-wing views about the merits of trying to redistribute a nation's wealth to better fund a social welfare programme. It is likely that there is going to be disagreement; and a recourse to 'the economic facts of the matter' will not resolve the dispute, as it is unlikely that each side will agree with the other's interpretation of the facts, even if they are able to agree on what the facts are. And it is important to mention that we don't have to be embroiled in a political argument to be aware that our co-interactants may be inclined to dismiss our claims: sometimes even the most innocuous of remarks might receive sceptical responses.

However, there are occasions when people make explicitly controversial or extraordinary claims, for example the kinds of reports of paranormal or supernatural phenomenon which we discussed in the last chapter. Accounts of such experiences are likely to be met with a sceptical response: the experience was delusional; it was a case of misperception of an ordinary phenomenon, the person making the report is trying to glamorize their lives, and so on. These sceptical responses all work to undermine a claim to have encountered a truly paranormal phenomenon which had an objective existence in the world.

So there is a variety of circumstances in which speakers will be sensitive to the likelihood that their claims may receive sceptical or possibly hostile responses. This raises two issues for investigation: first, we can begin to document the use of discursive resources through which speakers can ensure that claims are warranted, reasonable or factual; and second, we can examine the ways in which utterances have been built so as to anticipate and minimize the effectiveness of specific kinds of counterclaims. This issue will concern us in the second part of the chapter.

Although the use of a conversation analytic approach to the study of factual discourse is a relatively novel development, an interest in the constitutive properties of language use has been a more long-standing concern in other areas of the social sciences. For example, sociologists interested in the study of scientific knowledge have examined the ways in which scientists' discourse reproduces the independent and objective status of the objects or processes they study (Gilbert and Mulkay 1984; see Woolgar 1988 for a succinct account of the way in which sociologists of science became interested in scientific discourse). Foucault's socio-historical studies also relied on the idea that the features of discourse constrain the shape and development of specific ways of thinking about, and acting in, the everyday world (Foucault 1977).

However, the study of factual language use has primarily emerged in an area of social psychology called discourse analysis (Potter and Wetherell 1987; Edwards and Potter 1992). Discourse analysts have been critical of the ways in which social psychology has tended to treat language as a passive or neutral means of communication. Drawing from conversation analysis, ethnomethodology and semiotics, they have argued instead that language is a functional and constructive medium. Consequently, one of the main concerns of discourse analysis has been to develop a research programme in social psychology which takes full account of the dynamic properties of language use, both spoken and written. The study of factual discourse as a topic in its own right has been one of the consequences of this programme.

Potter (1996) provides an important account of the interdisciplinary history of the study of factual discourse, and reviews several important studies in the area. He proposes that research in factual discourse falls into one of two categories which correspond to the two main themes we have identified in this chapter. First there is a concern with the *action orientation* of factual language: this focuses on the 'why this now' feature of factual utterances, and examines the ways in which they can be used to accomplish specific kinds of interactional or inferential tasks. Second, there is the study of the *epistemological orientation* of factual utterances, in which we can begin to investigate the ways in which accounts can be built to warrant the objective existence of the events or objects being reported, or to establish the validity of claims being made.

The action orientation of factual statements

Even the most mundane statement can be used to perform a range of important work in social interaction. We can illustrate this by examining Potter's (1996) account of the following utterance: 'Neil you've got shoes on'. An initial reaction to this utterance might be that it is a simple report of what someone is wearing, and therefore an unlikely vehicle for delicate interactional work. However, this simple report comes from the following sequence in which some young people are discussing a noise they can hear outside their flat.

(1) **[From Potter 1996: 108]**
Becky: oi (.) sh shh (.) it could have been that
Neil: NO ʃthat's not making a noise
Alan: ʟno (.) something outside
     (0.4)
     it was definitely outside
Diane: Neil you've got shoes on

What happens after this is that there is an explicit discussion about who should go outside and investigate the cause of the

noise. So what we find is that the placement of a simple observation about Neil's footwear in a *sequence* of turns concerned with
a mysterious noise is deeply consequential, because it constitutes
a request or suggestion that he should go and investigate. An
apparently neutral observation about the world has been used to
do a specific kind of interactional work.

This illustrates how participants' interpretations of the work
done by factual utterances will be informed by their reasoning
about the context in which they are used. In extract (1), the
observation about Neil's footwear can be seen to constitute a
request for him to do something by virtue of the topic of the preceding talk. However, topic may not be the only relevant context:
the kinds of discursive actions participants are engaged in may
also establish a sequential context in which apparently neutral
factual observations can perform delicate interactional work. The
following extract comes from a telephone conversation in which
one person (Ilene) is trying to obtain a lift from another person
(Charlie) when he drives to Syracuse. However, Charlie can't go
unless he has somewhere to stay. At the start of the extract Charlie has just finished explaining that the person he had intended to
stay with is now going away.

(2)   **[Trip to Syracuse:2]**
    1   Charlie: So tha: ⌈:t
    2   Ilene: ⌊k-khhh
    3   Charlie: Yihknow I really don't have a place tuh sta:y.
    4   Ilene: hhOh::::::.h
    5   (0.2)
    6   Ilene: .hhh So yih not g'nna go up this weeken?
    7   (0.2)
    8   Charlie: Nu::h I don't think so.
    9   Ilene: How about the following weekend.
   10   (0.8)
   11   Charlie: .hh Dat's the vacation isn't it?
   12   Ilene: .hhhhh Oh:. .hh ĀLright so:- no ha:ssle, (.)
   13   s⌈o
   14   Charlie: ⌊Ye:h
   15   Ilene: Yihkno:w::
   16   ( ):   .hhh
   17   Ilene: So we'll make it fer another ti:me then.

Charlie has explained that he is unable to make a trip on a
date which had been previously arranged. As an alternative,
Ilene proposes another date – 'How about the following weekend' (line 9). After the pause Charlie refers to the revised pro-

posal for the trip: 'Dat's the vacation isn't it?' We may note, first, that in this utterance Charlie has redescribed the occasion which Ilene had suggested as the revised date for the trip. He has substituted 'next weekend' with 'vacation', thereby indexing a range of conventions associated with public holidays, but not with 'just any weekend', for example, that it is a time for family activities. Ilene then says, 'Oh:. .hh ALright so:- no hassle', and 'So we'll make it fer another ti:me then', indicating that she treats this simple description as indicating that Charlie won't be able to make the trip on the date she had suggested earlier, an interpretation which is implicitly confirmed when Charlie does not produce a subsequent utterance saying, for example, that that was not what he meant. So this simple factual statement marks Charlie's unavailability, and this action orientation is informed by the activities performed in the immediately prior utterances concerning the trip: negotiating the possibility of obtaining/giving a lift.

In the context of a nervous discussion about the cause of suspicious noises outside a bedroom window, the work done by the utterance 'Neil you've got shoes on' was relatively transparent. In extract (2) the work performed by 'vacation' was more subtle, as it allowed the recipient to infer its interactional significance by virtue of the fact that it invoked conventions associated with holidays. However, the inferential orientation of factual descriptions can be even more subtle. Consider the following data, which come from the transcript of a rape trial. In these extracts the counsel for the defence (C) is cross-examining the prosecution's main witness (W), the victim of the alleged rape. These data have a special relevance to this chapter in so far as a courtroom case is an environment in which versions of events may be routinely contested or undermined. Note that both parties produce what might be termed competing factual versions of ostensibly the same event. Each version has been designed, however, to do a different kind of work: the counsel's questions refer to events in such a way as to undermine the witness's claims that she was raped, and the witness's answers refer to the same events so as to warrant her claim that she could not be accused of encouraging the man who was alleged to have attacked her.

(3)   **[From Drew 1992: 489]**
1   C: ((referring to a club where the defendant and
2   the victim met)) it's where uh (.) uh gi:rls and fella:s
3   meet isn't it?

```
       4       (0.9)
       5   W:  People go: there.
```

(4)   [From Drew 1992: 489]
```
       1   C:  An during the eve:ning: (0.6) uh: didn't mistuh ((name))
       2       come over tuh sit with you
       3       (0.8)
       4   W:  Sat at our table.
```

In extract (3), the counsel builds a question through a description of one specific feature of the club in which the defendant and the witness met on the night of the alleged attack. The counsel does not refer to the patrons of the club as 'men or women' or 'local people', but as 'fellas' and 'girls'. Furthermore, he describes the club as a place where males and females meet each other. This description invokes the sense of young people out in the evening to make contact with members of the opposite sex. This in turn establishes the basis for the inference that people go to the club with a view to meet others for sexual purposes. This simple description works to undermine aspects of the witness's account which are crucial if her version of events is to be believed; for example, that in no way could it be suggested that she was encouraging any sexual relations between herself and her alleged attacker. Her reply 'People go: there' reformulates the 'function' of the club to escape the inference that it is a place in which males and females come together for sexual purposes. This is achieved primarily through the way she refers to the patrons as 'people': whereas a sexual division is emphasized and exploited by the counsel, she provides a gender neutral classification.

Similar concerns inform the sequence in extract (4): the question 'didn't [he] come over tuh sit with you' portrays a friendship between the witness and the alleged attacker; but by replying that the defendant 'Sat at our table' the witness is able to establish that his behaviour was not prompted by any special relationship with her in particular, but was due to a familiarity with that group of people of which she was only one member.

In extracts (1) to (4) we examined how ostensibly neutral and apparently uncontentious descriptions can be designed and used to perform a range of subtle interactional and inferential tasks aimed at establishing the validity of one version of events over another. However, there are many kinds of everyday circumstances in which the factual status of an utterance or account may be contentious and subject to explicit scepticism or rebuttal. In such cases, there is a variety of discursive practices through which speakers can establish the factual or warrantable status of their claims and accounts.

The epistemological orientation of factual statements

In this section we shall first examine some systematic properties of one way in which we can use language to minimize the likelihood that our claims may be met with a sceptical response. We shall then go on to examine the importance of negotiating category membership and personal interests, or 'stake', in the production of factual statements. Finally we will examine some interview data to see how these various resources and issues intersect in the speaker's report of a violent episode following a punk rock concert.

Extreme case formulations

When we try to convince people of the validity of our opinions, or when we defend ourselves against accusations or complaints, or even if we simply attempt to sell something, we are engaged in the business of persuading. In these (and many other) everyday circumstances, we are attempting to ensure that the people we are talking to will arrive at certain conclusions: for example, in conversation, if we express our opinions, we want our co-interactants at least to see that they are reasonable opinions to hold, or perhaps even to adopt them for themselves. One resource in the business of persuading is the way we formulate descriptions: a state of affairs (such as an opinion or an excuse or a complaint) may be portrayed as compelling and believable in the way in which the description of it is designed.

Pomerantz (1986) studied some of the linguistic resources people use to warrant their claims. In particular she has examined 'extreme case formulations'. These are simply ways of referring to an object or event which invoke its maximal or minimal properties. For example, 'never', 'always', 'brand new', 'forever', 'everyone' and so on are extreme case formulations. Pomerantz looked at ordinary conversations where one of the participants was engaged in activities such as accusing, defending, justifying and complaining. In these circumstances, she found extreme case formulations tended to be used to do one of three kinds of work.

First, she found that they could be used to defend against possible challenges to the complaint or accusation a speaker is making. Pomerantz examines the following extract. Here the speaker, Ann, is talking on the telephone to Bill, who has called to speak to Ann's husband, George. However, George is not in. Although Ann does not know Bill, she begins to tell him about her husband's affair with another woman.

(5) **[From Pomerantz 1986: 220]**
   Ann: And so when he went way on Mother's Day and .hh he went
          away on Saturday evening of (0.3) Mother's Day .hh he spent
          the night (.) with her and all day Sunday and came home
          around about nine o'clock Sunday night . . .

Ann does not explicitly condemn her husband for his behaviour. However, Pomerantz claims that the description of this incident is designed so that Bill will come to see George's culpability. For example, she describes that George was seeing the other woman on Mother's Day. She could have merely stated the date, or 'last weekend' (or whenever it was). But by identifying it as Mother's Day she is able to invoke conventions regarding appropriate family behaviour on such days, and thereby amplify the nature of his offence: it wasn't just that he went to see his other woman, but that he went to see her on a day on which he should have been honouring Ann (as mother to his children).

Clearly then Mother's Day/Sunday is crucial to the complaint Ann is making. And when she comes to characterize that portion of Mother's Day during which her husband was absent she says 'he spent the night (.) with her and all day Sunday and came home around about nine o'clock Sunday night'. 'All day' is an extreme case formulation, and in so far as it points to the unreasonable amount of time George was away, it further exacerbates the extent of his misbehaviour.

However, Ann has a tricky problem. Bill has called to speak to George. So although Ann does not know Bill, Bill certainly knows George in some capacity. Consequently they may be friends, and Bill may even have some sympathy for George.

Pomerantz argues that Ann's use of an extreme case formulation addresses the possibility that Bill may try to reconstruct George's actions so as to lessen the degree of the offence. So she is making it clear that it was not simply the case that at some point in the day George went away. The extreme formulation of that portion of the day George was away presents it as an unwarrantably long absence. Thereby this small description works to undermine one way in which the severity of the offence could be minimized by someone who was sympathetic to her husband.

The second set of circumstances in which extreme case formulations can be used involves a speaker attributing a cause to an object or person. This is illustrated in the following extract, in which the speaker (C) is talking to his wife about a week at work during which time the speaker's office co-manager (the 'he' referred to) was away.

(6)   [From Pomerantz 1986: 224]
C: We got so much done (.) and more than that but everyone had
     this feeling that we were .hhhh c-complishing things, you know we
     all felt real progress going on, .hhhh it's just so amazing,
     whenever he's around (.) he's utterly disparaging of our efforts,
     (.) and (.) he's c-completely disruptive.

The speaker here uses 'everyone' and 'we all' to mark a general positive response to the absence of the co-manager. The speaker is thereby able to attribute the cause of problems at the office to the co-manager's personality and attitudes.

The speaker has had personality clashes with the co-manager; consequently, it would be possible to suggest that the difficulties in the office have something to do with the speaker and not just his co-manager. But by using extreme case formulations the speaker demonstrates that everyone in the office performs better in the absence of the co-manager, and not just the speaker. As Pomerantz puts it, 'The lay logic is something like: if others react the same way to the co-manager, then the co-manager is responsible for the difficulties' (1986: 224).

Finally, Pomerantz shows how extreme case formulations may be used to invoke the rightness (or wrongness) of a state of affairs or action. This is illustrated in extract (7) which comes from a call to a suicide prevention centre in the United States. 'A' is the agent of the centre who took the call, and 'C' is a female caller.

(7)   **[From Pomerantz 1986: 225]**
```
1       A:   Do you have a gun at home?
2            (0.6)
3       C:   A forty fi:ve,
4       A:   You do have a forty fi:ve.
5       C:   Mm hm, it's loaded.
6       A:   What is it doing there, hh Whose is it.
7       C:   It's sitting there.
8       A:   Is it you:rs?
9            (1.0)
10      C:   It's Da:ve's.
11      A:   It's your husband's hu:h?=
12      C:   =I know how to shoot it,
13           (0.4)
14      A:   He isn't a police officer:r,
15      C:   No:.
16      A:   He just ha:s one.
17→     C:   Mm hm, It-u-Everyone doe:s don't they?
```

Even in the United States, where it is legal for citizens to own firearms, a gun is the type of possession for which you might be required to have a reason. And in this extract the member of the centre's staff tries to find a reason for the caller's possession of a gun by asking whether her husband is a police officer. As police officers in the United States are armed, this would account for why the caller has a gun in the house. But in this case, the caller's husband is not a police officer, so that account for possessing a gun does not hold. Her subsequent turn in line 17 'Everyone doe:s don't they' is a defensive utterance, in that it is oriented to the absence of a good 'official' reason for having a gun; and the design of her utterance is done with respect to that defensive action her turn is accomplishing. The point of using 'everyone' rather than, say, 'most people' or 'many people round here' is not that she's making a strict claim that every single individual in the world has a gun. Rather, the import of that description is that it proposes that this is a common practice and therefore something for which she does not have to offer a mitigating explanation.

Pomerantz's work is important for three reasons. First, it draws attention to the way in which the activity of persuading can underpin a variety of routine conversational circumstances: complaining, accusing, justifying and so on. Second, she highlights the subtlety of the persuasive techniques which can be employed. That is, in these cases it is not simply that people are trying to persuade their co-participants: they are also designing their talk in anticipation of a sceptical or unsympathetic response. But perhaps most important, Pomerantz's examination of these descriptive sequences leads us to consider the relationship between language and states of affairs or events in the world which are being described. Consider extract (5), and Ann's description of her husband's infidelity. Her use of an extreme case formulation, together with the use of 'Mother's Day' to refer to the date of the incident she is reporting actually constitutes the grounds for her complaint. That is, she has produced this version of the world in such a way that it supports the kind of conversational action she is engaged in.

Category entitlement

Consider other kinds of categories we have for referring to and describing people: 'man', 'woman', 'husband', 'wife', 'son', 'daughter', 'punk', 'skinhead', 'Catholic', 'Conservative, 'liberal', 'Canadian', 'widower', 'student', 'factory worker' and so on. All of these are membership categories: we are all members of a potentially large range of categories such as these. These categories are culturally available resources which allow us to describe, identify or make reference to other people or to ourselves. And the interesting thing is that they are not exclusive. For example, it is not hard to imagine a single individual who could be accurately described as a mother, daughter, accountant, divorcee, Piscean, Protestant and so on. This means that when we come to describe other people or ourselves, there is an issue of selection: why did we characterize our social identity, or the social identity of someone else, in that particular way at that particular time?

In thinking about this issue it is important to bear in mind that categories are not neutral descriptions: they are what Sacks called inference rich – there are strong expectations and conventions associated with them. For example, look at these two sentences, which come from a story told by a small child: 'The baby cried. The mommy picked it up' (Sacks 1972c: 330). The vast majority of readers will have interpreted 'the mommy' as being the mother of the baby; similarly, the baby crying will have been read as the reason why the mother picked it up. Neither set of information is contained in the sentence itself; however, we all arrive at the same interpretation because of the commonsense expectations associated with categories like mother (for example, that they will, or should, care for their children when they are distressed), and the way in which categories are grouped in relation to other categories (Sacks 1972c).

Categories, then, do not merely provide us with convenient labels which allow us to refer to persons; they also provide a set of inferential resources by which we can come to understand and interpret the behaviour of persons so designated. That is, 'Membership categories may conventionally be seen as having category-bound predicates ... they are loci for the imputation of conventional expectations, rights and obligations concerning activities (for instance) which it is expectable or proper for an incumbent of a given category to perform' (Watson and Weinberg 1982: 60). What this means is that the assignment of a person to a category ensures that conventional knowledge about the behaviour of people so categorized can be invoked or cited to interpret or explain the actions of that person. Furthermore, in everyday conversation it is common to find sequences in which speakers clearly display their sensitivity to the inferential implications of category ascription.

There are two interesting examples in the following data, which is an extended sequence of an extract we considered in the previous chapter.

(8)   [From Sacks 1992, vol. 1: 44]
```
1   A:   Corliss, the g-this chick I'm hanging around with now
2        she's real nice she's got a real good personality,
3        she's not – y'know she's just a real cute kid
4   B:   mm hm
5   A:   And last night we went to the Mardi Gras together
6        and we were both well we were both pooped because
7        I I ran in the track meet yesterday. And she
8        she's in the girls' tumbling team. I mean she
9        doesn't like it she's just on it for the credits.
```

What happens here is that in lines 7 and 8 speaker A characterizes his girlfriend in terms of her membership of the school tumbling team. Immediately after that, however, he explains her membership of the team by reference not to her interest in gymnastics, but because she needs school credits. By accounting for her membership of the tumbling team in this way the speaker appears to be sensitive to the kinds of inferences which may be drawn about his girlfriend by virtue of her membership of the category 'girls' tumbling team': it is likely that for teenagers being a member of a school tumbling team might not be seen as 'cool', but in fact quite the opposite. However, his account for her membership is a way of indicating that common knowledge about that category does not apply in this case. The speaker's account for his girlfriend's activity is evidence that, as he was telling this little anecdote, he was monitoring its production to assess the kinds of conclusions about his girlfriend which might be inferred by the recipient. What he has done is acknowledge his friend's membership of a category and then establish that the inferences which are normally associated with that category do not apply in this instance.

We have taken a relatively lengthy digression to illustrate how tacit knowledge and expectations about people and their actions are stored by reference to conversational categories. We can now begin to see how these associations are relevant to establishing a warranted or factual account.

Consider the following data, from a call to the 911 emergency service in the United States. This call to the emergency switchboard (SB) comes from a hospital. We know this because in the first utterance of the caller (C) is 'This is General', which is a shorthand term for the name of a city hospital. By virtue of this institutional identification the caller categorizes himself as an employee of the hospital, rather than, say, someone who just happens to be calling from the hospital premises.

(9)   **[From Whalen and Zimmerman 1990: 483]**
    SB: Mid City emergency
    C: Hi .hh this iz General – there's been an over dose (.)
          twenty six twenty six .hh Columbia: hh upstairs apartment
          num:::ber two
    SB: O:kay thank you
    C: umhm bye

Here the caller makes a specialized kind of claim: to be able to identify that someone has taken an overdose at least implies medical knowledge about the toxic properties of a drug when large quantities are ingested, what counts as 'a large dose' compared to the recommended dosage, possible effects of an overdose and so on. As soon as the switchboard says 'thank you', what has happened is that she has processed the call and emergency services are being despatched. So this call gets an instantaneous response. Note that the switchboard operator does not question the caller's competence to declare that the medical problem is an overdose. This is because of the expectations associated with membership of the broad category of medical personnel: people who identify themselves professionally with a hospital would in all likelihood be competent to evaluate medical problems and make appropriate diagnoses.

In the next extract, however, the caller makes a similar kind of specialized claim when he identifies that a certain kind of crime is being committed. What is different here, though, is that the caller is a member of the public.

(10) **[From Whalen and Zimmerman 1990: 473]**
```
SB:   Mid City emergency
C:    Would you send the police to eleven six oh Arvin Avenue
      North
SB:   Eleven six oh Arvin Avenue North?
C:    Yes there's been raping goin' on
SB:   WHERE
C:    Eleven six ⌈oh
SB:          ⌊Inside or outside?
C:    Inside the house
SB:   There's somebody being RAPED?
C:    Yup=
SB:   How do you know this?
C:    I live next door. Two ladies bein raped, eleven six oh=
SB:   =Di-How do you know they're being raped inside that house.
```

Unlike the previous extract, in this call the appropriate emergency service is not despatched immediately. Instead the operator seeks further details and then explicitly questions the basis of the caller's authority to make a claim about a rape.

What seems to be crucial in determining how seriously the operator treats the claims is the caller's category membership. The claims of the caller who establishes membership of a category of people who would be expected to be able to make specialized claims are dealt with unquestioningly. Thus one powerful resource in producing a factual or warranted report is to establish membership of a category, incumbency of which is associated with specific kinds of skill, knowledge or expertise.

In his study of accounts of paranormal experiences, Wooffitt (1992) examines how category membership is invoked by speakers to establish their authority and reliability, and to undermine the likelihood of sceptical responses. In the following extract, for example, the speaker describes her reactions to the onset of a series of anomalous noises in such a way as to invoke her membership of the category 'ordinary' person.

(11) **[EM A 286]**
```
 1   S:   every time I walked into
 2        the sitting room (0.3) er:m. (0.7)
 3        right by the window (0.3)
 4        and the same place always
 5        I heard a lovely (0.3) s:ound
 6        like de↑de↓dede↑dedede↓dededah
 7        just a happy (.) little tu:ne (0.5)
 8        a:nd >of course<
 9        I tore apart ma window
10        I tore apart the window frame
11        I >did Everything<
12        to find out what the hell's causing that
```

Here the speaker claims she searches for the cause of the noise. This is a perfectly reasonable reaction to the sudden appearance of weird noises; indeed, it is easy to imagine that the occurrence of such an anomaly which did not precipitate a search for a cause would itself be a reportable matter. The search is described in a way which portrays the normality of the speaker's thoughts and actions in these circumstances: that she conducted her search with urgency ('I tore apart', lines 9 and 10), and that it was exhaustive ('I >did Everything<', line 11). As 'ordinary' people do not immediately come to the conclusion that every odd event is the product of supernatural forces, her identity as an 'ordinary' person is warranted also in the way she reveals that she looked for a physical cause of the noise.

In the following extract the speaker describes his actions prior to encountering an anomalous phenomenon in such a way as to index his membership of a specific occupational category, that of police officer.

(12) **[AY]**
```
 1   S:   it was:: (.) it was not a stop check
 2        on a night y'know
 3        yuh jus' drove past it
 4        we'd 'ad a lot of thieves (.)
 5        yu know a couple of years ago
 6        so (°yus°) (.) y' know (.)
 7        look for any strange vehicles really
```

```
8        (1.3)
9        un' driving fairly slowly
10       having checked the school (0.3)
11       on the other side of the road
12       (1)
13       er:m:
14       (1)
15       un something caught me eye
         ((goes on to describe experience))
```

By revealing that he was looking for strange vehicles, and that he 'checked the school', the speaker invokes the duties associated with the category of 'police officer'. As police officers are expected to be level-headed and not prone to fantasy or delusion, membership of this category is a valuable inferential resource with which to establish the speaker's reliability and the authenticity of the experience.

So far we have seen how the relationship between categories and their associated expectations and activities are crucial in building the authority of a speaker's claims. However, the same kind of relationship can also be exploited to discount or undermine the factual status of claims and reports. Potter (1996) uses the following example which comes from a famous radio interview between the BBC broadcaster Brian Redhead and Nigel Lawson, who was then the Chancellor of the Exchequer in the Conservative government.

(13)   [From Potter 1996: 145]

> Lawson: ... Unemployment will go on falling throughout the
>   course of this year.
> Redhead: But much of that fall is the creating of special
>   measures. You may have heard ↑mister Hattersley
>   talking about young people being invited to job clubs.
>   to play games under the supervision of nursery school
>   teachers. Creation of- two thirds of the new jobs are
>   low paid part time jobs. These aren't real jobs that
>   you used to talk about way back in nineteen seventy
>   nine and eighty.
> Lawson: .hhh Well you've been a supporter of the Labour Party
>   all your life Brian .hh so I I expect you to say
>   something like that ...((goes on to defend
>   government's record))

Prior to this extract, Lawson has just been boasting about the government's record on unemployment. Redhead then makes some critical comments about the government's record, to which

Lawson replies 'Well you've been a supporter of the Labour Party all your life Brian .hh so I I expect you to say something like that'. What we have here is the ascription of category membership – being a supporter of the Labour Party – to undermine the factual status of Redhead's critical assessment of the Conservative government's schemes for job creation. This has a powerful rhetorical appeal, as it portrays Redhead's criticism of the government's record as being motivated by his commitment to the Labour Party, rather than on the basis of a neutral or objective assessment of the facts.

Stake management

The way in which Lawson rebutted Redhead's criticisms illustrates the inferential significance of a stake or personal interest. The status of one's claims can be very effectively undermined if they can be portrayed as simply reflecting personal interest. Consequently, stake management can be a central concern when producing an account which is intended to be authoritative or factual. Potter (1996) has documented some of the discursive strategies through which people inoculate themselves against the invocation of a stake. There is, for example, stake confession, in which speakers may actually draw attention to circumstances or category membership which could be invoked to account for their claims, thereby portraying themselves as being aware of, and able to stand aside from, their own personal interests.

Alternatively, speakers can display indifference towards that object, state of affairs or account in which they do clearly have a vested interest. Consider these extracts.

(14)   [From Wetherell and Potter 1992: 96]
     Jones: There have been a lot of ideas put, what is it, that
               the majority of rapes are committed by Islanders or
               Maoris and . . .

(15)   [From Potter 1996: 131]
     Jimmy: Connie had a short skirt on I don't know. . . .

The first of these two extracts comes from interviews with white New Zealanders to discover the extent of racist attitudes towards native Maori people, who, like the Aborigines in Australia, constitute an oppressed group. Racist rhetoric often emphasizes that the (usually white) majority are regularly subject to violent attacks committed by members of the (usually black) minority, a belief which is rehearsed in this extract when the speaker refers to the idea that Maori men regularly rape white women.

The second comes from a recording of a counselling session between a husband and wife concerning problems in their relationship which stem from his jealousy and possessiveness. His observation about the length of his wife's skirt is made when he is recalling one specific incident in a longer narrative in which he claims that Connie flirts with other men.

In both cases, the speakers are in an inauspicious environment: the points they want to raise have a sensitive character in that they could be the basis for negative assessments about the speaker's character. That is, on the basis of their utterances they leave themselves open to accusations of bigotry and pathological jealousy. In each case, however, the sensitive issues – a racist remark, or an observation about the length of a partner's skirt – are produced in tandem with expressions of uncertainty: 'what is it' and 'I don't know'. These phrases might seem entirely casual interjections, but their use allows the speakers to establish that they have no stake in, or commitment to, the sensitive issues they have just introduced.

For example, Jimmy's use of 'I don't know' portrays him as not really noticing his wife's dress precisely at the point in the account when it becomes an issue for him. A sceptical recipient of this account might attribute a negative motive to Jimmy for making this observation: that he is unwarrantably jealous and possessive, and therefore he would have a stake in monitoring the length of his wife's skirt. Furthermore, the ascription of such an interest would undermine his claim that indeed her skirts were unnecessarily revealing. But by using 'I don't know' to characterize his uncertainty about, or indifference to, his wife's clothes, he is able to inoculate himself against the charge that the grounds for his grievances are not derived from his partner's actual behaviour, but are more a reflection of his own psychological problems.

So far we have looked at extreme case formulations, category entitlement and stake management as discrete issues. However, it is quite easy to find instances of language use in which all these devices and issues intersect. In the next section we will show how in the space of a short account of a violent incident, a speaker draws on his tacit knowledge of various discursive resources to construct the factual status of his version of events.

Accounting for violence

This extract is taken from Widdicombe and Wooffitt's (1995) study of accounts from members of youth subcultures, and comes from an interview with three punks. In this segment one of the speakers is describing events which occurred after a gig by a famous punk rock band.

(16) **[2P:M/F:T8SA (CM)] (MR speaks with a strong Scots accent)**
```
 1   MR:   and the police were all outside there,
 2         (.) (ehr) at the co:ncert,
 3         there wasnae a bit of trouble 'part fro(m) 'nside
 4         one or two wee scra:ps, you know?
 5         (0.2)
 6   MR:   But that happens=ev'ry one- every gig
 7         ⌈there's a scrap?
 8   FR:   ⌊°mm°
 9   MR:   >(th)'s all's< somebody doesnae like somebody else.
10   FR:   Mm:
11   MR:   dunna mattah w:ha:t it is (0.4) i's always happenin',
12         .hh  y' know you cannae sto:p that?
13         (0.6)
14   MR:   an' (.) we go outside. and there they are.
15         (0.8)
16   MR:   fucking eight hundred old b'll,
17         (0.2)
18   MR:   just wai:tin' for the cha:nce,
19         (0.3)
20   MR:   riot shields truncheons (0.2) and you're ↑not
21         doin' nothin' you're only trying to get doon
22         to the tube and gae hame .hh
23         so what do they do?=you're walk(n) by 'en
24         they're pushing you wi'tha' (.) truncheons
25         an' .h they star(t) hattin' the odd punk
26         here and there,
27         (0.3)
28   MR:   and what happens?=the punks rebe-rebel, they
29         don' wanna get hit in the face with a truncheon
30         ↑nobody does .hhh so what do you do,=you push
31         yer copper back and (>then<) wha' happens?
32         ten or twelve of 'em are beatin'
33         the ⌈pure hell out of some poor bastard
34   FR:      ⌊mm
35   MR:   who's only tried to keep somebody off his back,
36         (0.7)
37   MR:   Now:* that started a ↓riot.
```

The gist of the speaker's account is that it was the police, not the punks, who initiated the violence. However, he has some very obvious problems in establishing this. First, there is the issue of category membership: punks and punk rock emerged in the mid-1970s and tabloid press coverage focused on and glorified the more extreme characteristics of their lifestyle and the music – rejection of societal convention, self-mutilation as decoration, violence, uncleanliness, rebellion and so on. Consequently, the speaker is providing an account which emphasizes the innocence of the punks when 'common knowledge' about the category would depict them as potential troublemakers. A related issue is that for whatever reason, the speaker does not deny that violence happened on this occasion. This is a potentially damaging confession in that it could lend at least some credence to the negative expectations associated with punks. Finally, the speaker is a member of that category of people he is defending, and therefore his version of events could be glossed as a simple reflection of self-interest and group loyalty, and not a factual account of the incident.

How does the speaker deal with these problems in the design of his account? We begin by examining the use of extreme case formulations.

Recall that the speaker concedes that there were 'one or two wee scraps' at the concert. He then says:

```
 6  MR:   But that happens=ev'ry one- every gig
 7         ⌈there's a scrap?
 8  FR:   ⌊°mm°
 9  MR:   >(th)'s all's< somebody doesnae like somebody else.
10  FR:   Mm:
11  MR:   dunna mattah w:ha:t it is (0.4) i's always happenin',
12         .hh y' know you cannae sto:p that?
```

Observe the work that the use of extreme case formulations does here. 'Every gig there's a scrap' portrays violence as being related to a general kind of social occasion, namely, rock concerts. Note that he does not say that these violent incidents occur at every punk rock gig. Rather it is the 'gigs' that are associated with the disturbance, and not the gigs of bands whose following comes from a specific youth subculture. The second extreme case formulation 'there's always somebody who doesn't like somebody else' characterizes violence as arising inevitably from interpersonal conflict. Such conflicts are portrayed as having their roots in idiosyncratic clashes of personality, irrespective of the social groups to which individuals may belong. Finally, 'it's always happening' marks such conflicts as a recurrent and consistent feature of human existence, and not peculiar to specific sections of the community.

In reporting the violence which occurred at the concert, the speaker makes no reference to the fact that the combatants were punks. Indeed, he does considerable work to portray the incident as something which occurs routinely at rock gigs generally, or which arises from two people's dislike for each other, and which is endemic in human society. In so doing, he minimizes the relevance of the social identity of the combatants as 'punk rockers', and thus implies that their subcultural membership is merely incidental to this violence and not the reason for it.

The speaker's sensitivity to the possible inferential implications of category affiliation also informs his account of the events leading up to the eventual violence. Note that the first reference to the punks' behaviour is a very minimal description of what they did after the concert: 'and we go outside'. The second reference provides a further characterization of the unexceptional nature of their behaviour: 'doing nothing' and simply 'going home'. It is interesting to note that the speaker's reference to the punks changes in the course of the segment. He says firstly that 'we go outside' but then he reports their subsequent behaviour as 'you're only trying to [go home]'. There is a sense in which 'we' clearly marks the speaker as a member of a specific group or collectivity. But the characterization of their attempt to go home as 'you're only trying ...' does not invoke such a clear affiliation. Indeed, it appeals to 'what everybody does' or 'what anybody would do'. This has two inferential consequences. First, the category affiliation of the people coming out of the gig is minimized, in that they are not engaged in activities specifically associated with the category punks: they are doing things that any ordinary person would do. Second, those activities are so mundane and unremarkable that the police's presence, and their subsequent actions, are portrayed as entirely unwarranted.

As we mentioned earlier, the speaker does concede that violent episodes did occur at the concert. However, subtle inferential work informs the way that this information is introduced into the account. For example, consider the numerical evaluation 'one or two wee scraps'. A first point is that 'one or two' clearly registers the 'occurring more than once' character of the incident being described. Referring to a number of violent incidents could easily be used by a sceptic to undermine the general thrust of the speaker's claim that the police presence after the concert was unwarranted. However, 'one or two' provides the most minimal characterization of 'more than one'. Secondly, note that the speaker does not say 'one' or 'two', but 'one or two'. In one sense, this marks the speaker as 'not knowing' the precise number of incidents. More important, however, is that the display of 'not knowing' marks the precise number as not *requiring* clarification, and therefore as being relatively unimportant. Consequently, the speaker is displaying his lack of interest in, or indifference to, precisely those events which have a crucial significance to the way that his version of events will be received. In this sense he is engaged in a form of stake inoculation.

Throughout this account the speaker is using a variety of resources to establish the factual status of his account. One feature of his efforts is to build his case so as to undermine a range of sceptical responses. For example, his use of extreme case formulations allows him to portray the violence which preceded the police involvement as an intrinsic property of gigs in general (and therefore not just punk rock gigs). Consequently he is using extreme case formulations to construct the 'out-there-ness', or objective reality, of the events as he is describing them. In this sense, they can be used as *externalizing devices*.

Externalizing devices

The significance of externalizing devices has been charted in various ethnomethodologically informed studies. Of particular importance is Dorothy Smith's (1978) analysis of a report which charts the apparent decline towards mental illness of a young woman, 'K'. Her analysis reveals the work done by the opening sequence of that account, in which the person telling the story, K's friend, states that 'I was actually the last of her close friends who was openly willing to admit that she was becoming mentally ill' (1978: 28.). Thus K's 'mental illness' is established as a fact, which is gradually 'realized', and 'accepted' by her friends. It is thereby established as a quality of K, independent of the perceptions, personal motivation and judgements of those who encountered her behaviour.

Smith's analytic concerns were later developed by Woolgar (1980) in his examination of part of a scientist's Nobel Prize lecture address. Woolgar was primarily concerned to develop arguments concerned with methodological issues in the sociological study of scientific knowledge. He focuses on the rhetorical practices through which the objectivity of the physical phenomenon known as a pulsar was established. This was in part constituted by the opening part of the scientist's lecture: 'The trail which ultimately led to the first pulsar ...' (Woolgar 1980: 253). This metaphorical description of the process of research and discovery has much in common with other phrases which are available to characterize scientific research and the acquisition of knowledge: 'the road to truth', 'the path of discovery' and so on. They each imply *motion* towards a goal or target. Woolgar argues that this feature of the speech warrants the reader/hearer's understanding of the objective existence of the pulsar. He states:

> We would suppose that an entity of our own creation might be fairly readily at hand at the time when it was first noticed as existing. But 'the first pulsar' is to be understood as having a pre-existence, a quality of *out-there-ness* which required that it be *approached*. (1980: 256; original emphasis)

In the last chapter we saw how we could track some broader organizational patterns in data from unstructured interviews with people who claimed to have experienced a range of paranormal phenomena. One of those patterns concerned the use of reported speech. In the next section we will see how aspects of reported speech provide a resource through which speakers can establish the objective reality of a phenomenon.

Active voicing

Speakers may formulate information so that it can be heard as reported talk when in fact it is unlikely, or in some cases impossible, that the words so reported were actually said in that way (Wooffitt 1992). Consequently, it is useful to begin with the assumption that the speakers are designing certain utterances to be heard *as if* they were said at the time. Therefore, it is more accurate to refer to 'active voicing' rather than reported speech.

Active voices can be used in a number of ways to warrant the factual status of claims and undermine the possibility of sceptical responses. One powerful argument which can be made about a claim to have encountered an anomalous phenomenon is that the person experiencing it was mistaken, and that what she might claim to have seen was not *actually* what she saw. One variant of this sceptical position is to assert that the phenomenon was in some way the product of the person's own imagination. Active voices may be used to counter this position in a variety of ways. In the following extract, active voices are used to demonstrate that the phenomenon was visible to people other than the person who is giving the account.

(17) **[From Wooffitt 1992: 163–4]**
(The speaker is describing one of a series of encounters with a malevolent spirit.)
1   tha:t night: (1.5) I don't know what
2   time it was: (1.3) my: husband (.) and I
3   both woke up: (0.7) with the mo:st (.)
4   dreadful (0.5) feeling of (1.7) hhh °well°
5   being (nyrie) smothered (0.3) but the powerful
6   smell .h and a blackness (0.3) that ws that
7   was (0.2) blacker than black I can' describe it
8   like (.) anything else (.) hh it was the most
9   penetrating (0.3) type of blackness .hh and there
10   was this (1.7) what I assumed to be th-
11   the shape of a man (.) in a cloak (2)
12   it was the most (0.3) formidable (1.2) sight
13   (1) my husband said 'my God what is it' (.)
14   an' I just said 'now keep quiet and say the Lord's
15   prayer'

Here the speaker invokes the urgency of the encounter by dealing with various features of the shape. Immediately after this elaborate and evocative descriptive work, she introduces her husband's utterance 'my God what is it' (line 13). This establishes that he could see the figure, and also corroborates the description provided by the speaker. That is, the severity of the husband's verbal reaction confirms that the thing in the room, and the associated sensations, were as powerful and alarming as the speaker had reported. This in turn works to confirm the speaker's reliability as an accurate reporter of the event.

Finally, in the following extract the speaker uses an active voice to confirm the paranormality of the event.

(18) [From Hufford 1982: 186]
(The speaker is reporting an experience she had while staying with a friend. The morning after the night of the experience she questioned her friend about the history of the house.)
1 she says
2 'Did you feel something?'
3 'Damn <u>right</u> I felt something!'
4 I said,
5 'There's a ghost up there.'
6 She says,
7 'Yeah, we know.
8 We didn't want to tell you
9 because we didn't want to
10 unnecessarily frighten you.'

In this extract an active voice is used to confirm that the speaker's assumptions about the nature of her experience were correct. Through the construction of the account in this way she portrays herself as arriving at a conclusion about the experience independent of any prior knowledge. It is only later that her assumptions about the experience are proved to be correct.

In this chapter we have introduced some of the main themes in the study of factual accounts informed by a conversation analytic approach. To conclude, we will identify one of the principal implications which arises when we cease to view language as a passive reflection of an objective, independent world and instead approach it as the site in which the factual status of events can be actively constructed, undermined and negotiated.

In so far as we have examined how language is used to construct the factual status of its referents, we have adopted a broadly ethnomethodological line of inquiry. This means that we have treated 'members' accounts, of every sort, in all logical modes, with all their uses, and for every method for their assembly [as] *constituent features of the settings they make observable'* (Garfinkel 1967: 8; emphasis added). Garfinkel's argument is that we realize or constitute the sense of our social actions through 'lay' procedures of practical reasoning. These procedures are language based and embedded in the activities we perform in language: 'describing', 'referring', 'accounting', 'judging', 'explaining', 'persuading' and so on.

The constitutive feature of language use, however, is not

merely an 'issue in conversation analysis' and therefore limited to research conducted within that domain. Rather, it is a feature of all *social* activities: quite simply, occasions in which people employ the sense-making interpretative procedures which are embodied in the use of natural language. This has very important implications for any social science research which employs people's accounts as investigative resources. It means, for example, that when people are asked to provide reports of their social lives in ethnographic research projects, or when people are required to furnish more formal answers to interview questions about attitudes and opinions, they are not merely using language to reflect some overarching social or psychological reality which is independent of their language. Rather, in the very act of reporting or describing, they are actively building the character of the states of affairs in the world to which they are referring. This raises serious questions about the status of findings from social science research projects which trade on the assumption that language merely reflects the properties of an independent social world.

CHAPTER 9

The Practical Relevance of Conversation Analysis

This book has introduced the perspective, methods and findings of CA, and discussed its impact on various fields of social scientific inquiry, including sociology, linguistics and social psychology. One thing which should be clear by now is that CA is an evolving field of inquiry. Developing from Sacks's initial studies of the organization of calls to a suicide prevention centre, it has become established as the pre-eminent social scientific method for the analysis of ordinary conversational interaction. And since then, researchers have applied the principles of CA in the analysis of forms of talk which are far removed from everyday conversation. For example, Atkinson and Drew's (1979) pioneering analysis of courtroom interaction was only the first in a continuing series of studies which focus on talk in institutional and work settings (Drew and Heritage 1992a). Furthermore, CA continues to evolve as an interdisciplinary field of study, contributing to questions that emerge in specific disciplines but turn out to have a wider relevance.

To conclude the book, we return to the interdisciplinary nature of CA's impact on the social sciences, looking at how its methods and findings have been applied in fields such as political communication, human–computer interaction and the treatment of language disorders. In the process, this chapter will illustrate something of the practical relevancies of the conversation analytic approach. Like many qualitative research methods, CA is often accused of having little relevance for issues and problems in the 'real world': the world outside of academic social science. This is not a view that we share, and in this final chapter we use the evolving nature of CA to show how it addresses 'real world' issues.

In a sense, we have already started to examine the practical relevance of CA. We have discussed its use in the academic study of various forms of talk-in-interaction which seem far removed from everyday conversation, such as institutional interaction and interview interaction; and in the previous chapter we saw how CA can inform a broader concern with the construction and properties of factual discourse. In this chapter we extend the scope of the discussion to include some of the more practical benefits to be gained from the application of conversation analysis. Specifically, we want to show how CA's findings and analytic orientation may have implications for the development of policies and practices in three arenas of social activity: the production of political rhetoric, the design of information technology, and the treatment of speech disorders. First, then, we will discuss the work of Max Atkinson to show how CA can reveal the systematic interactional properties of persuasive and effective political discourse. Second, we consider the ways in which CA has been used by researchers in the field of human–computer interaction in general, and by designers of speech-based interactive computer systems more specifically. To conclude, we examine how a conversation analytic perspective is beginning to illuminate the orderly basis for 'disorderly' talk: speech problems associated with people with aphasia.

The interactional organization of political rhetoric

We are all familiar with political rhetoric. In many countries some of the business of government and legislative bodies is broadcast live on radio or television, and broadcast news regularly includes excerpts from and assessment of political speeches. Especially during important local or national elections, political speeches, or parts of them, are broadcast on television and radio, and reproduced in the print media.

During election campaigns and at party political conferences, politicians speak to a large-scale, co-present audience which usually responds by clapping and cheering at numerous points during the course of the speech. Intuitively, it seems reasonable to assume that applause which appears during such speeches is a display of the audience's approval of the point or sentiment expressed by the speaker: that is, that applause is a response to the content of the speech. However, research carried out by Atkinson (1984a; 1984b) suggests that the way in which a point is presented may also influence the likelihood of applause.

Atkinson studied video and tape recordings of political speeches, and the transcripts of those recordings. In his transcriptions he used the letter x to convey the duration and intensity of audience applause. This is illustrated in the next extract, which comes from a speech by Margaret Thatcher, who was then leader of the Conservative Party and British Prime Minister.

(1)   **[Conservative Party Conference 1980]**
       Thatcher: Soviet Marxism is ideologically, politically
                         and morally bankrupt
       Audience: ⌐xxXXXXXXXXXXXXXXXXXXXxx-x
                                              | (9 seconds) |

In this case, the audience begins to show its approval even before Mrs Thatcher has finished speaking. The transcript indicates that the applause is loud (represented by the upper case letter x) and continues for nine seconds before dying away.

The next example illustrates the use of lower case letter x's separated by hyphens, which is a convention used to characterize weak and intermittent applause.

(2)   **[UK General Election 1979]**
       Shore: it's one thing to sell to sitting tenants, (0.7) and it's quite
                        an↓other to keep hous↑es ↓empty (0.4) while they're
                        ↑HAWKED ar↓ound to find ↑some ↓purch↑aser (0.2)
                        who could just as well ↓buy (0.7) in the open market (0.2)
                        like any ↓other owner occupier ↓does. (1)
       Audience: -x-   (0.2)   x xx-xxxxx-xx-x
                                    | 5 seconds |

Here, a point seems to receive only half-hearted approval: there is a one-second gap after the end of the point before the audience begins to applaud, and then the clapping is rather weak and hesitant, and lasts for only five seconds.

It is important to remember that in both these cases the speakers were addressing audiences composed of supporters of their respective parties. They were also both taken from party conferences which were broadcast by the media, and in which the general tendency is for a political party to display its unity around basic policy questions. Thus the poor response of the audience in the second extract cannot be easily explained by reference to the audience's hostility to the speaker or the broader political values he represented.

Atkinson (1984a) began to study this kind of data to see if there were any recurrent characteristics of those parts of speeches which immediately preceded enthusiastic audience applause. He discovered that there were indeed consistencies in the way these successful points were organized and packaged. He identified various rhetorical formats which seemed to be particularly effective at eliciting audience applause, and we shall consider two of them in detail: three-part lists and contrast devices.

A three-part list is simply some point made via the use of three specific components. In extract (1) above Mrs Thatcher denounces Soviet Marxism by claiming it is ideologically, politically and morally bankrupt. Extracts (3) and (4) provide further examples produced by the same speaker.

(3) [Conservative Party Conference 1980]

    Thatcher: I am however, very fortunate in having a
               marvellous deputy, who's wonderful
               in all places,   1
               at all times,   2
               in all things   3
               Willie Whitelaw
    Audience: ⌊x-xxXXXXXXXXXXXXXXXXXXXXXXXXXXxxx-x
                       ∣   (8 seconds)   ∣

(4) [Conservative Party Conference 1980]

    Thatcher: This week has demonstrated (0.4) that we
               are a party united in
               ↑purpose   1
               (0.4)
               strategy   2
               (0.2)
               and re↓so⌈lve   3
    Audience: ⌊Hear⌈hear
                             ⌊x-xxXXXXXXXXXXXXXXXXXXXXXXXXXXXxx-x
                       ∣   (8 seconds)   ∣

On each of these occasions, as in extract (1), it is noticeable that the audience's applause is coordinated very closely with the production of the third part in the list. In fact, in extracts (1) and (4), the onset of applause overlaps with the final syllable of the third list part (in extract (3) the audience waits for the naming of the politician who is referred to in the preceding three-part list before applauding). For some reason, then, three-part lists appear to be very effective in generating applause. Why is this?

One of the reasons why three-part lists are so effective is that making three specific points can strengthen or affirm a broader, overarching position or argument. In the next extract, Mrs Thatcher is making a general self-congratulatory statement about the Conservative Party's behaviour in government, and she underlines that claim by stating three aspects of the government's behaviour.

(5)   [UK General Election 1983]

Thatcher:	There's no government anywhere that is tackling the problem with more	
	vigour,	**1**
	imagination and	**2**
	determination	**3**
	than this conservative government	
Audience:	Hear⌐hear	
Audience:	└x-xxXXXXXXXXXXXXXXXXXXXXXXXXXXxx-x	
	| (8 seconds) |	

As this extract indicates, a staple of political speeches is a critical attack on opposition parties and their policies: pointing out the deficiencies of other groups is an effective way for politicians to affirm implicitly the value of their own party or approach. However, politicians can positively evaluate their own position in a much more explicit way, while at the same time still criticizing another position or set of policies. This can be done through the second of the major rhetorical devices we want to mention: contrast devices, in which one argument or approach is contrasted with another in such a way that the speaker's favoured position is seen to be superior. In the following extract the speaker is advising his own (opposition) party on the best way to contest Mrs Thatcher's government.

(6)   [Labour Party Conference]

Osborn:	the way to fight Thatcher	
	(0.4)	
	is not through the silent	**A**
	conformity of the graveyard	
	(0.5)	
	but by putting party	**B**
	policies (0.2) powerfully and determinedly	
	from the front bench	
Audience:	xxXXXXXXXXXXXXXXXXXXXXXXXXXXXXXXXxx	
	| (8 seconds) |	

Extract (7) comes from a debate at the 1981 Labour Party conference about the needs of disabled people in society.

(7) **[Labour Party Conference 1981]**
Morris: Governments will argue (0.8) that resources
are not available to help disabled people
(1.3)
The fact is that too much is spent on the   A
munitions of war
(0.6)
and too little is spent ⌈(0.2) on the munitions   B
                   ⌊of peace.
Audience: XXXXXXXXXXXXXXXXXXXXX
      | (9 seconds) |

Again, in these examples, close coordination is evident between the completion of the contrast and the audience's applause. Indeed, in the last extract, the audience begins applauding at a point where it is simply clear that the second part of a contrast is being made (after 'too little is spent'), without waiting to hear what 'too little is spent' on. This brings us to the key point about why such devices are so effective.

An audience is composed of hundreds, perhaps thousands, of people who do not know each other, and whose behaviour is unrehearsed and, therefore, unlikely to be coordinated. This poses a problem for the speaker who wishes to coordinate the audience's applause for specific points he or she is making. Social psychological research (and intuitive reflection) shows that audience members feel uncomfortable about applauding in isolation (though this is apparently not the case for its opposite, booing; see Clayman 1993); thus audience members need to be under the impression that others will also applaud at the same time as they do. Atkinson's data show that applause typically does not begin in an isolated manner and then build to a crescendo; therefore it is unlikely that audience members rely on taking their 'cue' from a few more courageous or less apprehensive individuals. Rather, applause characteristically begins as a 'burst'. How is this kind of collective response organized?

Rhetorical formats like lists and contrasts solve this problem because they project their own completion: as they are being built, they signal when they are going to end. The devices themselves provide the audience with a cue for when to clap and thus allow collective displays of affiliation. In this sense, we can say that devices like lists and contrasts are audience management devices. Let us look again at three-part lists.

Lists are not only found in political speeches; they are a common phenomenon in ordinary conversation. Jefferson shows that when people produce lists in conversation, they routinely do so using three parts. The following extracts come from Jefferson's (1990) study of the interactional properties of listing, and all occurred in everyday conversation, either on the telephone or in face-to-face interaction.

(8)　[Jefferson 1990: 64]
　　　Sydney:　　While you've been talking to me I mended,
　　　　　　　　two nightshirts,　　　　　　　　　　　　　1
　　　　　　　　a pillow case?　　　　　　　　　　　　　　2
　　　　　　　　enna pair'v pants　　　　　　　　　　　　3

(9)　[Jefferson 1990: 64]
　　　Maybelle:　I think if you
　　　　　　　　exercise it　　　　　　　　　　　　　　　1
　　　　　　　　an' work at it　　　　　　　　　　　　　　2
　　　　　　　　'n studied it　　　　　　　　　　　　　　3
　　　　　　　　you do become clairvoyant.

In these next extracts speakers have produced two parts of a list, but either have exhausted the relevant items which could be used to extend the list, or cannot find an appropriate word with which to complete it. In each case they use an item such as 'or something', 'things like that' and so on to complete the list as a three-part unit (as indeed our list was just completed).

(10)　[Jefferson 1990: 66]
　　　Heather:　And they had like a concession stand at a fair
　　　　　　　　where you can buy
　　　　　　　　coke　　　　　　　　　　　　　　　　　　1
　　　　　　　　and popcorn　　　　　　　　　　　　　　2
　　　　　　　　and that type of thing.　　　　　　　　　3

(11)　[Jefferson 1990: 66]
　　　Sy:　　　　Take up
　　　　　　　　m:Metsecal er,　　　　　　　　　　　　　1
　　　　　　　　Carnation Slender　　　　　　　　　　　　2
　　　　　　　　er something like that.　　　　　　　　　3

These extracts tell us something very interesting about three-part lists. Note that in each case the third part is not actually another item like the two that went before. Instead, it is a general term, such as 'and that type of thing'. Where a specific third component does not come to mind, speakers can use a general term in order to still end up with a three-part list. By using these 'generalized list completers' (Jefferson 1990) speakers in extracts (10) and (11) are displaying their sensitivity to a maxim of conversation which runs something like: 'if doing a list, try to do it in three parts.'

This means that in ordinary conversation, when one speaker is producing a list, a co-participant can anticipate that when the third item is produced, then the list is likely to be complete. As Jefferson shows, speakers recurrently treat the end of the third part of a list as a legitimate transition-relevance place.

(12) **[Jefferson 1990: 74]**

Matt:	The good actors are all dyin out.
Tony:	They're all- they're all
	dyin out ⌐yeah.
Matt:	⌐Tyrone Po:wuh. Clark Gable, Gary Cooper,
Tony:	Now all of 'em are dyin.

Here, Matt's list could easily have been extended: it is not the case that these three names constitute an exhaustive list of good-but-dead actors. Thus Tony's decision to start talking displays his understanding that Matt's list was possibly complete upon the provision of a third item.

Just as third items in conversation are conventionally taken to be possible utterance completion points, so too are they treated as possible completion points in speeches. An audience can see that a politician is making a list, and their tacit sensitivity to conventions of everyday conversation enables them to anticipate that it will be completed not after two points, and not after four, but after three. Each individual member of the audience can therefore predict the end of a specific point and is thereby provided with a resource, intrinsic to the speech, through which their behaviour can be coordinated with the other audience members' to provide a 'next turn' in the form of a collective response.

The completion point of a contrast device can be anticipated partly because both parts tend to be constructed and presented in the same ways: for example, some words or phrases may be mirrored in both parts. The following extract is a particularly clear example:

(13) **[Labour Party Conference 1981]**

Morris: Governments will argue (0.8) that resources
are not available to help disabled people
(1.3)
The fact is that too much is spent on the
munitions of war
(0.6)
and too little is spent ⌈(0.2) on the munitions
⌊of peace.
Audience: ᴸXXXXXXXXXXXXXXXXXXXX

There are several points where the second part mirrors the first.

too much is spent on the munitions of war
too little is spent (0.2) on the munitions of peace.

There are numerous words in common, and in fact the only words that differ are the key contrastive items in each part: 'much' versus 'little' and 'war' versus 'peace'. Moreover, these contrastive items are emphasized in the same way in both parts of the contrast.

The audience's awareness that certain words and phrases are being repeated will alert them to the fact that a contrast is being set up; they can recognize that what is being said now echoes the structure of what was just said before. But more importantly, if the second part of a contrast closely mirrors the first, having already heard the first part, members of the audience can predict more or less precisely when the second part of the contrast will end. This in turn means that the audience will be provided with a signal as to when the point being made via a contrast will be complete, and when, therefore, it is appropriate to clap.

The symmetry between the two parts in a contrast is thus very important. If there are major differences, the effect on audience applause can be striking. In the following example, Mr Heath, an ex-leader of the British Conservative Party, is arguing that the influence of the trade unions on government policy-making should be restrained. This anti-union stance was a central theme of Conservative government policy throughout the late 1970s and 1980s. As he was speaking to an audience of Conservative Party members and supporters, we might expect Mr Heath's remarks to receive unequivocal support and enthusiastic applause.

(14) [UK General Election 1979]
     Heath: In my view
                 it is right that the government should consider   **A**
                 these matters and take them into account.
                 (1)
                 What is entirely unacceptable (0.8) is the view that
                 parliament never can (0.6) and never should approve
                 any legislation (0.8) nor should a government pursue   **B**
                 any policy (0.8) unless first of all the trades unions
                 themselves (.) approve of it.
    →   (0.5)
                 THAT is entirely unacceptable
     Audience: Hear⌈hear
     Audience: ⌊x-xxXXXXXXXXXXXXXXXXXXXXXXXXXXXxxx-x
               | (8 seconds) |

Note here that despite the fact that Mr Heath is espousing a sentiment widely supported by the audience, the end of his point is greeted not with closely coordinated applause but, at least initially, with silence (at the arrow). Indeed, it is only when he 'recompletes' his point (Atkinson 1984b; Hutchby 1997) by saying 'THAT is entirely unacceptable', thereby explicitly indicating to the audience that he has finished making a point, that the audience starts applauding.

The momentary absence of any applause can be seen as arising from the failure of Mr Heath to build a symmetrical contrast. The first part of the contrast is neat and short. The second part, however, meanders somewhat, and clearly does not match the first part. Consequently, when Mr Heath has finished, the audience remains silent: they have not been able to use the design of the contrast to help them anticipate when they should start clapping.

Three-part lists and contrasts, among other devices identified in subsequent research by Heritage and Greatbatch (1986), project their own ending; thus they allow the audience to anticipate when the device, and the point being made, will end, thereby ensuring that the audience may provide collective displays of affiliation. In this sense, these rhetorical patterns solve the tricky interactional problem of ensuring that a collection of unrehearsed, disparate individuals can be coordinated in their behaviour as a group.

The appeal of the work initiated by Atkinson is that it exposes to conscious and public scrutiny the largely tacit ways in which language can be used in the sequential organization of public speeches. Although the audiences at political meetings or rallies are, by and large, in support of the person who is speaking, or the party he or she represents, political speeches remain a very important vehicle by which a politician can garner the support and affiliation of a wider audience. This suggests the possibility that Atkinson's findings could prove illuminating in the study of more overtly persuasive language in which speakers (or indeed, authors of written texts) build arguments for recipients who may be decidedly more unsympathetic than the audience at most contemporary political conferences and rallies. Furthermore, it provides an insight into a form of language use to which the majority of people in the Western world will be exposed at some points in their lives, and which may be consequential for the way in which individuals reach decisions about possible political allegiances (see Atkinson 1984a, ch. 5). But Atkinson's work is also important for its contribution to the study, and practice, of rhetoric.

Academics and intellectuals have long been concerned with the properties of effective rhetoric. Indeed, in ancient Greek society, judicial rhetoric was important because it was expected that all citizens should be able to represent themselves in legal debate. Later, scholars such as the Roman statesman and orator Cicero tried to articulate the most effective way to present cases in a speech in law courts. However, these attempts to lay bare the rules of effective rhetoric tend to be couched in terms of the discrete components of specific arguments and their relationship to each other. So for example, Cicero argued that legal presentations should have six parts: the exordium, narration, partition, confirmation, refutation and conclusion, and these components should occur in this order.

While these traditional assessments of rhetoric, and persuasion more generally, have been insightful, they have provided no more than arguments in principle for the way in which persuasive rhetoric works. The application of CA to the study of political speeches, however, has made three major advances. First, it established the significance of a fine-grained empirical investigation of rhetoric. This provided the stimulus for other researchers to apply the same analytic method in the study of other forms of rhetoric: for example, Keith and Whittenberger-Keith's (1988–9) analysis of Martin Luther King's famous 'I have a dream' speech; some recent analyses of advertising (see Myers 1994); or studies of how ordinary citizens rely on similar rhetorical devices in their contributions to debates in public spaces such as 'soapbox' corners (McIlvenny 1996) or audience participation shows on television (Hutchby 1998). Secondly, it has revealed that a small number of robust devices seem particularly effective in eliciting audience approval, and that these devices are not necessarily peculiar to a specific genre of speech event, such as the political speech: the three-part list, for example, is a routine feature of everyday conversational interaction, as well as being used in the other settings mentioned above.

Finally, this work has shown that even in large-scale mass meetings there are sound interactional bases for the production and coordinated display of affiliation and approval. Relatedly, as Clayman (1993) has since shown, a similar approach to Atkinson's can be applied to disaffiliative responses such as booing, although it appears that the interactional dynamics of booing are substantially less coordinated than applause. One intuitive reason for this is that speakers themselves do not actively seek jeers in the way that they seek applause.

CA, human–computer interaction and software design

We turn now to another specialized application of CA, in the field of human–computer interaction (HCI), which is itself a sub-field of computer science. Despite its name, much of computer science is essentially an engineering discipline concerned with the design and construction of artefacts, albeit often only in computer code. Like practitioners of many engineering disciplines, computer scientists are keen to draw on ideas from other areas of academic research. The field of artificial intelligence in computer science, for example, has always had a parasitic relationship with cognitive psychology. And software engineers in the UK are increasingly looking to some branches of mathematics for new approaches to the specification of systems (for example, Cohen, Harwood and Jackson 1986).

As Suchman (1987) observed, operating a computer is a process related less to mechanistic techniques and more to linguistic techniques. For example, computers are not operated on the basis of pulling levers with some physical result, as is, say, a car. Rather, we use some common language to specify operations, make requests, issue commands, and assess their outcomes. That language takes the form of the interface, which is some kind of an amalgamation of ordinary English words and phrases, icons, a cursor operated through a mouse, and virtual buttons which can be pressed using the cursor. As a result, system designers tend to talk of what goes on between computers and their users in terms of 'interaction', 'dialogue' and 'conversation'. It seemed, then, a natural progression for system designers to turn to research in the social sciences which was directly concerned with the organization of conversational interaction. Consequently, during the late 1980s and early 1990s, many system designers became keen to explore ideas from sociology, and conversation analysis in particular (see Button 1993; Luff, Gilbert and Frohlich 1990; Thomas 1995). This reflected the increasing influence of the idea that in order to design computer systems which can either simulate or, more ambitiously, reproduce the nature of human communication, it is necessary to know about the ways in which everyday interaction is organized.

Interacting with computers

A key moment in this 'turn to sociology' in system design was the publication of Lucy Suchman's *Plans and Situated Actions* (1987), in which she drew from conversation analysis to offer a critique of the model of human communication with which most system designers and programmers tend to work.

The prevailing idea within the community of computer systems developers is that the individual is a plan-based actor. Essentially this represents a 'computational' metaphor of human action: we act on the basis of intentions and plans, which our co-participants in a given situation have to decipher or compute, in order to understand what we are doing and act in concert with us.

It is relatively easy to see how this model can be incorporated in a machine. The computer also has intentions and plans; although in this case they are really the intentions and plans of the programmer. This means that there are two basic problems for computer system design. First, the system must be designed in such a way that the user can adequately comprehend its activities, which generally come in the form of instructions as to what to do in order to get the machine to work in a desired way. To use Suchman's term, computer systems are constructed to be *self-explicating machines*: the machine is an 'expert' in its own use, while the user is a 'novice'. The expert–novice metaphor is one that is widely relied on by designers, and the assumption is that the system should be able to explain its own use to a novice user.

The second problem, however, is much more important: the system itself must be designed so as to comprehend the activities of its user. The assumption here is that users come to the system with goals in mind, and the system needs to have the capability to 'discover' what these are and respond appropriately.

Suchman studied pairs of novice users operating a simple 'expert help' system on a photocopying machine. She was interested in two questions: to what extent can we say that there is successful communication, on the basis of mutual intelligibility, between the users and the system? And what happens when that mutual intelligibility breaks down? How do the participants (users and system) manage that situation?

On the basis of her analysis, Suchman argues that the user models employed in cognitive and computer science depend on users starting with and sticking as closely as possible to a plan. But actual human interaction, with machines as well as with other humans, is essentially ad hoc. This distinction is succinctly captured in the title of her book: the difference is one between plans and situated action. Designers attribute plans to users, and systems work well whenever the actions undertaken by the user can be linked to prior assumptions about what the user is doing. But problems soon occur when those assumptions about users' goals and plans do not match with their actual, situated actions.

For example, a user may be aware of what the machine requires her to do to achieve some specific objective; however, the situated actions by which she tries to achieve that objective – particularly, the sense she makes of what the system requires her to do – are not available to the machine. Neither do the user's situated actions match the system's idealized model of the 'plan' that the user has in mind. Furthermore, the user has no access to this model, but has to make sense of the system's requirements within the context of her particular situation and in the light of her understanding of previous actions. At the same time, the system has no access to the 'sense' she has made of those prior actions, on the situated level, and proceeds by assuming that she has understood in the way the designer's user model predicts.

Suchman concludes that a model of interaction based on the idea of people with discrete plans and goals in their heads is unhelpful in the design of interactive computer systems. Instead she suggests that it is necessary to view user interaction with computer systems as an emergent and situated activity. In particular she emphasizes the way in which participants' orientation to the sequential ordering of interaction provides resources for establishing mutual intelligibility and the identification and repair of troubles in communication.

Suchman's work has had an important impact on the field of system design. Not only did it propose a strong critique of the model of the user as plan-following and goal-seeking, but it introduced the significance of conversation analysis, and sociological approaches more generally, to the community of system developers. To many designers, CA appeared to provide a coherent and principled view of communication which avoided many of the problems associated with the model of goal-driven and plan-led interaction. In particular, it was felt that CA offered a set of empirical findings which might, by analogy, be applied to the design of the interface between people and computers. For a designer of complex computer systems, the interface with the human user often presents particular difficulties. For practical and commercial reasons, systems need to have a high degree of usability: it is generally accepted that interfaces should be easy to learn, quick to operate, give rise to low rates of error and be pleasant to use. Speech is the optimum medium for computer interfaces: most people can speak, and speech-based interfaces do not require users to be familiar with keyboards, or skilled in the physical manipulation of on-screen instructions and icons.

Another reason why CA was so readily adopted by system designers was that it offered a perspective on human–computer interaction which is independent of the technology used to implement systems and independent of the specific psychological characteristics of individual users (Norman and Thomas 1990). Consequently, while CA has been used in the design of screen-based interfaces (Frohlich and Luff 1990), it has been primarily used by researchers designing speech-based interactive computers. Indeed, it seems intuitively sensible for system designers to consider whether it would be possible to develop a system that it is informed by some knowledge of the organization of conversation.

However, this is a contentious issue. Some conversation analysts have been critical about the extent to which CA is a useful
resource in the design of natural language interfaces (for example, Button 1990; Button and Sharrock, 1995). The main point of
contention concerns the notion of rules. It is a common assumption that if a computer is to work it needs to be programmed with
formal rules. And it has appeared to some computer scientists
that many of the findings of CA, such as the turn-taking system
and basic sequential phenomena such as adjacency pairs, are
amenable to being specified in terms of formal rules which a
computer program could instantiate.

Yet CA's perspective emphasizes that talk-in-interaction is not
rule *governed*; rather it is informed by a sensitivity to the normative propriety of certain patterns of behaviour. Moreover, people
orient to these communicative 'rules' not as causal constraints
but as interpretive resources by which to make sense of their
ongoing interaction with others. Recall, for example, our discussions of turn-taking and conditional relevance in the early chapters of this book. A basic 'rule' is that on the provision of the first
part of an adjacency pair, an appropriate second part is condi-
tionally relevant. However, analysis of occasions in which second
parts do not appear shows that speakers use that 'rule' to draw
context-tied inferences about the intentions of co-speakers, or
about some features of the immediate circumstances, which
make sense of that absence: the other person didn't hear, was
being reluctant to answer a question or accept an offer, and so
on. In this, speakers display an awareness of, or sensitivity to, the
'rule' that following the production of a first pair part, the appropriate second is due. Furthermore, these rules (or 'norms', 'procedures', 'maxims' and so on) are available only through analytic
inspection of the empirical materials which display a sensitivity to
them; hence it is asserted that they are embodied in actions, not
determinants of action. Computer scientists have responded that
this view rests on a limited appreciation of the sophistication of
programming techniques: contrary to the impression that one
would gain from most of the literature debating the topic, rule-
based computer programs are only one type and alternative
designs which include nothing that is recognizably a rule are
quite feasible (Hirst 1991).

However, in the literature which draws on CA as a resource
for the design of interactive systems, there has been an unfortu-

nate tendency to discuss aspects of conversational organization, such as turn-taking and paired actions, in the abstract, removed from empirical materials (for example, Cawsey 1990; Finkelstein and Fuks 1990). This tendency has, ironically, resulted in an impoverished appreciation of the complexity of talk-in-interaction among those in the HCI community keen to explore the utility of findings from conversation analytic research.

CA and system design

It is clear, then, that the extent to which the results from conversation analytic studies of ordinary conversation can be usefully adapted in the design of interactive systems is by no means a straightforward issue. What seems less contentious, however, is the claim that the analytic stance of CA can sensitize researchers in the HCI community to the detail of practical reasoning which underpins those forms of language use which are to be mimicked by, or modelled into, computer systems.

This approach was adopted in the SUNDIAL project (Speech UNderstanding in DIALogue), a European Commission funded initiative to develop a computer system capable of 'conversing' with members of the public over the telephone to answer simple queries, such as the time of arrival of a particular airline flight or the times of trains. One of the possibilities in designing this system is to make it emulate as closely as possible the human enquiry clerk. (For an overview of the SUNDIAL project see Wooffitt et al. 1997.)

It was felt that the researchers could not anticipate the kinds of features of calls to public information services through intuition alone. Consequently, at the very start of the project, corpora of real-life exchanges between members of the public and agents of information services were collected; the researchers in the UK obtained a corpus of calls to the British Airways flight information service, and the first 100 calls were transcribed. The enquiries made by callers to this service were broadly similar in purpose to the calls that a fully operational speech-based computer information service would be expected to deal with. Thus it was hoped that a conversation analytic examination of these data would reveal aspects of both callers' and agents' communicative competencies which would have to be addressed by an interactive speech-based computer system. To illustrate, we will make some observations about the ways in which agents engage in correcting callers who have made erroneous inquiries.

In calls to the flight inquiries service, callers' errors such as getting the flight details wrong or calling the wrong number for the required kind of information occurred regularly. Analysis of these events showed that service agents use a basic verbal pattern in producing their corrections of callers' errors. One possibility is that such a naturally occurring verbal pattern could be modelled into a system which would thus be provided with capacities for correcting callers in a 'graceful' or natural-seeming manner.

Callers have two basic ways of formulating their initial inquiries: we will call them 'no problem' and 'possible doubt' types of inquiry. While sometimes 'possible doubt' inquiries pre-monitor, in their design, the possibility of a problem (see extract (16) below), in fact both these forms can result in errors being made and corrections undertaken.

In the 'no problem' request, the flight about which the caller is inquiring is identified in a way that exhibits no doubt on the caller's part as to the correctness of the flight identification details they provide. Extract (15) is an example (throughout these transcripts, C = caller, A = agent):

(15) **[Tape 2:1235 (37)]**
```
    1  C:   good afternoon I'm inquiring about (.)
    2       bee ay flight bee ay (.) nin:e
    3       six ni:ne from hamburg (0.3) can you tell
    4       me what time this flight got in please
    5  A:   yes just one moment I'll check for you
```

The request formulation (lines 1–4) proposes that the caller is identifying an actual plane that possesses the quoted flight number (flight BA969) and is flying from the quoted airport (Hamburg). In this extract, that appears adequately to do the work of identifying the flight for the agent, and she immediately undertakes a search procedure with the database (line 5).

In the second type of request formulation, callers indicate a degree of uncertainty as to the flight identification details they have, or the specific kinds of flight information that can be obtained on this number. Frequently in such cases, the trouble that the caller's 'possible doubt' request form appears to pre-monitor rapidly materializes. For instance:

(16)   **[Tape 3:Side A:1897 (51)]**
```
1   C:   can you >tell me if< the
2        flight from ibiza is it bee eye ay
3        four five one six i-(s) is arriving
4        on time,
5   A:   not british airways flight number I'm afraid we
6        don't fly from ibiza madam
```

In this case the caller incorporates markers of doubt into his request. The caller is uncertain about the number of the flight, and incorporates a question as to the accuracy of his information into the request: 'the flight from Ibiza *is it* bee eye ay four five one six'.

In fact, it turns out the caller has called the wrong number. The agent indicates this by stating that the flight number that was given is not one that his database contains ('not British Airways flight number I'm afraid'). Thus, even when callers begin by displaying some possible doubt about their inquiry, the problems that arise in callers' initial inquiries set up the situation in which agents will have to correct these mistakes.

However, as we remarked above, it is not just in 'possible doubt' calls that problems materialize and correction needs to be undertaken. It turns out that in extract (15), in which the initial inquiry takes the 'no problem' form, a problem in fact emerges: that is, the flight details the caller has given do not refer to an actual flight in the database. This results in the agent having to correct the caller by re-identifying the flight (lines 18–19):

```
1    C:   good afternoon I'm inquiring about (.)
2         bee ay flight bee ay (.) nin:e
3         six ni:ne from hamburg (0.3) can you tell
4         me what time this flight got in please
5    A:   yes just one moment I'll check for you
6         (5.3)
7    A:   hello:,
8    C:   hello:
9    A:   yes I haven't got a flight nine six
10        nine from hamburg I'll just check it for
11        you hold on please
12        (5.0)
13   A:   hello nine six fi:ve,
14        (0.3)
15   C:   (yu-) bee ay nine six (.) f-<ni:ne
16        (0.3)
17   A:   no:o(r)h I've got a nine six fi:ve from er
18        hamburg into london
```

```
19  C:   yeah
20  A:   and uhm:: (0.3) that arrived (.)
21       it's scheduled to arrive at eleven o'clock
22       this morning I'⌈ll just check that for yo⌈u
23  C:              ⌊yes                        ⌊yeah
24       °thank you°
```

Beginning at line 9, the agent indicates that the flight number she has been given appears to be incorrect. At line 13 she produces a turn that stands as a possible alternative suggestion. The caller initially takes this not as a correction, but as a 'checking move' by the agent – a turn in which the agent checks that she has correctly heard the number from the caller – and responds by repeating his original number (line 15). Subsequently, the agent exhibits that she in fact was correcting him by informing him that the flight from Hamburg in the database is numbered nine six five rather than nine six nine (lines 17–18).

A suggestion that arises here is that the 'no problem' form of initial inquiry may lead to the caller being resistant to correction by the agent (Wooffitt 1991). That could be useful information to incorporate into a metastrategic model for a computer system. Having detected a no-problem formulation in the original request, the system may then be sensitized to possible resistance on the part of the user to any correction it may be necessary to make.

When agents do make corrections in the human inquiries corpus, those corrections routinely consist of two basic components: (1) a negation, and (2) an alternative suggestion. In all the cases of correction in the data corpus, these two components are recognizably produced, and always in that order. However, in some cases callers respond or react to the negation component, which proposes error on their part, prior to the production of the alternative suggestion component. In these cases callers seek to mitigate or account for their error, and often follow up that mitigation attempt by actively requesting the alternative suggestion.

The following extract provides an example of the two components being produced with no intervening talk (arrows point to the two components, negation and alternative suggestion).

(17) [Tape 3:Side B:1143 (58)]
```
1   C:   oh good afternoon could you give me
2        any details please on flight (.) tee ee
3        two
```

```
4→    A:  I haven't got any information on air
5          new zealand
6→         I can give you their enquiry number?
```

In the next example, the caller produces some talk between the negation and alternative suggestion components. What can we say about the properties of that intervening talk?

(18) [Tape 4:Side A:1860 (74)]
```
1      C:  yes can you tell me please if air ukay three
2          ni:nety is coming in at fifteen twenty
3          five still
4      A:  I'm sorry we're british airways (we) don't
5          handle air ukay
6          (0.4)
7→    A:  ⌈thee-
8→    C:  ⌊er: >well it just says in the book<
9          heathrow seven five nine two five
10         two five
11→   A:  that's british airways heathrow
12     C:  oh (.) what number do I need then
13     A:  seven five nine
14         (0.3)
15     C:  yeah
16     A:  four three two one and they'll
17         put you through
```

Notice that a gap of 0.4 seconds (line 6), left by the agent after his negation component, allows the caller to judge that perhaps this negation is all that is going to be produced. While at the first arrow (line 7) the agent appears to embark on the beginnings of an alternative suggestion ('thee-' may be the start of a turn such as 'the enquiry number for air ukay is ...'), this is overlapped by a turn in which the caller appears to be mitigating his 'error'. This is done by referring to an authoritative source – 'the book' (the telephone directory) – as the place from which he got his apparently erroneous information. Subsequently (line 11) the agent responds by again indicating the caller's error. Notice here that while (or perhaps because) the agent does not move immediately to the production of an alternative suggestion, the caller embarks on explicitly requesting that information: 'oh (.) what number do I need then'.

Returning to extract (16), we find a similar phenomenon of the caller attempting to mitigate or downgrade the error:

```
1  C:  can you >tell me if< the
2      flight from ibiza is it bee eye ay
3      four five one six i-(s) is arriving
4      on time,
5  A:  not british airways flight number
6      I'm afraid we don't fly from ibiza
7      madam
8  C:  you don't o⌐h >so wha(t)-< What⌐
9  A:             ⌊You  sure  it's  not  B⌊ee eye ay
```

In this extract, the caller hears the negation component (lines
5–7), and immediately embarks on a turn that begins with the
words 'you don't oh'. What this utterance seems to be doing is
displaying the caller's recognition of her mistake. We can specu-
late that the reason why the caller may want to make it clear she
recognizes her mistake has to do with one typical cultural reaction to being in error. Proposing that someone is in error can be a
'face-threatening act' (Brown and Levinson 1987). In other
words, it can represent a threat to a person's sense of himself or
herself as a competent social agent. In most cases in the British
Airways data, mitigation of that threat is provided by the production of the second component in the agent's correction: an alternative suggestion. But in this case the caller responds to the face
threat herself by proposing that the agent's announcement that
British Airways do not fly from Ibiza is 'news' to her: 'you don't
oh'. The use of the item 'oh' is key here. As Heritage (1984b) has
shown, 'oh' is routinely used in conversation as a change-of-state
marker, a way in which speakers indicate that they have undergone some change in their current state of knowledge or awareness. By drawing attention thus to her changed state of
knowledge, the caller downgrades her 'error' by implying that
she had reason to believe that British Airways did in fact fly from
Ibiza.

The caller's turn then progresses to what looks like the request
for a possible alternative source for the required information:
that is, in context, 'so wha(t)- What' strongly appears to be a start
on a request such as 'What number should I call?' This request is
abandoned as the agent embarks on producing an alternative
suggestion in overlap with the caller's utterance (line 9). In this
case, then, the caller's intervening talk operates again to downgrade the error she has made.

Parenthetically, it turns out that the agent's alternative suggestion in this case, 'You sure it's not Bee eye ay', shows that she in

fact had misheard the caller's original request, which had indeed been about flight 'bee eye ay four five one six' (see lines 2–3). This is suggestive of the format's potential for the recovery of speech recognition errors. If we imagine that the agent here is a machine that has made a speech recognition error, mistaking an actual flight number (say, BIA 4516) for a non-existent number (say, BI 4516), then the alternative suggestion strategy would allow that mistake to be gracefully recovered, subject only to the caller 'sanctioning' the system by saying something like: 'That's what I said in the first place.'

It seems, then, that if callers embark on talk at some point between the first and second components in an agent's correction move, they do so in order to mitigate or account for their error; and part of that mitigation involves requesting the alternative information that, in other cases, is volunteered by the agent as the second component in a correction move.

While these observations are not intended as a full-blown analysis, they do suggest that even the most routine kinds of exchanges between callers and agents are rich in detail. What conversation analysis can offer is a description of the orderly basis of these interactions, and the inferences which human participants are capable of drawing from them. It is the task of the system designer to use these insights in the development of increasingly user-friendly and, perhaps, genuinely interactive speech-based computer interfaces.

While conversation analytic examination of forms of human interaction can provide information which may be useful for system designers trying to develop computers to do the same kinds of work as humans, there is an even more intriguing use of CA in HCI. Whether or not these kinds of insights are drawn on in the development of interactive systems, and unaffected by debates about whether it is possible in principle to build a conversing computer, system designers will continue to develop new technologies and refine existing systems. Consequently, it seems reasonable to suggest that in the near future, verbal exchanges with speech-based computer interfaces will be a common feature of everyday life. People will be using such systems regardless of the extent to which they accurately mimic human speech skills or embody patterns of interaction derived from the study of everyday conversation. The task will be, then, to study the ways in which people interact with these systems, and to see how everyday communicative competencies inform the ways in which human users make sense of their dealings with increasingly sophisticated interactive computer technology.

The order in 'disorderly' talk

Conversation analysts have described the social organization of a wide range of *everyday* conversational phenomena. Consequently, there has been a tendency to focus on interaction between people with normal speech capacities. In the past few years, however, there has been a growing interest in the use of conversation analysis to investigate the interactional capabilities of people who, for neurological, physiological or psychological reasons, have speech difficulties. For example, Gardner (1994; 1997) has produced sophisticated studies of interactions involving children with speech difficulties talking to their mothers and their speech therapists.

There are two immediate benefits of this development. First, the analytic approach of CA seeks to describe the *competencies* which inform the production of utterances in interaction; this is true even when one or more of the participants might be regarded as somehow deficient in their normal verbal and interactional skills. While being sensitive to the physiological or psychological difficulties people face, the focus of CA emphasizes the subtle and sophisticated range of skills which people with speech problems nevertheless employ in their interaction with others; a range of competencies which might be lost to an analysis motivated by, and embodying the assumptions of, a model of the speaker as intrinsically deficient (Gardner 1997). Such an approach to the investigation of speech problems is therefore not only positive, but potentially liberating, in that analysis of interaction involving people with speech problems is not in the first instance propelled or constrained by underlying assumptions of (for example) asymmetry in the verbal endowment of the participants.

The second benefit is more practical. Speech therapists can draw from the findings of conversation analysis to identify the precise basis of specific forms of problem in the verbal patterns of people who have some form of speech difficulty. This is illustrated by Wilkinson's (1995) study of a spate of interaction between a speech therapist and a person with aphasia.

For Wilkinson, CA offers an alternative to more traditional methods in aphasiology in that it emphasizes the importance of naturally occurring data, and focuses on the properties of sequences of turns. He begins from the basic conversation analytic position that utterances are both context shaped and context renewing: that is, an utterance will be understood in relation to the prior turn; similarly, it will then constitute a context for the next turn. During interaction between speakers without speech difficulties, this relationship enables speakers to interpret an utterance in terms of its sequential relevance, or as Wilkinson puts it, they can ask: 'why this now?' This, of course, is a key resource for participants to arrive at an understanding of the relevance of a particular utterance. The feature Wilkinson focuses on to illustrate some of the problems is the phenomenon of repair.

As we saw in chapter 2, an other-initiated self-repair sequence will involve the use of next turn repair initiators, such as the partial repeat of a prior turn, or utterances such as 'what?' or 'huh?' Speakers can analyse the sequential placement of an NTRI and infer that it marks that a problem has occurred in the prior turn; indeed, the NTRI may even indicate the precise nature of the trouble. In so far as an NTRI identifies a trouble without attempting repair, the producer of the trouble source can infer that it establishes the relevance of *self*-repair.

Of course, participants in conversation do not assess NTRIs merely to locate their sequential relevance: the question 'why this now?' is an inferential step which underpins speakers' analysis of each successive contribution to conversation. It is this observation which allows Wilkinson to identify some of the problems which emerge in part of a session between an aphasic and a speech therapist.

The aphasic patient was attending a session with his speech therapist at a preliminary meeting before the start of a new period of therapy after a lengthy break. The session consisted of a short conversation between the therapist and patient, followed by a series of more formal tasks to assess the patient's verbal development. The session was video recorded.

Wilkinson observes that most attempts to understand the problems generated by aphasic language have tended to examine

utterances in isolation from the context in which they were produced. Through analysis of the following instance, however, he
makes an empirical case for the importance of understanding the
ways in which specific difficulties, such as misunderstandings,
may be traced to the sequential context in which they were
originally produced.

In the early part of the conversation the topic was the patient's
interest in flower arranging ('T' is the therapist, 'P' is the patient).

(19) [Wilkinson 1995]
```
 1  T:   how about your flower arranging?
 2       (.) °is ⌈that uh°
 3  P:         ⌊uh actually: (.) still (.) only now and then,
 4  T:   ⌈mm hmm
 5  P:   ⌊but uh:m uh:m (0.5) I think me and more more:, (1.8)
 6       uh:m >I mean< no. only now and then
 7       but maybe (.) °ah: right!° maybe (.) not plain
 8       but also speckled and (.) much (.) better
 9  T:   ⌈mm.
10  P:   ⌊and also (.) uh flowers much (0.2) pretty or something.
11       ⌈>you know?< but uh:
12  T:   ⌊oh right! sounds interesting.
13  P:   >I mean< maybe maybe not I ⌈don't know⌉ you know
14  T:                               ⌊right    ⌋
15  T:   so the speckled flowers is that uhm something ⌈you'd ( )⌉
16  P:                                                  ⌊n-no     ⌋
17       but no uh:m (0.3) vase
18  T:   oh::!
```

In this sequence it emerges that there is some confusion over the
referent of the adjective 'speckled', used by the patient in line 8.
The therapist misinterprets this word as referring to 'flowers', a
perfectly reasonable interpretation given that the topic of the
talk was flower arranging. It is only when the therapist explicitly
refers to 'speckled flowers' that the patient can see that there is a
problem, at which point he produces a repair and clarifies the referent of 'speckled' as a vase, or vases (it subsequently transpires
that he was talking about painting vases). The problem can be
traced to two events. First, the patient's utterance in lines 5 to 8
had changed the topic from flower arranging to painting vases
without making that shift explicit. Second, the therapist
attempted to locate the sense of the word 'speckled', and indeed
the trajectory of the interaction, by interpreting it in terms of its
sequential and topical context.

Wilkinson makes a similar argument about a sequence which

occurs during a later part of the conversation. The patient has trouble finding a word when he is providing an account of something that is going to happen in the future.

```
49   P:   and uh:m uh:m last (0.3) m- uh year
50        (.) and uhm >very famous<
51        not England but (2.0) °hm° (0.8) °terrible° (0.8)
52        uh:m (4.0) I think (4.0) uh:m (3.0)
53        °not England° but (2.0) °not Scotland° but (.)
54        Wales right?
55   T:   °right°
56   P:   and uh one:, (1.5) °oh God almighty (0.8) one (1.0)
57        uh:m (3.0) ↓town.
58   T:   ((nods))
```

At the start of this extract, when he is providing an account of something that is going to happen in the future, the patient has trouble finding a word.

It subsequently transpires that the patient is trying to locate the name of a city. It is noticeable that he tries to engage the assistance of the therapist by establishing the kind of word he is looking for: 'not England' and 'not Scotland' indicating that the unforthcoming word is the name of a place. Eventually, he is able to convey that he is seeking the name of a town in Wales. However, the therapist merely provides minimal verbal and non-verbal encouragement to the patient (lines 55 and 58). In keeping with common practice she is encouraging the patient to self-repair, even if that process is extended over several turns and takes some time. The following exchange then occurs.

```
59   P:   uh:m (.) and >obviously< uh:m people (0.5) uh
60        every (.) part of the (.) country.
61   T:   mm hm=
62   P:   =uh:m and >sorry< and uh:m (2.0)
63        an- and (3.0) car or van or something (.)
64        what the word? >I mean< what the (1.0) uh:m (1.0)
65        very famous or very, (3.5)
66   T:   are these this people round the country go to somewhere
67        in Wales, with (.) are they=
68   P:   =or ⌈yes        ⌉
69   T:        ⌊what⌋ what do they go there for?
70   P:   hh ⌈right     ⌉
71   T:      ⌊is that⌋ to ⌈something⌉ to do with driving?
72   P:                   ⌊uh:m    ⌋
73   P:   yes ⌈right right⌉
74   T:       ⌊for people⌋ who (.) dis ⌈abled?⌉
75   P:                                ⌊no    ⌋>no no<
```

In this segment the search for a place name has been abandoned as the patient attempts a different strategy to tell his story.

Eventually, however, the patient says, 'what the word?' (line 64), thereby inviting the therapist to help him. But it soon becomes apparent that the therapist is having difficulty in helping the patient. For example, when she offers the category 'disabled' as a candidate target of the patient's reference to 'people', the patient is quick to indicate that that is not the group he is talking about. Eventually, the attempt to remedy this trouble is also abandoned.

Wilkinson identifies the basis for the therapist's difficulties in helping the patient in his word search. In a subtle analysis he shows how the therapist's problems lie in the fact that she has not understood the previous part of the patient's narrative in which this word search difficulty is embedded. Consequently two problems become conflated: the patient's search for the appropriate word, and the therapist's lack of understanding of the context in which that search is taking place. Again, then, the root of the problem is contextual: because of the patient's aphasic language the therapist does not have access to a necessary understanding of the sequential context for which this particular story is being told; and without that understanding she has no basis on which to offer help appropriate to the patient's efforts to locate a specific word.

As Wilkinson notes, these kinds of analytic observations could provide the basis for therapeutic programmes. For example, it may be possible to develop the patient's metalinguistic awareness of how and why psycholinguistic impairments cause problems for interactants at particular points in the interaction. That is, if conversation analytic studies of everyday interaction provide a resource which allows us to chart comprehensively the distressing effects of speech problems in everyday life, then they may in turn furnish the basis for more sophisticated and effective means of treatment. Equally important, however, the application of CA to these kinds of data can provide deeper insight into the precise nature of the difficulties faced by people with aphasia, and other forms of speech problems. Studying decontextualized instances of aphasic speech to determine the ways in which physiological conditions impair articulation is not in itself sufficient: whatever problems a person may have, and whatever their organic cause, they are still most keenly felt in real-life interaction. In that sense, Wilkinson's study represents a fitting final illustration of the conversation analytic perspective, for, like CA in general, it emphatically shows how those difficulties become manifest, and attain their significance, in relation to the web of normative expectations and inferential processes which underpin everyday conversational activity, and in which they are inextricably embedded.

References

Atkinson, J. M. (1984a) *Our Masters' Voices: The Language and Body Language of Politics*. London: Methuen.

Atkinson, J. M. (1984b) Public speaking and audience response: some techniques for inviting applause. In Atkinson and Heritage (1984), pp. 370–409.

Atkinson, J. M. and Drew, P. (1979) *Order in Court: The Organisation of Verbal Interaction in Judicial Settings*. London: Macmillan.

Atkinson, J. M. and Heritage, J. (eds) (1984) *Structures of Social Action: Studies in Conversation Analysis*. Cambridge: Cambridge University Press.

Austin, J. (1962) *How to Do Things with Words*. Oxford: Oxford University Press.

Beattie, G. (1983) *Talk: Analysis of Speech and Nonverbal Behaviour in Conversation*. Milton Keynes: Open University Press.

Becker, H. (1953) Becoming a marijuana user. *American Journal of Sociology*, 59: 41–58.

Beimer, P. P., Groves, R. M., Lyberg, L. E., Mathiowetz, N. A. and Sudman, S. (1991) *Measurement Errors in Surveys*. New York: Wiley.

Black, M. (1965) *Philosophy in America*. London: Allen and Unwin.

Blount, B. and Sanchez, M. (eds) (1975) *Sociocultural Dimensions of Language Use*. New York: Academic Press.

Boden, D. (1994) *The Business of Talk*. Cambridge: Polity Press.

Boden, D. and Zimmerman, D. (eds) (1991) *Talk and Social Structure*. Cambridge: Polity Press.

Brown, P. and Levinson, S. (1987) *Politeness*. Cambridge: Cambridge University Press.

Brown, P. and Yule, G. (1982) *Discourse Analysis*. Cambridge: Cambridge University Press.

Button, G. (1990) Going up a blind alley: conflating conversation analysis and computational modelling. In Luff, Gilbert and Frohlich (1990), pp. 67–90.

Button, G. (1992) Answers as interactional products: two sequential practices used in interviews. In Drew and Heritage (1992a), pp. 212–34.

Button, G. (ed.) (1993) *Technology in Working Order*. London: Routledge.

Button, G. and Casey, N. (1984) Generating topic: the use of topic initial elicitors. In Atkinson and Heritage (1984), pp. 167–90.

Button, G. and Lee, J. R. E. (eds) (1987) *Talk and Social Organisation*. Clevedon: Multilingual Matters.

Button, G. and Sharrock, W. (1995) On simulacrums of conversation: towards a clarification of the relevance of conversation analysis for human–computer interaction. In Thomas (1995), pp. 107–25.

Cawsey, A. (1990) A computational model of explanatory discourse. In Luff, Gilbert and Frohlich (1990), pp. 221–34.

Chomsky, N. (1965) *Aspects of the Theory of Syntax*. The Hague: Mouton.

Clark, H. and Haviland, S. (1977) Comprehension and the given-new contract. In Freedle (1977), pp. 1–40.

Clayman, S. E. (1988) Displaying neutrality in television news interviews. *Social Problems*, 35: 474–92.

Clayman, S. E. (1992) Footing in the achievement of neutrality: the case of news interview discourse. In Drew and Heritage (1992a), pp. 163–98.

Clayman, S. E. (1993) Booing: the anatomy of a disaffiliative response. *American Journal of Sociology*, 58: 110–30.

Coates, J. (1995) *Women Talk*. London: Routledge.

Cohen, B., Harwood, W. T., and Jackson, M. I. (1986) *The Specification of Complex Systems*. Wokingham: Addison-Wesley.

Coulter, J. (1982) Remarks on the conceptualization of social structure. *Philosophy of the Social Sciences*, 12: 33–46.

Couper-Kuhlen, E. and Selting, M. (eds) (1996) *Prosody in Conversation: Interactional Studies*. Cambridge: Cambridge University Press.

Cuff, E. and Payne, G. (1984) *Perspectives in Sociology*. London: Allen and Unwin.

Davidson, J. (1984) Subsequent versions of invitations, offers, requests, and proposals dealing with potential or actual rejection. In Atkinson and Heritage (1984), pp. 102–28.

Dijk, T. van (ed.) (1985) *Handbook of Discourse Analysis, Volume 3: Discourse and Dialogue*. London: Academic Press.

Drew, P. (1984) Speakers' reportings in invitation sequences. In Atkinson and Heritage (1984), pp. 129–51.

Drew, P. (1987) Po-faced receipts of teases. *Linguistics*, 25: 219–53.

Drew, P. (1992) Contested evidence in courtroom cross-examination: the case of a trial for rape. In Drew and Heritage (1992a), pp. 470–520.

Drew, P. and Heritage, J. (eds) (1992a) *Talk At Work: Interaction in Institutional Settings*. Cambridge: Cambridge University Press.

Drew, P. and Heritage, J. (1992b) Analyzing talk at work: an introduction. In Drew and Heritage (1992a), pp. 3–65.

Drew, P. and Wootton, T. (eds) (1988) *Erving Goffman: Exploring the Interaction Order*. Cambridge: Polity Press.

Drummond, K. (1989) A backward glance at interruptions. *Western Journal of Speech Communication*, 53: 150–66.

Edwards, D. and Potter, J. (1992) *Discursive Psychology*. London: Sage.

Ellis, D. and Donohue, W. (eds) (1986) *Contemporary Issues in Language and Discourse Processes*. Hillsdale N. J.: Erlbaum.

Finkelstein, E. and Fuks, H. (1990) Conversation analysis and specification. In Luff, Gilbert and Frohlich (1990), pp. 173–86.

Foucault, M. (1977) *Power/Knowledge*. Hemel Hempstead: Harvester.

Frankel, R. (1984) From sentence to sequence: understanding the medical encounter through microinteractional analysis. *Discourse Processes*, 7: 135–70.

Frankel, R. (1990) Talking in interviews: a dispreference for patient-initiated questions in physician–patient encounters. In Psathas (1990), pp. 231–62.

Freedle, R. O. (ed.) (1977) *Discourse Production and Comprehension*. Hillsdale, N.J.: Erlbaum.

Frohlich, D. and Luff, P. (1990) Applying the technology of conversation to the technology for conversation. In Luff, Gilbert and Frohlich (1990), pp. 187–220.

Garcia, A. (1991) Dispute resolution without disputing: how the interactional organization of mediation hearings minimizes argument. *American Sociological Review*, 56: 818–35.

Gardner, H. (1989) An investigation of maternal interaction with phonologically disordered children as compared to two groups of normally developing children. *British Journal of Disorders of Communication*, 24: 41–61.

Gardner, H. (1997) Social and cognitive competencies in learning: which is which? In Hutchby and Moran-Ellis (1997), pp. 115–33.

Garfinkel, H. (1956) Conditions of successful degradation ceremonies. *American Journal of Sociology*, 61: 240–4.

Garfinkel, H. (1963) A conception of, and experiments with, 'trust' as a condition of stable concerted actions. In Harvey (1963), pp. 187–238.

Garfinkel, H. (1967) *Studies in Ethnomethodology*. Englewood Cliffs: Prentice-Hall.

Garfinkel, H. and Sacks, H. (1970) On formal structures of practical actions. In McKinney and Tiryakian (1970), pp. 338–66.

Giddens, A. (1984) *The Constitution of Society: Outline of the Theory of Structuration*. Cambridge: Polity Press.

Gilbert, N. and Mulkay, M. (1984) *Opening Pandora's Box: A Sociological Analysis of Scientists' Discourse*. Cambridge: Cambridge University Press.

Givon, T. (ed.) (1979) *Syntax and Semantics, Volume 12: Discourse and Syntax*. New York: Academic Press.

Goffman, E. (1959) *The Presentation of Self in Everyday Life*. New York: Doubleday.

Goffman, E. (1961) *Encounters*. New York: Bobbs-Merrill.

Goffman, E. (1971) *Relations in Public*. New York: Basic Books.

Goffman, E. (1981) *Forms of Talk*. Oxford: Blackwell.

Goffman, E. (1983) The interaction order. *American Sociological Review*, 48: 1–17.

Goldberg, J. A. (1990) Interrupting the discourse on interruptions: an analysis in terms of relationally neutral, power- and rapport-oriented acts. *Journal of Pragmatics*, 14: 883–903.

Goodwin, C. (1981) *Conversational Organisation: Interaction between Speakers and Hearers*. New York: Academic Press.

Goodwin, C. (1984) Notes on story structure and the organisation of participation. In Atkinson and Heritage (1984), pp. 225–46.

Goodwin, C. (1986) Between and within: alternative sequential treatments of continuers and assessments. *Human Studies*, 9: 205–17.

Goodwin, M. H. (1990) *He-Said-She-Said: Talk as Social Organisation among Black Children*. Bloomington: Indiana University Press.

Graddol, D., Cheshire, J. and Swann, J. (1994) *Describing Language*. Milton Keynes: Open University Press.

Greatbatch, D. (1992) On the management of disagreement between news interviewees. In Drew and Heritage (1992a), pp. 268–301.

Greenberg, J. (ed.) (1963) *Universals of Language*. Cambridge, Mass.: MIT Press.

Gumperz, J. and Hymes, D. (eds) (1972) *Directions in Sociolinguistics*. New York: Holt, Rinehart and Winston.

Harvey, O. J. (ed.) (1963) *Motivation and Social Interaction*. New York: Ronald Press.

Heath, C. (1992) The delivery and reception of diagnosis in the general practice consultation. In Drew and Heritage (1992a), pp. 235–67.

Helm, J. (ed.) (1966) *Essays on the Verbal and Visual Arts*. Seattle: University of Washington Press.

Heritage, J. (1984a) *Garfinkel and Ethnomethodology*. Cambridge: Polity Press.

Heritage, J. (1984b) A change-of-state token and aspects of its sequential placement. In Atkinson and Heritage (1984), pp. 299–345.

Heritage, J. (1985) Analyzing news interviews: aspects of the production of talk for an overhearing audience. In Dijk (1985), pp. 95–119.

Heritage, J. (1989) Current developments in conversation analysis. In Roger and Bull (1989), pp. 21–47.

Heritage, J. and Greatbatch, D. (1986) Generating applause: a study of rhetoric and response at party political conferences. *American Journal of Sociology*, 19: 110–57.

Heritage, J. and Greatbatch, D. (1991) On the institutional character of institutional talk: the case of news interviews. In Boden and Zimmerman (1991), pp. 93–137.

Heritage, J. and Sefi, S. (1992) Dilemmas of advice: aspects of the delivery and reception of advice in interactions between health visitors and first time mothers. In Drew and Heritage (1992a), pp. 359–417.

Heritage, J. and Watson, D. R. (1979) Formulations as conversational objects. In Psathas (1979), pp. 123–62.

Hirst, G. (1991) Does conversation analysis have a role in computational linguistics? *Computational Linguistics*, 17: 211–27.

Hopper, R. (1989a) Conversation analysis and social psychology as descriptions of interpersonal communication. In Roger and Bull (1989), pp. 48–65.

Hopper, R. (1989b) Speech, for instance: the exemplar in studies of conversation. *Journal of Language and Social Psychology*, 7: 47–63.

Hopper, R. (1992) *Telephone Conversation*. Bloomington: Indiana University Press.

Houtkoop-Steenstra, H. (1991) Opening sequences in Dutch telephone conversation. In Boden and Zimmerman (1991), pp. 232–50.

Houtkoop-Steenstra, H. (1995) Meeting both ends: standardisation and recipient design in telephone survey interviews. In ten Have and Psathas (1995), pp. 91–106.

Hufford, D. (1982) *The Terror that Comes in the Night: An Experience-Centred Study of Supernatural Assault Traditions*. Philadelphia: University of Pennsylvania Press.

Hughes, E. (1970) *The Sociological Eye: Selected Papers*. New York: Aldine.

Hutchby, I. (1992a) The pursuit of controversy: routine scepticism in talk on talk radio. *Sociology*, 26: 673–94.

Hutchby, I. (1992b) Confrontation talk: aspects of 'interruption' in argument sequences on talk radio. *Text*, 12: 343–71.

Hutchby, I (1996a) *Confrontation Talk: Arguments, Asymmetries and Power on Talk Radio*. Hillsdale, N.J.: Erlbaum.

Hutchby, I. (1996b) Power in discourse: the case of arguments on talk radio. *Discourse and Society*, 7: 481–97.

Hutchby, I. (1997) Building alignments in public debate: a case study from British TV. *Text*, 17: 161–79.

Hutchby, I. (1998) Rhetorical strategies in audience participation debates on radio and TV. *Research on Language and Social Interaction*, 31, forthcoming.

Hutchby, I. and Moran-Ellis, J. (eds) (1997) *Children and Social Competence: Arenas of Action*. London: Falmer Press.

Jefferson, G. (1972) Side sequences. In Sudnow (1972), pp. 294–338.

Jefferson, G. (1973) A case of precision timing in ordinary conversation: overlapped tag-positioned address terms in closing sequences. *Semiotica*, 9: 47–96.

Jefferson, G. (1978) Sequential aspects of storytelling in conversation. In Schenkein (1978), pp. 219–48.

Jefferson, G. (1979) A technique for inviting laughter and its subsequent acceptance/declination. In Psathas (1979), pp. 79–96.

Jefferson, G. (1980) On 'trouble-premonitory' response to inquiry. *Sociological Inquiry*, 50: 153–85.

Jefferson, G. (1981) The abominable 'ne?': a working paper exploring the phenomenon of post-response pursuit of response. Occasional Paper 6, Department of Sociology, University of Manchester.

Jefferson, G. (1983) Notes on some orderlinesses of overlap onset. Tilburg Papers in Language and Literature 28, Department of Linguistics, Tilburg University.

Jefferson, G. (1985) An exercise in the transcription and analysis of laughter. In Dijk (1985), pp. 25–34.

Jefferson, G. (1986) Notes on latency in overlap onset. *Human Studies*, 9: 153–83.

Jefferson, G. (1987) On exposed and embedded correction in conversation. In Button and Lee (1987), pp. 86–100.

Jefferson, G. (1989) Notes on a possible metric which provides for a 'standard maximum silence' of one second in conversation. In Roger and Bull (1989), pp. 166–96.

Jefferson, G. (1990) List construction as a task and resource. In Psathas (1990), pp. 63–92.

Jefferson, G., Sacks, H. and Schegloff, E. A. (1987) Notes on laughter in pursuit of intimacy. In Button and Lee (1987), pp. 152–205.

Keith, W. M. and Whittenberger-Keith, K. (1988–9) The conversational call: an analysis of conversational aspects of public oratory. *Research on Language and Social Interaction*, 22: 115–56.

Kelly, J. and Local, J. (1989) On the use of general phonetic techniques in handling conversational material. In Roger and Bull (1989), pp. 197–212.

Kendon, A. (1982) The organisation of behaviour in face-to-face interaction: observations on the development of a methodology. In Scherer and Ekman (1982), pp. 440–505.

Kendon, A. (1990) *Conducting Interaction*. Cambridge: Cambridge University Press.

Knorr-Cetina, K. and Cicourel, A. V. (eds) (1981) *Advances in Social Theory and Methodology*. London: Routledge.

Knorr-Cetina, K., Krohn, R. and Whitley, R. (eds) (1980) *The Social Process of Scientific Investigation*. Dordrecht: Reidel.

Kotthoff, H. (1993) Disagreement and concession in disputes: On the context-sensitivity of preference structures. *Language in Society*, 22: 193–216.

Labov, W. (1972) *Sociolinguistic Patterns*. Philadelphia: University of Pennsylvania Press.

Labov, W. and Waletsky, J. (1966) Narrative analysis: oral versions of personal experience. In Helm (1966), pp. 12–44.

Lamoreux, E. (1988–9) Rhetoric and conversation in service encounters. *Research on Language and Social Interaction*, 22: 93–114.

Levinson, S. (1983) *Pragmatics*. Cambridge: Cambridge University Press.

Levinson, S. (1992) Activity types and language. In Drew and Heritage (1992a), pp. 66–100.

Lindstrom, A. (1994) Identification and recognition in Swedish telephone conversation openings. *Language in Society*, 23: 231–52.

Local, J. (1996) Conversational phonetics: some aspects of news receipts in everyday talk. In Couper-Kuhlen and Selting (1996), pp. 177–230.

Luff, P., Gilbert, N. and Frohlich, D. (eds) (1990) *Computers and Conversation*. London: Academic Press.

Lukes, S. (ed.) (1986) *Power*. Oxford: Blackwell.

Lynch, M. and Bogen, D. (1994) Harvey Sacks' primitive science. *Theory, Culture and Society*, 11: 65–104.

McHoul, A. (1978) The organisation of turns at formal talk in the classroom. *Language in Society*, 19: 183–213.

McIlvenny, P. (1996) Popular public discourse at Speaker's Corner: negotiating cultural identities in interaction. *Discourse and Society*, 7: 7–37.

McKinney, J. C. and Tiryakian, E. A. (eds) (1970) *Theoretical Sociology*. New York: Appleton-Century-Crofts.

Maynard, D. W. (1991) Interaction and asymmetry in clinical discourse. *American Journal of Sociology*, 97: 448–95.

Maynard, D. W., Schaeffer, N. C. and Cradock, R. M. (1995) A preliminary analysis of 'gatekeeping' as a feature of declinations to participate in the survey interview. Unpubl. MS.

Mead, G. H. (1934) *Mind, Self and Society*. Chicago: University of Chicago Press.

Mishler, E. (1984) *The Discourse of Medicine: Dialectics of Medical Interviews*. Norwood, N.J.: Ablex.

Moerman, M. (1972) Accomplishing ethnicity. In Turner (1972), pp. 54–68.

Moerman, M. (1977) The preference for self-correction in a Thai conversational corpus. *Language*, 53: 207–29.

Moerman, M. (1988) *Talking Culture: Ethnography and Conversation Analysis*. Philadelphia: University of Pennsylvania Press.

Montgomery, M. (1986) Language and power: a critical review of *Studies in the Theory of Ideology* by John B. Thompson. *Media, Culture and Society*, 8: 41–64.

Myers, G. (1994) *Words in Ads*. London: Edward Arnold.

Norman, M. and Thomas, P. (1990) The very idea: Informing HCI design from conversation analysis. In Luff, Gilbert and Frohlich (1990), pp. 51–66.

Ochs, E. (1979) Transcription as theory. In Ochs and Schieffelin (1979), pp. 43–72.

Ochs, E. and Schieffelin, B. (eds) (1979) *Developmental Pragmatics*. New York: Academic Press.

Park, R. (1952) *Human Communities: The City and Human Ecology*. New York: Free Press.

Parret, H. and Verschueren, J. (eds) (1992) *(On) Searle on Conversation*. Amsterdam: John Benjamins.

Parsons, T. (1937) *The Structure of Social Action*. New York: McGraw-Hill.

Perakyla, A. (1996) *AIDS Counselling: Institutional Interaction and Clinical Practice*. Cambridge: Cambridge University Press.

Perkins, M. and Howard, S. (eds) (1995) *Case Studies in Clinical Linguistics*. London: Whurr.

Pomerantz, A. (1978) Compliment responses: notes on the cooperation of multiple constraints. In Schenkein (1978), pp. 79–112.

Pomerantz, A. (1980) Telling my side: 'limited access' as a 'fishing' device. *Sociological Inquiry*, 50: 186–98.

Pomerantz, A. (1984a) Agreeing and disagreeing with assessments: some features of preferred/dispreferred turn-shapes. In Atkinson and Heritage (1984), pp. 79–112.

Pomerantz, A. (1984b) Giving a source or basis: the practice in conversation of telling 'how I know'. *Journal of Pragmatics*, 8: 607–25.

Pomerantz, A. (1986) Extreme case formulations. *Human Studies*, 9: 219–30.

Pomerantz, A. (1988–9) Constructing skepticism: four devices for engendering the audience's skepticism. *Research on Language and Social Interaction*, 22: 293–313.

Potter, J. (1996) *Representing Reality: Discourse, Rhetoric and Social Construction*. London: Sage.

Potter, J. and Wetherell, M. (1987) *Discourse and Social Psychology*. London: Sage.

Psathas, G. (ed.) (1979) *Everyday Language: Studies in Ethnomethodology*. Hillsdale, N.J.: Erlbaum.

Psathas, G. (ed.) (1990) *Interaction Competence.* Washington D.C.: University Press of America.

Psathas, G. and Anderson, T. (1990) The 'practices' of transcription in conversation analysis. *Semiotica,* 78: 75–99.

Roger, D. and Bull, P. (eds) (1989) *Conversation.* Clevedon: Multilingual Matters.

Roger, D., Bull, P. and Smith, S. (1988) The development of a comprehensive system for classifying interruptions. *Journal of Language and Social Psychology,* 7: 27–34.

Sacks, H. (1963) Sociological description. *Berkeley Journal of Sociology,* 8: 1–16.

Sacks, H. (1972a) An initial investigation of the usability of conversational data for doing sociology. In Sudnow (1972), pp. 31–74.

Sacks, H. (1972b) Notes on police assessment of moral character. In Sudnow (1972), pp. 280–93.

Sacks, H. (1972c) On the analysability of stories by children. In Gumperz and Hymes (1972), pp. 325–45.

Sacks, H. (1975) Everyone has to lie. In Blount and Sanchez (1975), pp. 57–80.

Sacks, H. (1979) Hotrodder: a revolutionary category. In Psathas (1979), pp. 7–14.

Sacks, H. (1984a) Notes on methodology. In Atkinson and Heritage (1984), pp. 21–7.

Sacks, H. (1984b) On doing 'being ordinary'. In Atkinson and Heritage (1984), pp. 413–29.

Sacks, H. (1987) On the preferences for agreement and contiguity in sequences in conversation. In Button and Lee (1987), pp. 54–69.

Sacks, H. (1992) *Lectures on Conversation,* ed. G. Jefferson. 2 vols, Oxford: Blackwell.

Sacks, H. and Schegloff, E. A. (1979) Two preferences in the organisation of reference to persons in conversation and their interaction. In Psathas (1979), pp. 15–21.

Sacks, H., Schegloff, E. A. and Jefferson, G. (1974) A simplest systematics for the organisation of turn-taking for conversation. *Language,* 50: 696–735.

Sapir, E. (1921) *Language: An Introduction to the Study of Speech.* New York: Harcourt Brace and World.

Schaeffer, N. C. (1991) Conversation with a purpose or conversation? Interaction in the standardised interview. In Beimer et al. (1991), pp. 367–91.

Schegloff, E. A. (1968) Sequencing in conversational openings. *American Anthropologist,* 70: 1075–95.

Schegloff, E. A. (1972) Notes on a conversational practice: formulating place. In Sudnow (1972), pp. 75–119.

Schegloff, E. A. (1979a) The relevance of repair to syntax-for-conversation. In Givon (1979), pp. 261–88.

Schegloff, E. A. (1979b) Identification and recognition in telephone conversation openings. In Psathas (1979), pp. 23–78.

Schegloff, E. A. (1980) Preliminaries to preliminaries: 'Can I ask you a question?' *Sociological Inquiry*, 50: 104–52.

Schegloff, E. A. (1982) Discourse as an interactional achievement: some uses of 'uh huh' and other things that come between sentences. In Tannen (1982), pp. 71–93.

Schegloff, E. A. (1984) On some gestures' relation to talk. In Atkinson and Heritage (1984), pp. 266–96.

Schegloff, E. A. (1986) The routine as achievement. *Human Studies*, 9: 111–52.

Schegloff, E. A. (1987a) Recycled turn-beginnings. In Button and Lee (1987), pp. 70–85.

Schegloff, E. A. (1987b) Analysing single episodes of interaction: an exercise in conversation analysis. *Social Psychology Quarterly*, 50: 101–14.

Schegloff, E. A. (1988a) Presequences and indirection: applying speech act theory to ordinary conversation. *Journal of Pragmatics*, 12: 55–62.

Schegloff, E. A. (1988b) Goffman and the analysis of conversation. In Drew and Wootton (1988), pp. 89–135.

Schegloff, E. A. (1988c) On an actual virtual servo-mechanism for guessing bad news: a single case conjecture. *Social Problems*, 32: 442–57.

Schegloff, E. A. (1988–9) From interview to confrontation: observations on the Bush/Rather encounter. *Research on Language and Social Interaction*, 22: 215–40.

Schegloff, E. A. (1991). Reflections on talk and social structure. In Boden and Zimmerman (1991), pp. 44–70.

Schegloff, E. A. (1992a) Introduction. In Sacks (1992), vol. 1, pp. ix–lxii.

Schegloff, E. A. (1992b) To Searle on conversation. In Parret and Verschueren (1992), pp. 113–28.

Schegloff, E. A. (1992c) Repair after next turn: the last structurally provided defense of intersubjectivity in conversation. *American Journal of Sociology*, 97: 1295–345.

Schegloff, E. A. and Sacks, H. (1973) Opening up closings. *Semiotica*, 7: 289–327.

Schegloff, E. A., Jefferson, G. and Sacks, H. (1977) The preference for self-correction in the organisation of repair in conversation. *Language*, 53: 361–82.

Schenkein, J. (ed.) (1978) *Studies in the Organisation of Conversational Interaction*. New York: Academic Press.

Scherer, K. R. and Ekman, P. (eds) (1982) *Handbook of Methods in Nonverbal Behaviour Research*. Cambridge: Cambridge University Press.

Searle, J. (1965) What is a speech act? In Black (1965), pp. 221–39.

Searle, J. (1969) *Speech Acts*. Cambridge: Cambridge University Press.

Searle, J. (1986) Introductory essay: notes on conversation. In Ellis and Donohue (1986), pp. 7–19. Repr. in Parret and Verschueren (1992), pp. 7–29.

Sinclair, J. and Coulthard, M. (1975) *Towards an Analysis of Discourse*. Oxford: Oxford University Press.

Smith, D. (1978) 'K' is mentally ill: the anatomy of a factual account. *Sociology*, 12: 23–53.

Suchman, L. (1987) *Plans and Situated Actions*. Cambridge: Cambridge University Press.

Suchman, L. and Jordan, B. (1990) Interactional troubles in face-to-face survey interviews. *Journal of the American Statistical Association*, 85: 232–41.

Sudnow, D. (ed.) (1972) *Studies in Social Interaction*. New York: Free Press.

Tannen, D. (ed.) (1982) *Analysing Discourse: Text and Talk*. Washington D.C.: Georgetown University Press.

ten Have, P. (1991) Talk and institution: a reconsideration of the 'asymmetry' of doctor–patient interaction. In Boden and Zimmerman (1991), pp. 138–63.

ten Have, P. and Psathas, G. (eds) (1995) *Situated Order: Studies in the Social Organisation of Talk and Embodied Activities*. Washington D.C.: University Press of America.

Terasaki, A. (1976) Pre-announcement sequences in conversation. Social Sciences Working Paper 99, University of California at Irvine.

Thomas, P. (ed.) (1995) *The Social and Interactional Dimensions of Human–Computer Interfaces*. Cambridge: Cambridge University Press.

Thompson, J. B. (1984) *Studies in the Theory of Ideology*. Cambridge: Polity Press.

Turner, R. (ed.) (1972) *Ethnomethodology*. Harmondsworth: Penguin.

Watson, R. and Weinberg, T. (1982) Interviews and the interactional construction of accounts of homosexual identity. *Sociological Analysis*, 11: 56–78.

Weinreich, U. (1963) On the semantic structure of language. In Greenberg (1963), pp. 142–216.

Wetherell, M. and Potter, J. (1992) *Mapping the Language of Racism*. Hemel Hempstead: Harvester Wheatsheaf.

Whalen, M. and Zimmerman, D. (1990) Describing trouble: practical epistemology in citizen calls to the police. *Language in Society*, 19: 465–92.

Whyte, W. F. (1943) *Street Corner Society*. Chicago: University of Chicago Press.

Widdicombe, S. and Wooffitt, R. (1995) *The Language of Youth Subcultures: Social Identity in Action*. Hemel Hempstead: Harvester.

Wieder, D. L. (1974) *Language and Social Reality*. The Hague: Mouton.

Wilkinson, R. (1995) Aphasia: conversation analysis of a non-fluent aphasic. In Perkins and Howard (1995).

Wooffitt, R. (1991) Some observations on the organisation of problematic calls to the British Airways flight information service. Technical Report, Social and Computer Sciences Research Group, Department of Sociology, University of Surrey.

Wooffitt, R. (1992) *Telling Tales of the Unexpected: Accounts of Paranormal Experiences*. Hemel Hempstead: Harvester.

Wooffitt R., Fraser, N., Gilbert, G. N. and McGlashan, S. (1997) *Humans, Computers and Wizards: Analysing Human-(Simulated)-Computer Interaction*. London: Routledge.

Woolgar, S. (1980) Discovery: logic and sequence in a scientific text. In Knorr-Cetina, Krohn and Whitley (1980), pp. 239–68.

Woolgar, S. (1988) *Science: The Very Idea*. London: Ellis Horwood.

Index